ACROSS THE YEARS

1896 - 1936

Jane Bardsley's
Outback Letterbook
ACROSS THE YEARS
1896-1936

EDITED BY JOHN ATHERTON YOUNG

ANGUS
& ROBERTSON
PUBLISHERS

I would like to express my
appreciation to Dr Richard
Walsh and to Angus &
Robertson for their help,
and particularly to the
Publisher's Editor,
Ms Bryony Cosgrove.

ANGUS & ROBERTSON PUBLISHERS

Unit 4, Eden Park, 31 Waterloo Road,
North Ryde, NSW, Australia 2113, and
16 Golden Square, London W1R 4BN,
United Kingdom

First published in Australia
by Angus & Robertson Publishers in 1987

Copyright © John Atherton Young and
Robert Atherton Young 1987

National Library of Australia
Cataloguing-in-publication data.

Bardsley, Jane, 1877–1943.
  Across the years: Jane Bardsley's letters from far
  North Queensland.

  Includes index.
  ISBN 0 207 15456 2.

  1. Bardsley, Jane, 1877–1943 — Correspondence. 2.
  Ranchers' wives — Queensland, Northern — Correspondence.
  3. Ranch life — Queensland, Northern. 4. Queensland,
  Northern — Social life and customs. I. Young, John
  Atherton, 1936–   . II. Title.

994.3'009'94

Typeset in Baskerville
Printed in Singapore

CONTENTS

PREFACE

Despite being nearly seven years old when my grandmother died, I cannot recall her at all, although I can recall visiting Homefields in Mackay, where she lived after she had remarried. Nevertheless, her personality has long been well-known to me from the typescript copy of her volume of letters which she had given to my mother shortly before she died.

No-one now alive is certain when she actually wrote these letters. In their original form, which my grandmother destroyed, they comprised three handwritten volumes with a total length in excess of 100,000 words. Early in 1940, she asked her family solicitor to read them and to give her his opinion of them. He was a man with some literary interests of his own, and he offered her good advice — to shorten the text to 80,000 words, to change the sequences of the narrative here and there, to have the manuscript typed, and to offer it to Angus & Robertson. She took his advice concerning revision and typing and produced an illustrated volume that she entitled *Across the Years*, but the growing seriousness of the Pacific phase of World War II discouraged her from seeking a publisher. Instead, she assigned the volume to my mother with full authority to publish it after the war, or to destroy it if she saw fit. My mother had several copies prepared for limited circulation, but it is only now, almost half a century later, that my brother and I have finally decided to republish it for a wider readership, appropriately with Angus & Robertson as my grandmother herself had intended.

It is scarcely conceivable that my grandmother could have found opportunity, or perhaps courage, to have begun writing these letters when she first went to live at Midlothian station after her marriage to Thomas Arthur Atherton in 1895. I believe that she must have written them much later in her life, probably at Homefields in Mackay in 1938–1939, during the leisure time afforded her by the comfortable circumstances of her second marriage — to John Michelmore. Nevertheless, they still look like real letters that she might have written — in later life at least, she was a prolific and an accomplished letter writer. Most certainly she did have a cousin in Mackay called Althea — this was Vida Althea (or rather Althoea)

Cook (née Atherton, born 6 April 1875), a daughter of Richard Atherton, the youngest of my grandfather's uncles. Whether Althea Cook ever carried on a correspondence with my grandmother — they were of similar age — or whether she read the manuscript letters at all when my grandmother was preparing them for publication, I do not know. It is certainly conceivable that the letters we now have are based in part on a real correspondence between Jane Bardsley and Althea Cook: in those days one preserved interesting letters, often tied up in bundles and kept in old cigar boxes. Indeed, I have half a dozen of my grandmother's that were preserved in this way by my mother.

Nevertheless, whether based on real letters or not, the letters as they now exist are not to be treated as a literally accurate record. My grandmother has changed the chronology here and there in order to make the narrative clearer and more dramatic. The most notable example of this is in her description of the events preceding the death of my grandfather (10 February 1935) — she has altered the date of my mother's marriage (in reality 16 April 1935) and the birth of my first cousin, Thomas Arthur Atherton II (9 July 1935), so that they precede my grandfather's death. This was not a step made by an elderly writer whose memory was failing, but a deliberate decision of my grandmother's, a decision she was aware might evoke the disapproval of those who knew the real dates.

There are other interesting departures from strict truth in these letters. A most significant one concerns the circumstances of my grandmother's own childhood. Her mother, Jane Bardsley senior (1848–1925), must have been a rather formidable figure — stern, practical, conscious of the value of education, and rather class conscious. She came to Queensland as a child of fifteen in 1864 in the *Warren Hastings*, and in 1871, at Clermont she married John Bardsley, an immigrant saddler. John Bardsley had emigrated to Queensland in 1862 at the age of twenty-two in the *Sultana*, accompanied by an elder brother and an elder sister. The marriage was not very successful. John Bardsley, eight years Jane's senior, was something of a rolling stone and fond of alcohol. The couple moved from place to place, with John always seeking to make a fortune from gold digging or anything else that he thought promising, while my great grandmother endured nine pregnancies in as many years. Finally, John Bardsley deserted his wife and his three surviving children in Normanton, then even more of an isolated outpost than it is now. Jane Bardsley senior made a living as a seamstress and, on the proceeds of her labour, opened a hotel in Normanton. This venture evidently succeeded well, since two of the children were sent off to

Richard Atherton and his four daughters, Rose (top), Althea (left),
Ena (right) and Emily (bottom right). Althea (1875–1955), who was
about the same age as Jane (1877–1943), was her cousin by marriage
and may have been Jane's model for her imaginary correspondent.

boarding school to be educated — my grandmother to All Hallows Convent in Brisbane from 1889 to 1894 (a remarkable choice for my dourly Protestant great-grandmother), and my grand-uncle to the Ipswich Grammar School (1891 to 1893).

This remarkable effort on the part of my great-grandmother gave her daughter the education she needed to be able to write well. Interestingly, however, the daughter, in her book, chooses not to highlight the struggle faced by her mother in rearing her family, makes no mention of the hotel as their source of income, and passes discreetly over the question of why her father was not there to support them. Victorian mores required the suppression of these "unpleasant" facts while nevertheless permitting my grandmother, quite candidly, to describe how the Aborigines were exploited and ill-treated. In one sense, it is this changed social perspective that makes the letters so interesting.

The fact that my grandmother has tinkered with the chronology a little, and sanitised some of the realities of pioneer life, should not detract from their interest to the present day reader. Her life and personality still stand out clearly in what she has written, and neither I nor the publishers contemplated changing her text. She, and her times, can be assessed from her letters. They show us what she was like and, for that matter, what we also are probably like if we look behind the conventions of currently accepted standards.

A comment is necessary on my editorial approach to the text. Since the original hand-written version of the manuscript was destroyed by my grandmother, I have had to rely exclusively on the version she arranged to have typed in 1940–1941, despite its numerous typographical errors. Although most of the obvious errors had been corrected in the later version prepared by my mother in 1955, it had also been edited in an attempt to resolve some textual problems of the earlier version, so I preferred not to use it since such changes were clearly not authentic. I have, however, made a few grammatical corrections to the text myself (consistent with my grandmother's own style), and tidied up the spelling, particularly of place names (e.g. 'Maggieville' rather than 'Maggie Vale' station and 'Einasleigh' rather than 'Ainsley' River). Similarly, the publishers have substituted 'crocodile' for 'alligator', the word current in my grandmother's day (witness Alligator Point near the mouth of the Norman River and Alligator Creek near Sarina). In the letters where she describes my grandfather's overland journeys across North Queensland, journeys that she did not herself make, I have corrected what appear to be geographical mistakes. Thus, she had him zigzagging from Mareeba to Chillagoe, to Herberton, and on to Georgetown, whereas it seems much more likely that he went from Mareeba to Herberton, to Chillagoe, to Georgetown. In the same letter she places Green Creek telegraph station only "several miles" from Georgetown, whereas it ought to be about a hundred miles away. I have also attempted to eliminate some chronological inconsistencies in the letters dealing with what purports to be her first year at Midlothian: it appears to me that, as part of her attempt at shortening the manuscript, she must have revised a number of letters dealing with events taking place in later years to make them read as if they were all written in 1896. For instance, she writes that the rain "has gone for nine months" in one letter and then, in a later letter, in which she tells Althea that she is pregnant, she writes that it is just five months since she left her mother's home and came to Midlothian. Finally, to make reading easier, the text has been divided into twelve chapters and each given a short descriptive caption. For the benefit of any interested historian, the original manuscript including her illustrations will, in due course, be placed in the Oxley Library in Brisbane.

It was the realisation that these letters would be likely to have an appeal to a much broader readership than the members of our family and their friends, that led us to seek to republish them, and the approach of the Australian bicentenary year suggested to us that now is an appropriate time to do so. In addition, however, I have a very personal wish to help bring my grandmother's labour to fruition. Whenever I have read her final letter, with its reference to the birth, half a century ago, of my cousin Tom, with whom I grew up, I have been struck by the feeling that her book does indeed form a bridge across the years, a bridge linking her era to mine, and that it thereby makes her time one with my own. By publishing her remarkable record, I hope not only to perform an act of *pietas* but also to express my admiration for her and for the many like her who, by their struggles, created the country to which I belong inseparably.

JOHN ATHERTON YOUNG
Sydney, 4 May 1986

Right: In the case of those deceased persons who were not born in Queensland, the birth years have only been calculated from the information on the death certificates, cross-checked wherever possible from other secondary records. Consequently, some birth years may be incorrect by one year. (The table was compiled with the assistance of Mrs J. Harrison whose help is gratefully acknowledged.)

ACROSS THE YEARS

Family Tree

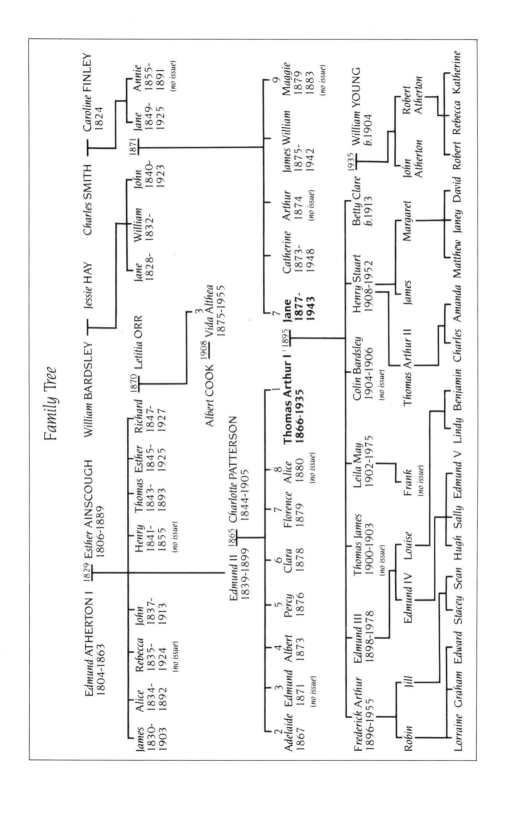

CHRONOLOGICAL TABLE

Below are set out the places where Jane lived (with dates in parentheses) and the dates of some of the major events in her life.

Copperfield, near Clermont, in a miner's cottage (1877–1886)
Jane was was born 7 March 1877 in Copperfield

Normanton, in a tent in a miners' camp (1887–1888)
The race riots in Normanton occurred on 14–15 June 1888

Brisbane, All Hallows Convent, Kangaroo Point (1889–1894)
Jane attended All Hallows Convent for 5 years

Normanton, in the house of Jane Bardsley senior (1895)
Jane married Thomas Arthur Atherton 4 December 1895 in St Peter's Church of England in Normanton

Midlothian, a large cattle station north-east of Normanton (1896–1901)
Frederick Arthur Atherton was born 6 September 1896 in Normanton
Edmund Atherton was born 17 October 1898 in Normanton
Thomas James Atherton was born 18 June 1900 in Normanton

Woonon, a cattle station at Plane Creek near Sarina (1901–1917)
Leila May Atherton was born 15 May 1902 in Mackay
Thomas James Atherton died 14 December 1903 in Mackay
Colin Bardsley Atherton was born 27 December 1904 in Mackay
Colin Bardsley Atherton died 8 November 1906 at Woonon
Henry Stuart Atherton was born 19 January 1908 in Mackay
Betty Clare Atherton was born 23 May 1913 in Mackay

Pretty Bend and Belmore cattle stations and Leyton (a farm house) in the Bowen district (1917–1919)

Maroona, a seaside house near Bowen (1920)

Tondara, a cattle station in the Bowen district (1921–1925)
Jane's father, John Bardsley, died 21 July 1923 in the Charters Towers Hospital
Jane's mother, Jane Bardsley senior, died 2 July 1925 in Cairns

Torrington, a dairy farm near Toowoomba (1926)

Taronga, a sugar farm at Bli Bli near Nambour (1926–1935)
Jane's husband, Thomas Arthur Atherton, died 10 February 1935 in the Maroochy Hospital

Homefields, John Michelmore's residence in Mackay (1937–1943)
Jane married John Michelmore 19 August 1937 in Mackay
Jane died 24 March 1943 in the Mater Hospital, Mackay

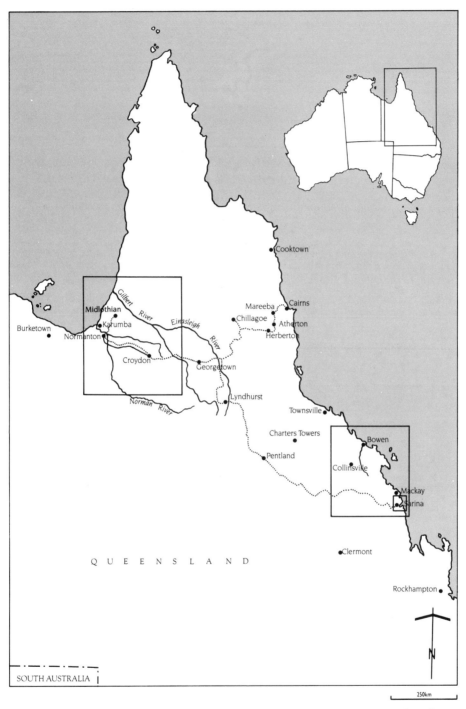

Map of Queensland showing the principal towns and stations mentioned in Jane Bardsley's letters. The dotted lines from Sarina to Georgetown, and from Cairns to Normanton, show the modern roads that correspond approximately to the overland journeys undertaken by Thomas Arthur Atherton I in the 1880s. The three outlined areas are enlarged on pp. 30, 141 and 187.

Jane's mother, Jane Bardsley senior (née Smith), circa 1905. Born in Maybole, Ayrshire, in 1849, she came to Queensland in the Warren Hastings *as a child of 15 years. She met John Bardsley at Copperfield, where they both lived, and married him on 29 April 1871 at Clermont. She lived at various times in Clermont, Normanton, Brisbane and, finally, Cairns, where she died on 4 July 1925.*

ACROSS THE YEARS

Clermont and Normanton
1886 to 1888

My Dear Althea,

We are leaving our dear little home in Clermont and our very own gardens for far distant lands, where Father[1] says the streets are strewn with gold.

Jim,[2] who is past twelve years of age, and I nearly eleven, are so anxious to gather it; but the days do take a long time to pass by, for us to make a start, I feel frightened they might alter their minds.

We shall buy the cricket set that he needs so badly. He says that Santy brings such a small set each year he is not able to use it. He is the best cricketer in his school. Mother[3] looks so worried when he cries about the mistakes Santy makes, and tells him he will have to use the bats that Father makes, and kerosene tins for wickets, a little longer, for we are not rich folk.

Father promises I shall have the pair of long lace-up boots, the ones that come almost to my knees — I have wanted them so badly for such a long time — and pretty dresses with lace and frills around the bottom and also around the sleeves and neck, to wear to Sunday school and Oh! a huge big doll like other little girls have, with buttons and buttonholes on the dresses so that I can have a doll's washing day. I do not want another like Santy brings every time. He does not understand what I want although I kneel and close my eyes so tight and pray so hard with my hands clasped in front of me. He still brings the same tiny little ones, just the same.

Mother says I shall have to be my big doll's dressmaker, learn to cut out and sew the seams very neatly before I spend the gold money I shall gather, as money is easily gathered and hard to spend properly.

At night while Mother is packing up, it is lovely to listen to Jim telling me what he is going to do when he gets his proper cricket set. I

---

[1] John Bardsley (1840–1923), a saddler, emigrated to Queensland accompanied by an elder brother and sister in the *Sultana* in 1862.

[2] James William Bardsley (1875–1942), son of John Bardsley and Jane Smith, was Jane Bardsley's elder brother.

[3] Jane Smith (1849–1925), daughter of Charles Smith and Caroline Finley, emigrated to Queensland with her mother and an elder sister, Annie (1855–1891), in the *Warren Hastings*, in 1864. She married John Bardsley at Clermont on 29 April 1871.

Above: Clermont, circa 1870. Clermont began as a mining boom-town. This view shows the bark and slab huts in which many of the miners lived. Others lived in tents just as the Bardsley family did when they moved to Normanton. John and Jane Bardsley met in nearby Copperfield, one of the actual mine sites, but they married in the more civilised surroundings of Clermont (29 April 1871).

Below: Winter & Lea's general store, Clermont, 1877. It would have been in a store like this that Jane's mother did her weekly shopping.

Above: School of Arts, Clermont, 1880. The School was a sign that the town was becoming respectable. These institutions, which usually housed a library, provided the town with a meeting hall.

Below: Wildcat Mine, Clermont, 1899. Although this photograph was taken long after the Bardsley family had left the district, it shows a typical landscape around the town at any time after its foundation.

think he will be a great batsman someday, as everybody calls out when he hits a good shot "well done, my boy", and I heard a lot of men say to Father, "You have bred a cricketer." What we cannot understand is that Father sings all the time he is helping to pack up, and seems so happy to be leaving to gather gold, and why Mother cries so. Sometimes she leaves the packing to lie down on the couch and cry, and then again, we can hear big sobs when she is burning letters and little clothes. Perhaps she is still sad at leaving Margaret,[4] our baby sister three years of age, who went to live with God only three years ago.

She always cries such a lot when we go out and put flowers on her grave on Sundays. Last Sunday we went out for the last time — as we are going in a few days — to see such a pretty little tombstone with Margaret Jessie Bardsley written in gold letters, and lovely iron railings painted black with shining silver tips. She cried more than ever and knelt on her knees with her eyes shut, for a very long time.

Mother said that it would be nice for Jim and I to kneel and ask God to look after our dear little sister, and to say lots of Lord's Prayers. I said the prayers over and over again, and must have fallen asleep, for when I opened my eyes I was in Mother's arms.

When we ask her why she cries so she just says, "I am leaving my little baby behind and all my old friends, and I am so afraid the gold might be gone when we get there."

Good night, and love from us all,

I remain, your fond friend,

JANE BARDSLEY

My Dear Althea,

We left our dear little home and our very own flower garden on 4th January 1887.

The trip to Rockhampton was over two hundred miles; the train was one of the first that entered that railway station, and it was the only one I had ever seen or travelled in. It was so wonderful to watch the trees all moving along, the clouds in the sky all passing by, and to see so many little towns, the houses mostly made of calico — I would not like to live in one of them — on the roadside.

[4] Margaret Jessie Bardsley (1879–1883), was the youngest of nine children born to John Bardsley and Jane Smith. Of the nine, only three survived to maturity — Catherine (1873–1948), James William (1875–1942) and Jane (1877–1943).

I could not understand that it was the train moving, and not the trees or sky, for quite a while.

For weeks Jim and I have listened to the arrangements talked over by Father, to secure our boat passages to the Croydon goldfields, and have listened to him reading aloud in the paper of large pieces of gold being found there. I am just longing to get there to pick some up, to play jacks. It will be lovely to play with yellow gold instead of sheep knucklebones.

Croydon is many miles away, it will take nearly three weeks to get there. It is situated about one hundred and sixty miles inland from the shores of the Gulf of Carpentaria.

Father tells me he was a wealthy man when I was born, but through our little town losing the copper trade, and the railway connecting our town with Rockhampton, it now has only a small living in it, and that he must move out for our sakes.

The packing up was most interesting; huge cases of drapery, sewing machines and shop fittings have all been sent to Rockhampton to go by boat to the Gulf.

Mother did not take any furniture, she says it will only bring back memories, and we had to give all our toys away for it would be too costly to pay the freight. Jim and I are not fretting about them, as they are all tiny little ones, and of course we shall not want them when we have bought the large ones with the gold money.

I have to hurry off to bed, as we are staying with Granny,[5] who says all little children must go to bed at half past seven.

Goodnight,

I remain, your loving friend,

JANE BARDSLEY

My Dear Althea,

We waited four weeks to embark in a small steamer that travelled the Fitzroy River, to meet a vessel of much larger size, well out to sea from the mud-laden shores of the coastline.

After the northern mails, passengers of all kinds and classes — including parsons, poets, lawyers, artists, labourers of all trades down to Chinese and other aliens — had been transhipped in the large vessel, we set off to find the gold.

I spent my first afternoon looking over the beautiful ship, and

[5] Caroline Finley (b. ca. 1824), wife of Charles Smith.

Clermont, 1876. The town had settled down to a modest prosperity by 1876.

comparing it with the boats I had seen in picture books. I watched the sailors running about, scrubbing the decks, polishing the brass, and was most interested in watching the different passengers. Some of the ladies had funny dresses on, and some had the lace and frills I want so badly. Other ladies had beautiful feathery fans, and lay back on the deckchairs while men fanned them.

The beautiful blue ocean of small and large waves, tossing and frolicking, crested with feathery foam, left me spellbound. The sea-gulls following the boat, swooping down, sometimes to ride on the waves and other times to catch fish or pick up scraps of food thrown from our boat, took up a great deal of my attention as I had never seen the beautiful seagulls before.

The day ended all too soon for me, and after I had eaten a good supper I was sent to bed. I felt the air hot and stuffy in the cabin, so different from on the deck. I could see the clothes hanging on the walls swaying backwards and forwards and I could feel something come up as far as my throat, then back again, while I was getting ready for bed. Lying on the berth I could feel my feet go up then my head go down and so on, until I could not control the lump in my throat. All went black, I was seasick and longed to be back home in our old-fashioned town. The sea had lost its charm.

I shall end now with love from us all.

I remain, your loving friend,

JANE BARDSLEY

My Dear Althea,

I am sure you will sympathise with me and my sickness, I am certain the feeling is next to death. I feel I shall never leave the Gulf, if I ever get there. I hope I shall not bore you with our trip up the coast, to me, I will always remember it. I have lost all signs of seasickness now.

After leaving Rockhampton our first stop was at Flat Top, an island with a flat top off the coast of Mackay, where merchandise was slung over to a small vessel which lay alongside our boat. To our horror the passengers were slung over, too.

Leaving Mackay, or I should say Flat Top, we were soon at the entrance to the Whitsunday Passage with beautiful islands standing all around us. The amazing tropical vegetation varied in colour with the light. The rich autumn gold shaded to palest primrose would be replaced in a few seconds by deep emerald and pastel green only to be succeeded by purple, mauve and shades of blue. It made our hearts glad and seemed to lure us on. This description of the scenery is not all mine, Mother is helping me to write all my letters.

She has been downstairs for two days and is so seasick. I have not been seasick again, but feel my stomach give a heave up every now and again.

We were sorry Mother could not go to the concert we had on deck one night. I stood on a chair and sang "Bonny Dundee", and "Hearts

Bowen Jetty, circa 1900. Although Jane describes Bowen Harbour as a "beautiful natural harbour", it is not very deep and the long jetty visible in the background was essential for loading and unloading cargo ships.

of Oak". Father stood near my chair dressed in his kilts, and I wore my very best Sunday white dress with a plaid sash. Father says that it would never do for me to wear kilts, as I have tent pole legs.

Mother said what a pity I did not sing a hymn, as she is tired of the rigmarole Scotch songs, and that she was thankful father cannot play the bagpipes.

I heard him call her a lowlander the other day and when I asked her what he meant, she said it was because she was born in Ayrshire. I often hear him call her "cutty sark", which I think must be a swear-word in Scotch, because she always cries. I have since learnt that it means a woman in a short shirt.

When I sang the two songs the people threw money on the deck near my chair, a steward picked it up and the captain handed it to me. When I gave it to Mother, she said, "It will go into your money box, it is the first start of gathering gold." I could not see any gold amongst it, as it was two shillings, one shillings and sixpences.

Our next call was Bowen, a most picturesque small town sloping back from the silver sands of the Pacific Ocean. The main streets start off from the water's edge. It has a beautiful natural harbour and lies well within the shelter of the Barrier Reef.

Leaving this small, almost asleep town behind, we passed through several passages in and around many islands and came to one in particular called Hinchenbrook I think. The island looked as if our forefathers had built fortifications there to guard the wonderful architecture of their castles, built in ages past on the steep cliffs against an invading enemy.

The glorious tropical sunsets were each day becoming more dazzling with their vivid colourings of mostly gold and purple. At times the sinking sun, hidden behind a dark cloud edged with silver, would sprinkle the horizon with gold dust, which Mother says makes her feel that our dream of gold was all too true.

Our next call was Townsville and here too our vessel lay well out under the shelter of the islands. The mails, passengers and perishable foodstuffs were taken ashore by small steamers, which returned a couple of hours later laden with a fresh consignment of human lives and mails. Lighters lay alongside our boat to receive the heavy cargo due for that port and the towns inland from Townsville.

Mother says that the noise from the bulwarks, the running about on the deck above our heads, the call of the tally clerks checking off the cargo, and the placing of new passengers into their respective compartments gives us all nightmares.

Before reaching Cairns the islands of the Reef became more dense

Atherton Township, Joss House, circa 1908. These temples were to be found in a great many country towns throughout North Queensland. After the mining boom collapsed, many of the immigrant Chinese miners remained in North Queensland and turned to market gardening and to running small businesses. The Joss House, a familiar sight in the back streets of each country town, served as a focus for the Chinese community.

with tropical growth of wild bananas, tree ferns, palms, tassel ferns, staghorns, elkhorns, orchids and many other beautiful varieties of plant life. Birds could be seen on some of the larger islands. It was their nesting time; here they felt safe to rear their little ones, far away from the reach of man.

Cairns was a small ordinary town, built on low-lying country; so low that the incoming tide from the ocean would leave pools of salt water in many places in the main street.

In daylight the town appeared a dirty, muddy place and was occupied by a good percentage of Chinese, who, when praying to their idols, burnt Joss sticks and smoked opium, the fumes from which clung constantly to the low-lying town. We had to hold our noses while inspecting the town.

At night the scene changed, as we imagined, to the home of Santy Claus — caused by the myriads of fireflies clinging to the branches of the mangrove bushes and illuminating the beach as far as the eye could see.

Cooktown was our next call. It is a charming little town of great natural beauty, built almost at the mouth of the Endeavour River and hidden away from the rough winds of the Pacific Ocean by Grassy Hill and Mount Cook — called after Captain Cook.

There is a monument erected in the main street in memory of Mrs Watson, who to get away from the wild tribes of aboriginals, put off to sea in a ship's tank from the island on which she lived — while her husband was away — with her baby of a few months and their china-man cook. The tank was picked up with a note lying beside their dead bodies, telling the tale of her last hope of escape.

Well, dear, I shall stop now for fear you might be bored with this long letter.

Love from,

JANE BARDSLEY

My Dear Althea,

I must start again for to me everything is so wonderful; we feel so happy, as everything points to our being rich soon.

Winding in and out the Reef islands we went through Albany Pass; so near did the land appear on both sides, one could imagine that by stretching out the hands, coloured leaves could be plucked from the tropical undergrowth. The peaceful looking station home Summerset, belonging to the old pioneer family Jardines, was next sighted on the mainland of Queensland. Black forms could be seen walking along the beach, which we learnt were Australian aborig-inals. The first blacks we had seen. Looking at the homestead we saw that quite a number of houses seemed to be amongst huge trees, and that all were built low on the ground, about one hundred yards off a white sandy beach.

Thursday Island was next sighted from our boat, which was anchored one mile off Cape York, the northern end of Queensland. Here many dark forms could be seen again. They were mostly New Guinea natives, dressed solely in very full grass skirts.

It was a pretty sight to watch the numerous little pearling boats pass out of sight. The natives on them, dressed in white skirts, red cummerbunds and little red caps to match, stood about as the boats sailed along, their white sails full of wind. Dozens of small boats came alongside ours, with coloured men all gibber-jabbering in their own language to each other, but not one of them came on board.

Small steamers took the passengers to the wharf on the island where the cargo was put into the lighters. After six hours of a most interesting voyage we entered the rough sea of the Gulf of Carpentaria. It took four long, weary days of seasickness before we sighted the first land in the form of a lighthouse at Karumba, the seaport for the Normanton and Croydon goldfields.

At Karumba we had to wait twenty-two hours; at this port the tide is every twenty-four hours, so if you were unlucky you missed it. We had to put up with mosquitoes and sandflies by the millions and look upon the sightless sea of the muddy Gulf waters.

After transhipping into a small steamer which carried all the perishables, we crossed the bar of sand at the mouth of the Norman River and started off on the long journey of sixty miles along low banks of mangrove and mud.

The dense mangroves, lapping the water to the beat of the waves made by our intruding steamer, awakened a huge crocodile about twenty-seven feet in length, who after eating his early breakfast was sunbasking on the mud banks. We saw him glide most gracefully into the river without making a ripple in the water.

The captain of the little steamer told us he had seen two white men, half-intoxicated, jump into the river for a wager and within a minute one of the men had the flesh torn from his back and died within an hour. Also, he had seen a horse with the whole of its jaw bitten off by a crocodile.

I am frightened already although Father tells us we are safe if we keep away from the water's edge. This will be hard to do as Jim and I have always paddled in the creek at the back of our Clermont home.

Mother is not very happy, she has started crying again. It is not the fear of the crocodiles as she had been doing it before she had heard what they can do.

Goodbye,

with love from,

JANE BARDSLEY

My Dear,

I am glad you are interested in our travels and experiences while you are on your holidays. I hope you will come to the Gulf just to see how the other towns live.

We reached the Margaret and Jane Wharf, two miles from Normanton, where most of the heavy cargo was unloaded as the tide was too low to reach the Normanton Wharf. Although two miles distant we could see the wharf, as the whole aspect was a claypan without one sign of vegetation.

It was midday when we arrived at the wharf, one of the Gulf days when the earth sent out rays of heat in a blaze of fire almost visible to the naked eye, with a dry temperature of one hundred and twenty in the shade.

The town, a half mile distant, was enveloped in a yellow mist of dust from the rolling of the bullock waggons, laden with timber merchandise, hogsheads of beer and cases of spirits for the goldfields, eighty miles distant.

The noise of the bullock drivers shouting and cussing at their weary-hearted animals, the cracking of whips, the groaning of waggon wheels, the tinkling of bells on spare horses, the barking of dogs following their masters and the caw-caw of hundreds and hundreds of black crows made Mother say we might be entering hell to gather the gold.

I feel too awful, and shall ask God to protect us tonight when I say my prayers.

This is only a short letter as we could only get the one room for Mother, Jim and me. Poor Father, I do not know where he is going to sleep. Mother says he will sleep well if he gets some of the Scotch whisky our boat brought to town.

Good night,

with love,

JANE BARDSLEY

My Dear,

Here I am with nothing else but woes. I forgot to tell you that during our voyage up from Rockhampton we met two most charming men. Father, whom you know was an old soldier of the Black Watch, has plenty in common with anything Scotch. Mr Davis and his son were truly Scotch and had only been in Australia a few months, hence a wonderful friendship sprang up.

The son had obtained a position as engineer on one of the river boats and the father was waiting his time to get a suitable position in Normanton.

Normanton is a busy centre with its six banks, fourteen hotels, a dozen stores, several commission and forwarding agents, three churches and a fair sprinkling of Government private houses, besides numberless calico houses and tents. The calico houses are made very comfortable by dividing them into rooms with gay cretonnes and using curtains for the doors. It took the inferiority complex from Jim and me when we found that other nice children lived in the same style of house.

Mr Davis, who lived in one of these homes, near the river, about a mile from us, walked up each evening to have a game of cards and to talk Scotland with Father.

Near his home was an ordinary tent in which two very respectable men were camped awaiting their seats in the twice-weekly coach to Croydon. This was the only transport apart from the ride on a bullock waggon or walk and carry your swag.

While they were reading their home mail one evening about eight o'clock, well tucked under their cheesecloth mosquito net, an alien entered their tent, the worse for liquor, and stabbed them both to death. Hearing their cries for help, and not knowing the ways of the aliens — who are very numerous in this town, employed mostly in hotels as cooks — our poor friend took his lantern in his hand and was found stabbed to death at the opening of the young men's tent.[6]

Oh dear! it was awful when I went to school the next day to hear the children talking about the murder, but when I found it was our only true Gulf friend, sobs burst from me and I ran wildly through the school gates. I already knew that Father had gone off to work and that Jim had got a position for a few weeks in Wilton Wood's Solicitor's office. Mother had heard the news and caught me in her arms to try to stop the tears and at last had to put me to bed, as I could not stop the big sobs coming.

The town of heat and noise now became a living hell. The white men took the law into their own hands. When night came shots from guns and rifles would rend the air. Poor Mother was distracted and held Jim and me in her arms, praying all the while for God to protect us, and to bring Father back, for he was one of the leaders out to avenge the death of his Scotch friend.

[6] See full account on p. 229.

Bachelors' Quarters, Normanton, 1885. This was presumably some kind of boarding house. It is groups of men such as are shown here who would have felt most threatened by the Chinese immigrant miners and it would have been from their ranks that many of the rioters were drawn.

Wharves on the Norman River, Normanton, circa 1898. For a few years, Normanton was a prosperous port supporting the exchange of goods and produce brought into and taken out of the district by ship. In 1888 many of the smaller boats, often used for fishing, were owned by Chinese and it was these that formed one of the targets for the rioters on the night of 15 June 1888.

Anyone with a tint of colour, apart from Chinese and aboriginals, when found was caught and put into the *Rapido*, which was stranded in midstream in the Norman River. At night when they were still hunting for the aliens, screams and yells from their wives and children were heard plainly from where we lived. Houses and tents were pulled down to catch the fleeing yellow man and some even set on fire.

Mother became so ill with fear that it was necessay to move her to a home that was much further away from the noise and shouting.

Stations for miles around the town were visited, and if their cooks resembled anything alien they would be driven as animals along the roads at a fair pace, to enter the *Rapido* with their mates, who were just cooped up like rats, waiting for the vessel to take them to Thursday Island, or so we supposed.

Goodnight dear, we wish we had never left our peaceful home.

JANE BARDSLEY

ACROSS THE YEARS

P.S.   Well, my parents have decided to send me down south to boarding school. I do not like leaving Mother, she seems to be so unhappy and cries at night when Father is away. I think she is delicate for the want of fruit and vegetables, as most of our meals in our other home were full and plenty, and we had such lovely milk three times a day too. Here, we use tinned milk and butter so salty that it has to be washed and washed to make it palatable. We never see fruit, Mother says they are only for the wealthy miners, but on Saturdays we get a shilling each to buy pressed dates which are four shillings a pound — to take the place of the fruit — to keep us in good health.

Both Father and Mother say that Jim, being a boy, can stand this awful life, but I must stay away until I am grown up. That will be a long time, as I am not quite twelve years of age yet.

J.B.

Schooldays
1889 to 1894

My Dear,

I have been at school[7] three years now and have never been home. Sometimes I wonder if I shall know Father and Mother. I saw Jim on his way to the Ipswich Grammar School. Father said the life in the Gulf would ruin a young boy's character, so packed him off, too. Do you remember how he dreamed of having a proper cricket set? It has come true, and I still hope to see him make a name for himself. He is the best cricketer at the school and hopes to win the bat this year.

I shall not be able to write many times, as we have to study hard to pass the Junior examination. So please dear, do not forget me, for when I leave school I shall write to you often.

Goodnight,

Your loving friend,

JANE BARDSLEY

P.S. I feel ashamed of this small letter, we never leave the grounds except on Sundays. I have never spoken to a man other than a priest and Jim.

When Jim came to see me I was not alone, as a nun sat reading in the room all the time. He says that I shall be lucky if I see him again, until we meet when I leave school.

J.B.

My Dear,

I forgot to tell you that Jim won the bat at school.[8] All my school are pleased because I am his sister and they all want to meet him, but there is no chance after his last visit, he was afraid of the nuns.

We went to Tenterfield to spend our Christmas holidays.[9] Jim was very proud of his bat and looked after it so much that I could have flung it out of the window.

[7] See full account on pp. 229–30.

[8] James William Bardsley (b. 18 June 1875, d. 23 April 1942) attended the Ipswich Grammar School between 5 October 1891 and 23 June 1893.

[9] This should be Christmas 1892, since Jim had left school by June 1893.

When we were returning to school the excise officer at Wallangarra railway station took possession of it, and would not release it until we paid the duty. Almost in tears, I tried to explain to the officer, who said we were trying to get away with it. Then a gentleman stepped forward and said "I saw this boy win it at the Ipswich School". We heard afterwards that he was the Member for that town. You may guess we were pleased as our pocket money was not very much.

Tenterfield was the place for fruit. We both got colic from eating too much. We wished Mother was there for them so she would soon get well.

This is a short letter, I really have no news, so I shall close,

Your loving friend,

JANE BARDSLEY

My Dear,

You will think me dreadful for not writing, but somehow I never seem to think of any letters but the weekly ones to Mother. There was studying for the Junior,[10] in which I failed, but the nuns wrote to Mother saying I suffer from stage fright and will never do well in examinations. Then there was music, singing, violin, drawing and painting and last but not least my weekly mending — which I did hate. You will be glad to know that I am grown up, and only have three more months to reach eighteen.

I did feel important when I was placed on board the boat by the old maid who looks after the girls and who never even looks across the road if it is a man passing by. She takes us girls to the dentist and keeps a strict eye on us so that we cannot look across the road.

Oh! I nearly forgot to tell you that when I went to All Saints Church every Sunday there was a nice choir man who used to look under his eyelids at me while he was praying, and of course it would have been rude if I had not looked back at him.

I could not have told you about this before, as all our letters were read by the nuns. If they found that I was making eyes in church I really do not know what would have happened, as I could not have

[10] This may have been at the end of 1891, or, more probably, 1892. Unfortunately, the Queensland Department of Public Instruction did not maintain records of candidates for the Junior Public Examination who presented from Catholic schools.

missed church.

After the strict old maid put me in the charge of a Mr and Mrs Catt, who lived in Normanton — Mr Catt works in the Burns Philp office — she left me saying "now be a very good girl till you get home".

You can never imagine how everything has altered. Rockhampton has a railway to a landing which is called Port Alma, from where all passengers, mails and cargoes are railed through most interesting country before reaching Rockhampton.

Flat Top has still the old flat top; mails, cargo and humans are thrown over the side in just the same old way.

Townsville, to accommodate the goldrush from Charters Towers and Ravenswood, has grown out of all recognition and is now a busy

All Hallows Convent, Brisbane, 1899. Established in 1863 by the Sisters of Mercy, the convent originally stood in Ann Street, Brisbane. The graceful building shown here was erected at Kangaroo Point overlooking the Brisbane River in 1881–1882 to the design of Andrea Strombucco, an Italian architect who was specially chosen for this job. A north wing was added in 1892, and both wings survive today, albeit overshadowed by rather less attractive neighbouring brick buildings. Jane, who studied here from 1889 to 1894, must have witnessed the construction of the north wing although she does not mention it in her letters.

commercial town. In order to have a harbour there they have spent thousands upon thousands building a breakwater, wharves and jetties.

Cairns has also grown considerably, from a dirty town — or so I thought — to a picturesque seaport of good size. I almost forgot to mention Bowen. Well, it is the same beautiful town, but to me it seems to be lying asleep.

Back in Normanton — Mother no longer cries — there is no busy town now, it is only a village which derives its livelihood from station folk, boiling-down meatworks and employees, and a few drovers.

The railway to Croydon has been opened. It took years to complete as the white ants would eat the wooden sleepers almost as quickly as they were laid down. The Philp Government[11] put down steel rails to cheat the white ants and bring Normanton down to where it is.

I cannot write any more today, but hope to have plenty to tell you in my next letter.

Love from,

JANE

My Dear,

I am absolutely shocked to death, I feel so grown up with embarrassment too. The native blacks are allowed into the town during the day to work for the white population for which they receive either old clothes or scraps of food.

I have nothing to do — we have black labour for all jobs — but practise music and singing, which gathers the natives from near and far. They think when I do singing exercises I am a Devil-devil. I enjoy them so much, I sing them until I am winded and Mother calls out "we have had enough for one day".

Oh! it is funny to see an old gin, fat and with a big stomach, dressed up in a discarded blouse and skirt. The bodice is well gored as it is made to fit size nineteen. I had to give one of my dresses away for

---

[11] Sir Robert Philp (1851–1922) was the M.L.A. for Townsville from 1886. As Secretary for Mines (from 1893) and Treasurer (from 1898) he achieved notoriety for the large sums he spent on railway construction. However, Jane is being anachronistic in referring to the Philp Government in 1894 — Philp did not become Premier until 1899 and was not yet a Minister at the end of 1894 when Jane was returning home from school.

which I am thankful. In fact I wish I could give all of them away, you have no idea how long I have to hold my breath to get into them. There is no need for me to practise deep breathing.

The black children under a certain age — usually eight or nine years — are allowed to walk the streets in the nude. At first I would feel my cheeks burn with shame and quickly look the other way, but now I am sophisticated and do not even shut an eye.

After reaching the age of nine, the children are supplied with clothing by the police — men's shirts for the big girls. These are never tried on but simply given, so at times one sees a little object with a shirt reaching to her ankles, at the back, while the front is just a nice length. Sometimes an overgrown child will have the tail of the shirt at the back of the knees and the front well up the thighs.

The boys get a strong pair of moleskin pants and a shirt from the Government. The poor little Mary-mary remains in the shirt until the white women get ashamed and take pity on them and give them old dresses.

There are quite a lot of different children in the blacks' camp now, and the abos are allowed to run in the town. There is a family of three who live up the hill with a white family, a Mr and Mrs Toby Walsh. Their mother is a full-blooded gin. They are known by the surname, Poindestre. Whether the gin mother was fascinated by the name or admired the handsome Government officer who patrolled the natives — dressed in spotless white moleskin pants, white shirt and red cummerbund — and who was no ordinary policeman but came from some special stock, she only knew.

The children were educated at the Normanton State School. The two boys got positions in the local post office. They were handsome lads, more white than black, and bore no features of the gin mother.

They both died from some awful epidemic in our town, and many others have gone, especially the poor niggers, who had not any attention except to lie by their campfires to keep warm.

The only girl, Bessie Poindestre, was very like the mother but of course half white. She married a snowy-haired white man, who was in charge of the lighthouse island in the Gulf of Carpentaria. Although well away from the reaches of the aboriginals, strange to say after they had lived on the island for twelve months Bessie's first baby was born jet black. Snowy was very disgusted and looked down on his wife for making such a mistake. I did hear he deserted her and went back to Germany.

I am lucky to be here as I have been very ill. That is one of the reasons I have taken so long to answer your letter. You did not take as

Aboriginal boys waiting at the ferry-house, Normanton, circa 1885.

long as usual to write; perhaps you are enjoying the different letters I am writing.

Oh dear! I am not as comfortable as I was at school, we were not allowed to wear corsets, but now I have to squeeze into number nineteen waist, when I really think by the agony I suffer I should wear size one yard. I am not at all slim, my weight is eight stone two and height five feet one, so you know that the fat has to go to some other part of the body when I get my waist to number nineteen. My fat seems to shoot up to my neck, I can easily rest my chin on it. I think it is much better to be round the neck than the stomach, don't you think so? Tell me if you are fat, and where does your fat go, up or down.

I shall now end,

With love from,

JANE

P.S. I hope you will not think me rude about the fat. You might be naturally size nineteen and so would not understand what I mean.

Aboriginal women waiting at the ferry-wharf, Normanton, circa 1885.

My Dear,

I have a wonderful secret to tell you, I have never breathed a word of it, not even to Mother, but I made a promise to a man on the boat coming home. I could just hear Mother saying "nonsense child, you are far too young for marriage", so I told my sweetheart if he even looks at me when my people are in sight it will be all off. I am so

afraid of Mother. Perhaps if I had seen more of her while I was growing up I should not have been deceitful.

However my fiancé insists that I shall wear his ring, so I have given him permission to ask Mother as Father has gone to Croydon to seek gold. He has made several attempts to ask, but comes back each time saying, "I'm blowed if I'm game to face her. She will look over her glasses and I can see her asking me what my business is."

SCHOOLDAYS

I met Tom Atherton at Flat Top, Mackay, when I was returning from school. He had been visiting his parents at Cliftonville station in Mackay, and was going back to their station — Midlothian — in the Gulf of Carpentaria.

This is a short letter — I am engaged — I seem to have lost my head. There are so many men looking for wives, and girls are so few, that I could have been married over and over again. One proposal happened like this. On Christmas morning a young man called to see me. He threw me a tin pannikin and merely said, "This is for you." When I caught it and looked inside there was a six-diamond gold ring wrapped up in a piece of newspaper. When I said I would not be allowed to take it, he looked sad and remarked, "I mean it for an engagement ring." This was cold-blooded for he never asked if I loved him.

I hope I have chosen wisely. Mother seems to damp my feelings by saying "Tom is a harum-scarum", but luckily adds, "that sort of man usually makes a good husband". I do not suppose I shall be able to write again until we are married a while.

Mother says I shall have to make all my undies and goodness knows what they will be like as I do not know one garment pattern from another. Jim says he is fairly good at putting puzzles together and has offered to give me a hand.

Love from your excited,

JANE BARDSLEY

P.S. This will be the last time I shall sign my nice old English name to you. I have always liked the little bit of English about me — I get so tired of Father and his Robbie Burns poems.

I almost forgot to tell you I met the man who made eyes in church. I went to the post office to post a letter to Tom and who should be there but he. I felt very guilty and ashamed, but recovered myself when he said, "I had no idea you lived so far away." I then said, "What are you doing up here?" He told me that he was going to Croydon to open a business as a lawyer, and that he would like to come down to Normanton to see more of me. I said, "Well there is no sense in that as I am to be married in a week's time."

I did not see him again as he got some high up Government position in New Guinea and died shortly afterwards.

First Year at Midlothian Station
1896

My Dear,

We were married just a year after I had left school.[12] Our wedding, which to me was wonderful, took place in the little Church of England. It was crowded to overflowing with station folk, business people and women and children, all wanting to see the girl bride who was going out amongst the natives, to strange country and doings so different to boarding school life, and the man who was game enough to take her.

I had a very pretty white, China silk dress with a long tulle veil and orange blossoms grown on the trees at Midlothian, my future home. Mr Amsden, the manager of Burns, Philp & Co., lent his drag and six white horses to take me to the church. The horses had white rosettes on their winkers and one of the bridal party held a white umbrella over my head while we drove to the church. Strange to say, I was not the least bit nervous but felt like a queen in fairyland. Tom was the nervous one, he actually turned round from the altar and said good day to some of his friends, and after the ceremony he got into the buggy on the wrong side.

I went up to the altar not realising whether I was in love or out, but after the marriage service, when we marched down the aisle to the strains of the *Wedding March* — played by the police magistrate's daughter Miss G. Zillman — I really knew I was truly in love.

Jim gave me away as Father was not at home. My bridesmaid was Miss Jean Currie, with whom I had gone to school for years and who was living with her aunt on Devoncourt station in the Cloncurry district. The best man was Reg (Paddy) Jones, accountant in the Joint Stock Bank. After the wedding came the breakfast. This was absolutely marvellous. The cake was a dream — Mother had it made in Brisbane — and there were plenty of sparkling wines and such a lot of other delicacies which I cannot enumerate for excitement. My dear, it looked like the table of a princess. All the menfolk were very gay —

[12] On 4 December 1895, in St Peter's Anglican Church, Normanton. Formal consent to the under-age marriage was given by Jane's mother, her father having deserted them by this time.

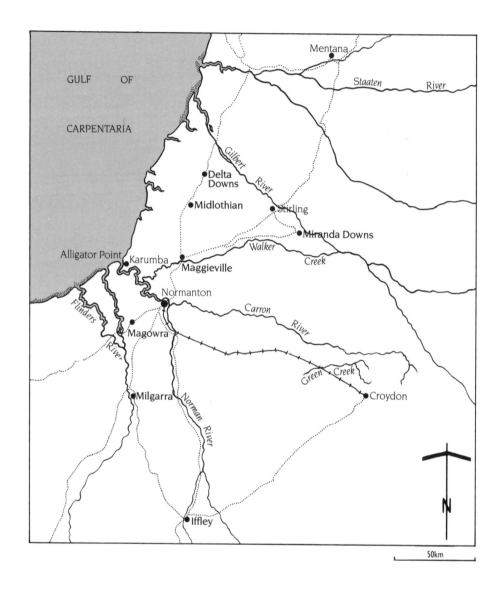

*Map of the Normanton district showing most of the Gulf Country
stations mentioned in Jane Bardsley's letters. The dotted lines indicate
modern roads but they appear likely to correspond to the original tracks
opened up by the settlers. The Normanton-Croydon railway line is also
shown. The area covered by this map is indicated on the general map
of Queensland shown on p. xiii.*

you can imagine this as, as I have told you, we had plenty of wine —
and as Tom was very popular they were all anxious to wish us
Godspeed.

We left in our little Abbott buggy for the punt which was to carry
us across the Norman River. Most of the employees of Burns, Philp &
Co. were in the street to wave us farewell. Some from the Customs
House office were there also to wish us good luck. The flag was flying
high from the Customs House.

When we arrived at the punt there were thirty or more of our
friends at the water's edge to wish us good luck. The first piece of
good luck was Tom's discovery, after the punt had moved out from
the land, that he had forgotten his pipe. Then there was an uproar
with everyone calling out, "Here's my pipe, don't turn back, it's bad
luck." I do not know how many pipes were thrown but Tom seemed
to have plenty to smoke for months. Some were almost new, while
others smelt of years and years of use.

With young fresh horses in our buggy, we simply flew over the first
twelve miles of almost level claypans and arrived at a waterhole,
where Homer our black boy was waiting with the pack and spare
buggy horses.

Our heated horses were quickly taken out of the buggy to have a
drink and a swim which is the customary thing to do in the Gulf,
where all horses suffer from a fever called the Puffs after being
worked a few hours in the heat.

Tom, with the aid of a blackfellow, caught the next pair of horses
for our buggy. I am sure they were praying all the while they were
trying to catch them from the gentle coaxing and whispers of "whoa,
whoa, you beauties", that I could hear. At last they were caught and
harnessed and gently put into the buggy. Not a murmur or a whisper
was allowed. The black boy held their heads, while I made a running
leap into the buggy. Tom, with the reins held firmly in his hands
called out "let go", and away we did go, at a full gallop. Now and
again I thought the horses would pull out of their collars, and then
again they would come back and almost sit on the swingle bars.

I closed my eyes and held my breath several times, and grabbed
the side of the buggy, thinking "Oh God, when is the end coming and
what a nice start for a honeymoon."

Tom was not in the least perturbed, but simply sat there with a
half-smile on his face. Looking at my rigid body, he quietly said,
"There is nothing to be frightened about dear, while I hold the
reins."

Maggieville was our first station call, the first I had ever seen.

There were black boys, gins, dogs, and piccaninnies everywhere. The gins wore men's shirts and the children were in the nude.

The bank had just taken over this property from Brodie and Haydon, two well-known pioneers from southern Queensland. The bank's inspector was giving an inventory and installing their new manager, a Mr Hetherington. The previous manager was also there and he looked like a grizzly bear; his whiskers and hair and bushy eyebrows all seemed to meet. He had a little Mary-mary piccaninny about two years old following him about who, although as black as the ace of spades, called him "Dadda".

A fat bullock had been killed the night before for the station meat supply. The chinaman cook knowing we were coming for dinner, had a huge roast, half a dozen vegetables — all grown on the place — and several puddings ready. Old Ross, the late manager, took the little piccaninny on his knee at the meal table and kept feeding her all the time.

Either from fear of the next pair of horses I could see being lassoed in the yard or the strangeness of it all, I could hardly swallow a morsel of food. Tom tried to persuade me to eat more saying we still had a long way to go. Oh dear, I did feel so shy amongst such a lot of men. To tell you the truth, I felt more like crying than eating and was ready to run back home.

All hands were out to see us start off. This time the horses' heads were held by two black boys who, at the words "let go", set free the

St Peter's Church of England, Normanton. In this church, Jane Bardsley and Tom Atherton were married on 4 December 1895.

ACROSS THE YEARS

horses and jumped clear of the buggy wheels. A boy had been sent ahead to open the station gates, and we went through at a gallop, just missing the gatepost with the buggy wheel by a couple of inches.

By this time I was limp with fear. When Tom said again "you are all right while I hold the reins", I wondered if there was a possibility of him letting the reins go, and I was quite ready to jump out and bolt home to Mother and away from the lonely bush.

Fifteen miles on we changed horses, and again the same performance went on. I could not hide my tears, but was thankful when Tom assured me that this pair of horses, after they settled down, could beat anything in the district. In my opinion they never settled down, at least not until I saw my future home in the distance. I began to think I would never get back to see Mother, as I certainly could not go through what I had experienced again.

The homestead, on the edge of a sun-dried plain — which I had seen first from a distance of one and a half miles — looked as if it was in harmony with the burning sun. There were hundreds of galah parrots, with their grey backs and rose-pink breasts, together with white corellas and cockatoos screeching and screaming their nesting calls, and casting another shadow of loneliness over my distracted mind. I was afraid and seemed so helpless in the midst of all this confusion.

I shall say goodnight,

with love from,

JANE ATHERTON

P.S. I cannot tell you yet if I like my new name as well as the one I left behind.

J.A.

My Dear,

I shall continue with the story of my arrival. Alighting from the buggy we entered the garden which is about one and a quarter acres. It is surrounded by five-inch diameter logs, standing five feet high.

The garden paths, which were swept clean every morning by the natives, were now a carpet of flaming red from the fallen flowers of five large poinciana trees out in full bloom. The fallen petals from the fragrant citrus tree blossoms looked like snow that had stolen in to cool the blaze of the red fire. The five-roomed house standing amidst this garden of Eden eased my frightened brain. I enclose a photo of my first home.

Midlothian Homestead, 1895. By the time Tom Atherton brought his bride to her new home in 1896, the house had been enlarged and a number of outbuildings erected.

Sim, the chinaman cook, had an afternoon tea ready — which was fit for the gods and enough for at least a dozen hungry people — set on a white sheet on the dining-room table. Tom said that he had tablecloths somewhere on the station but it was so long since he had used them that it might take hours to find them.

When Sim saw that we were not finishing the pies and tarts and a three-storied cake, which I suppose was meant for another wedding cake, he looked very hurt and remarked to me "what for you not eat plenty missus". I nearly looked round when he said missus; I thought he was talking to somebody else.

I seemed to be all in a daze when Tom whispered "eat, or we shall never see these cakes or tarts again". So we filled our pockets with what we thought enough to satisfy Sim's wishes and disappeared to throw them out of sight.

So far I had not seen a living soul, with the exception of Sim, who had a long pigtail and grass slippers which can be heard some distance going flip flop.

At times I fancied I could hear faint whisperings. My imagination proved to be correct for the whisperers made their appearance by looking round the corner of the dining room where I was sitting. Then they disappeared but after a few minutes ventured out again.

At last I became desperate and tried to catch them. When I managed to get near them I found they were two gins clad only in men's shirts.

Kitty, a tall gin of five feet seven inches and about twenty-five years of age, wore a shirt much too small for her. She came from the Cape York Peninsula and could only speak and understand a few words of English. She had a bright clear face and was inclined to be friendly at a distance. Annie on the other hand, a child of thirteen, was not nearly so pleasant. She had a sneaky expression and when I tried to catch her hand she yelled "what for white Mary" and ran away. She speaks and understands more than Kitty can and came from one of our neighbouring stations. Oh dear! I am afraid of her, although she is such a tiny mite, she has a face like a monkey.

After our long hot drive I felt I would like a bath so Tom beckoned to the gins and said this: "You two fellow fill up tub longa Mrs he (*sic.*) wantim bogey longa little fellow room (bathroom with slab walls and plenty of cracks) you hurry up you two black crows."

During my bath I fancied I could see eyes looking at me in the semi-darkness and I could hear muffled laughter. I felt frightened and hurried out and almost bolted to my bedroom to get ready for supper. When I opened the door I nearly dropped dead with fright — my nerves were so unstrung from the trying day — to find the two gins holding something at arm's length towards me. It looked like a dirty bundle of twine but I found out that it was a dillybag made from coloured wool. By spitting on the right hand, in which the wool is held, and rubbing it on the right thigh, it loses its colour and turns into a dirty black twine, from which the gins work in a mesh stitch to make these bags. They are used to keep onions fresh.

Oh dear, I was shocked when Annie, looking into my face and laughing, said, "When you been bogey me and Kitty look longa crack, you white Mary alright."

Our house has only iron walls and windows set very high, presumably to stop the niggers peeping in. Tom has furnished it very well. There is a nice suite of furniture in my bedroom; the sitting room has cane chairs, small tables and linoleum on the floor; the dining room has chairs, table and a sideboard, and the two spare rooms have beds and home-made furniture. Sim is a cabinetmaker as well as a cook.

I have had a busy day and shall be off to bed as soon as night sets in.

Love from

JANE ATHERTON

FIRST YEAR AT MIDLOTHIAN STATION

My Dear Althea,

The following morning I was awakened at six by the roar of a bullock bell being sounded by Sim for breakfast. I knew Tom had left the room as he had to fix drovers up with horses very early. Opening my eyes I saw the two gins standing at my door, looking spotlessly clean for they had had their early morning bath. They still wore men's shirts for dresses and their heads of matted curls were dripping with water.

Annie said, "Poor white Mary, you wantim nother bogey." I suppose they wanted to have another look at me. I could not stir. Every part of my body except my head ached from that dreadful drive, and my muscles were strained from clinging onto the buggy. Even my jaws were sore from clenching my teeth and at that moment I felt I hated everything on the place, and almost snarled at the gins to go away. I then took pity on the poor souls and tried to explain to them I was sick and had to stay in bed.

Tom had told Sim to send my breakfast to my room as he would be late. A tray arrived, carried by Kitty, loaded with three mince rissoles with a poached egg on top, a huge plate of curry and rice, hot scones and home-made bread and jam. Annie followed behind with a teapot, holding easily a gallon of tea, while Sim called from the verandah, "You eat him all up, it make you better, no good you sick."

The two gins stood near while I ate only a hot scone and drank a cup of tea. Remembering Tom's words when we first sat down to our afternoon tea, "eat or we may not see this again", I said to the gins, "You eat him all up." They did this in a few seconds and walked back to hand the empty tray — with an air of satisfaction — to Sim, who had given them a junk of salt beef and a pot of highly sweetened milkless tea for their breakfast.

We were expecting the Delta station manager to call for lunch. Tom said to me that it looked bad to be ill. He had a very hot bath ready for me, to ease my aching muscles, and he gave me a good rub-down with whisky as we had no methylated spirits.

Oh dear! I was shocked when I saw my white face in the looking glass and was glad when Tom left the room so that I could give my cheeks a rub with whisky to give them a bloom before I ventured forth.

I do not know that I enjoyed our visitor for he talked of nothing but fats and spayed cows. I wondered what he meant because he looked so shy whenever I spoke. When I found out from Tom what all his conversation was about I said, "He is a rude dirty man."

ACROSS THE YEARS

I do not know yet whether I like Atherton as much as Bardsley, all is so different out here.

I shall have to make something for my gins to wear apart from the men's shirts. It is really too embarrassing as we get such heavy winds that at times I am afraid I might find them shirtless.

This afternoon I put on my very best undies and one of my pretty muslin dresses which I have not seen for three weeks. I sent my luggage out beforehand by the carriers for fear of thunderstorms coming and preventing the waggons getting through. If I had not

Esther Atherton, née Ainscough. Esther was born in Lancashire in 1804 and married Edmund Atherton I in 1829 or early 1830. They came to Australia in 1844, settling first in Maitland, then in the Armidale district and finally at Mount Hedlow (originally spelled Hedloo) near Rockhampton in Queensland in 1860. She died there in 1889.

done this I would have had to wait five months — until the wet season was over — or run about in a man's shirt. We keep a stock in the storeroom.

When my lubras saw me they simply stared saying "budgeree", which means good. After they had walked round and round me several times, feeling the texture of my dress, to my amazement Kitty dropped on her knees and touched my pretty shoes. She traced the pattern of my black openwork stockings with her finger, and lifted the hem of my skirt and felt and admired my beautiful heavily starched petticoat with its frills and laces. She then came to another garment of which she made a thorough inspection. She called to

Henry Bell, husband of Alice Atherton (1834–1892). Henry Bell founded Plane Creek Station near Mackay in 1866.

The church at Mt Hedlow, near Rockhampton, circa 1870. The Atherton family settled at Mt Hedlow in 1860. From this church, Edmund Atherton I would have been buried following his death on 17 June 1863.

Annie, who had moved away a few paces, "By Chri! Missus got trousers on, you come look!"

I am sure I am going to like my new name and enjoy station life.

Love from,

JANE ATHERTON

My Dear,

It is a long time since your letter came but I have been trying to get my house in order, which I do not seem able to do. I am such a fool. One of the first things I did was to get a bundle of unbleached calico, with turkey twill for trimmings, and a simple pattern, to make dresses and underclothing suitable for my poor lubras.

Really I am sorry I ever started the dressmaking as I cannot get away from them and cannot get them to do any work for me as they are interested in every stitch I do. As it is all done by hand you can understand it is quite a business. Tom says that we shall buy a sewing machine when the times improve.

Since starting to sew I have already finished two dresses in princess style, trimmed with bands of turkey red — they love red — and two pairs of drawers, trimmed in the same way. The lubras are especially proud of these latter garments.

I had to bribe them to get their work done early by telling them they would get their dresses after dinner — one o'clock. So, won't there be plenty of excitement? I am longing to see them clothed in something other than men's shirts.

Later I gave them their dresses and as soon as I did so they raced off for their lives to the bathing hole to get clean before putting on their frocks. My dear, I can hardly write for laughing. These girls are screams. After their bogey they put on their clothes and came back to show me how they looked. They had forgotten to dry themselves and looked as though they had been through a heavy storm. You can imagine how funny they looked.

I have explained to them how to wash their drawers and to hang them on a barbed-wire fence, for we have no clothes pegs, and that they must not let white men see them on the line. You know dear, how our mothers would faint if we mentioned drawers in company, let alone see them flying high on a barbed-wire fence.

Every day brings some fresh amusement.

Love from,

JANE ATHERTON

FIRST YEAR AT MIDLOTHIAN STATION

Edmund Atherton II
(1839–1899). Born in
Lancashire, Edmund II came to
Australia with his parents in
1844 and trekked overland from
Armidale in New South Wales to
Mount Hedlow near
Rockhampton in Queensland in
1860. In 1865, he travelled
further north with his brother
Richard and his brother-in-law
Henry Bell to the Mackay
district, and, in 1866, founded
Cliftonville Station just north of
Mount Chelona. He died on 8
February 1899.

Richard Atherton (1847–1927).
Richard, the youngest son of
Edmund Atherton I and Esther
Ainscough, was the father of
Althea Cook, whose Christian
name seems to have been taken
by Jane for her fictitious
correspondent. When Edmund
Atherton II continued on to found
Cliftonville Station, Richard
remained behind to found Woonon
Station which was long known as
Atherton's Camp. It was this
property that Tom and Jane
Atherton bought in 1901; they
lived there from October 1901
until 1917 when they moved to
Pretty Bend near Bowen.

My Dear,

Some weeks have passed and I am still on the subject of hanging out the lubras' underclothing, for now they have each a chemise added to their wardrobe.

Kitty was not pleased with the place I had shown her to hang her drawers as she prefers to hang them where the wind has full play in filling out both legs. Judging by the number of times these articles are washed, I should say she likes seeing them on the line better than feeling them on her legs.

There is nothing left to do but eat, sleep and talk. The wet season has set in, so we shall not see town or a neighbouring station until the middle of April.

Tom is as good as any book with yarns of his grandfather and father, and his own pioneering days, and as there is nothing special just at present I shall write you something of their lives.

His grandfather was a Lancashire farmer and landowner and came out from England in 1844 with his wife and seven children, with the intention of settling in the then little-known continent Australia.[13]

The colony of New South Wales attracted his attention. They went first to Maitland where two other children were born: Ester, who afterwards became Mrs Haylock, and whose husband owned Sanomi in the Bowen district, and Richard.[14]

Wishing to acquire a larger run for their sheep and cattle, the grandparents and family moved into the New England district and took up land at Mount Pleasant, near Armidale. Later they acquired Bald Blair station further out.

In the mid-fifties James Atherton, the eldest son, came to Queensland and founded a sheep station called Rosewood on the Fitzroy River, in the Rockhampton district.

Queensland appealed to the grandfather and the other members of the family and so, in 1860, they left Armidale with all their possessions. They had three bullock waggons and one horse team.

[13] Edmund Atherton I, born 4 February 1804 at Blackrod near Wigan, Lancashire, married Esther Ainscough, who was born in the same village on 21 November 1806. They emigrated to New South Wales in the *Great Britain*, arriving in Sydney on 27 June 1844. He died at Mount Hedlow in Queensland on 17 June 1863.

[14] Richard Atherton (1847–1927), the youngest son of Edmund Atherton I and Esther Ainscough, was the father of Vida Althoea Atherton (known as Althea Atherton, later as Althea Cook, 1875–1955), perhaps the model used by Jane for her imaginary correspondent. Clearly, however, this passage was not written with Althea Atherton in mind since, in that case, it would surely have referred to Richard Atherton as "your father". In any case, the real Althea was married, whereas Jane's correspondent was a spinster.

The riders were in charge of two thousand head of shorthorn cattle.

A lovely big brolga strutted behind the waggons. He was too fond of grandma to stay with his own mates in New South Wales.

The journey through a country, practically without roads, and with all the disadvantages of the times, was a tremendous undertaking. It was, however, successfully accomplished in four months. They arrived at their destination and took up country in the Rockhampton district which they named Mount Hedlow, from the aboriginal word meaning mountain. The grandfather only lived two years after settling at Mount Hedlow, and then the whole family branched out.

John Atherton[15] took up Bomoyia and sold and delivered a mob of bullocks at the Palmer gold-diggings in 1870. So pleased was he with the north that he took up Cashmere and later Emerald End station, on which the town of Mareeba now stands.

Tom's father and Henry Bell — who married Tom's aunt, Alice — took up West Hill station in 1866, in the Mackay district. Here they were joined by Richard Atherton, who had been left at a boarding school in New South Wales.[16] Dissatisfied with the country around West Hill, they continued to blaze the trail along the coast towards the newly discovered Pioneer River, and the few tents and huts which comprised the new township of Mackay. As they rode along, the grass was so tall and thick they had to call out at times to keep trace of one another.

There were no other animals but the kangaroos and wallabies to keep the grass in check. Incidentally, I might mention that this was a wonderful covering for the wild blacks. Reaching a good creek with a nice open plain on the other side, the party decided to go to the nearest ridge to camp. Here they formed a station and shortly after arranged for each to take a run, as open untouched country was called in those days.

Henry Bell remained on at Plane Creek — as they named it. Edmund, Tom's father, went a few miles further north to the rocky Mount Chelona, and called his property Cliftonville.

Richard crossed the creek and took country between it and the sea, which through general usage became known as the Atherton Camp, then the Camp, and finally changed to Woonon.

[15] John Atherton (1837–1913), who was the second son of Edmund Atherton I and Esther Ainscough, gave his name to the Atherton Tablelands.

[16] Tom's father was Edmund Atherton II (1839–1899), the third son of Edmund Atherton I and Esther Ainscough. Alice Atherton (1837–1892) was his elder sister, and Richard Atherton (1847–1927) was his youngest brother.

Plane Creek Station, circa 1876. Founded in 1866 by Henry Bell.

I nearly forgot the pretty pieces about the forming of their places in the New England district. They brought from England a small pink monthly rose in a pot, and so far every Atherton in the family has a bush in his garden. The grandparents brought the weeping willows to Armidale and their sons planted slips in the creeks on the run, which, at the present time, make Armidale the picturesque town of New South Wales.

When Tom[17] left Brisbane Boys' Grammar School he accom-

[17] Thomas Arthur Atherton I, was born at Mount Hedlow in Queensland on 8 February 1866. He left school at seventeen and joined his father at Cliftonville in 1883.

FIRST YEAR AT MIDLOTHIAN STATION

panied his father on a search for fresh country as Cliftonville was overstocked, with fifteen thousand head of cattle.

A piece of country in the Gulf of Carpentaria attracted their attention. Leaving Mackay they travelled to Cairns by boat, purchased horses and a drover's outfit and crossed the main coastal range of Australia on to Tom's Uncle John's property, Emerald End.

They then followed a bridle track for ten miles through a dense scrub of lawyer-cane and stinging nettle, where majestic cedar trees stood like giants in the midst of the tangle. This place is now known as the Atherton Tablelands, after John Atherton of Emerald End.

They next reached Herberton, a small tin-mining settlement which received stores and sent out tin ore by packhorse, following the bridle track through the Atherton scrub. From here they passed through Chillagoe, another of John Atherton's properties. In after years this became a rich goldfield, and was called Chillagoe Township.

The small mining town of Georgetown was their next stop, then, about a hundred miles further on, Green Creek telegraph repeating station. After following a dry river for miles (the Carron River) they arrived at Normanton, only forty-five miles from their destination, on the York Peninsula. They had travelled nearly nine hundred miles to the tract of country they wished to inspect.

After they had made a good inspection they decided to purchase, and took up more adjoining land from the Government. They returned by boat to Mackay.

I had better stop writing all the dry stuff, but as you were a bush child I know you will not find it dull.

Love from,

JANE ATHERTON

My Dear Althea,

It is still raining. Our postman arrived in the middle of the night with six weeks' mail. So we have been reading all day and well into the night, and tomorrow we shall go through the advertisements in the papers and do all the puzzles. Even the children's page will give us pleasure, so dear, you can just imagine what life is like on a cattle station in the Gulf for nearly five months of the year. Of course it does

ACROSS THE YEARS

not rain all the time, but the country, being so low, becomes squashy and it is impossible to get a vehicle of any kind over the roads.

Our chinaman cook has gone and this morning we are short of a meal for our mailman who, when he comes late, gets his own breakfast and leaves before we have ours. This morning he finished up ten eggs, two loaves of bread and half the corned beef. You see he suffers from diabetes and has an enormous appetite. Luckily I have learnt to make scones cooked in fat, because otherwise we would have to wait until the oven is very hot, which is always an ordeal these muggy days.

All we do at present is sleep, eat and read so I shall continue with Tom's history.

In 1885, when Tom was nineteen years of age, his father started him with a mob of seventeen hundred cattle to stock the country they had acquired in the Gulf. He travelled with nine other white men, a team of bullocks, a waggon loaded with enough flour and medicine to last six months, and last but not least two aboriginal boys from Mackay called Charlie and Peter.

Everything pointed to a severe drought ahead of them. When they arrived at a little railway town called Pentlands — which was just a settlement with a couple of hotels, two stores, a butcher and a baker — pleura sickness broke out amongst the cattle, which caused great alarm. So they got a beast ready to be killed, in order to obtain the virus to inoculate the herd. They then found it was necessary to obtain agistment country as the drought had worsened, making it

Cliftonville Homestead, near Mackay. Founded in 1866 by Edmund Atherton II.

impossible to take their cattle further on.

They secured only sufficient ground to graze eight hundred head of cattle which they left in charge of two white men, while they journeyed on with the balance, about nine hundred, including the newly born calves, which made up for the pleura losses.

Lyndhurst was the first homestead they passed after leaving Pentlands. Here the drought had fixed the hand of horror on the plucky pioneers. The large waterholes, reduced to quagmires of sticky mud, were deathtraps to the hundreds of weak thirsty cattle who entered them in search of water, and remained bogged. They would then have to be shot by their owners and pulled to the top of the bank to be tombstones; reminders to the poor pioneers of the 1885 drought.

Here Tom met Frank Cobbald, manager of the Oaks station, near Carpentaria Downs station, and he advised him to follow the Einasleigh River to where the boiling springs are situated.

The track was rough and stony so their weary cattle were driven in short stages until they reached the next piece of agistment country they had secured.

I must describe the boiling springs. They are situated three miles off the banks of the Einasleigh River on a slight rise. The top spring, in the form of a well, has a temperature of boiling point. Tom cooked his meat, fish and potatoes by enclosing them in a handmade wire basket, and immersing it in the hot water until they were cooked.

I feel ashamed to tell you that we sleep so much, but all station people do the same for a few months while the rain is pelting down. Tom and the white stockman usually use this time for making all the hide ropes for branding and horse breaking, but by the look of things I am a bit in the way this year, so the poor stockman will have to do most of the work on his own.

I shall have to stop now,

With love from,

JANE

Dear Althea,

Another day has come and I shall have to write without receiving any letter from you. By the time the wet season is over you will have almost a book as there seems to be no end to Tom's experiences. He is talking about the aboriginals now and I am frightened for fear of what I may have to go through in the future.

While he was camped on the Einasleigh he could see fresh abo tracks around the hot springs where they too cooked their victuals. The tracks were there in hundreds, yet Tom did not see a sign of a darkie other than the footprints.

The water from the springs overflowed and after running some distance lost its mineral flavour and became soft and palatable.

The police patrol visited him twice during the six months he was camped there. His father went back to Mackay after a short stay and left him in full charge of the cattle and men in the midst of the fearful drought.

Two men travellers pitched their tent about six miles up the Einasleigh River. It was dusk when they lit their fire to boil the billy for tea. They had spread out their evening meal and taken off their boots to rest their weary aching feet — as they had walked many miles over very rough country — when suddenly they heard a noise which they supposed to be wild blacks. They were certain they could see a huge nigger armed with a spear coming towards them. They grabbed their rifles, fired several shots at him, and set off running towards Georgetown, thirty miles distant, bare-footed. They arrived in a state of nervous collapse, their feet torn and bleeding from running madly through rough mountainous country.

The patrol came to the camp to ask if they were troubled by the natives and to ask Tom's assistance in finding the spot from which the men fled as they knew he was a good bushman. After hunting for about an hour they came across it but instead of the body of a wild native, whom they meant to receive the bullets, there stood an old black tree trunk, bearing the marks of the travellers' shots.

After Tom's six months stay at the Einasleigh the drought broke and he could only muster two hundred and fifty cattle from the herd of nine hundred, and these were all males.

During the drought he and his men lived on johnnycake, which consisted of flour mixed with water and no rising, as they had run out of baking powder and salt. Their meat diet was from poor lean cattle, the flesh having been dried in the sun. The horses were too poor to travel back to Georgetown and the men were too weak to walk the long distance.

Now that the drought had broken Tom was expecting his father to arrive at any moment with a few luxuries. When he did arrive he found the men covered with nasty-looking sores from scurvy and in so low a condition that help had to be secured to take them to Georgetown for medical treatment.

I know you will understand by what I have written how the pioneers suffered, and how they were treated for their bravery in opening up the country. They were not given a scrap of help and were charged exorbitant prices for their tracts of country.

With only male cattle left there was no use in going further to stock up the Gulf country, so after Tom had recovered from his illness he left for Mackay. He travelled back this time by a different route. His father returned by boat from Normanton leaving a white man and the two niggers in charge of the camp and the two hundred and fifty cattle.

I shall stop now, but really dear, you cannot imagine how those trials have upset his nerves, he does get so irritable. We have a bed on the verandah where he rests at times and if I should want to wake him I have to touch him with a long cane — which I keep for the purpose — as he jumps out of his bed very suddenly and always strikes out. He is such a strong man, I feel sure that if I should get one of his blows there would be no more of me.

Goodnight, I shall have a bundle of scribble to post you next mail as I shall continue to write tomorrow. It is still teeming with rain. I have only one pair of shoes in good order now. I was shy at Tom seeing my bare feet, but at last realised it is better for him to see them than the folk I shall have to face when we return to civilisation, so I am now running about barefooted.

Love from,

JANE ATHERTON

My Dear,

Well here I am again to tell you some more of Tom's experiences.

The new country he travelled over when returning to Mackay was wild and rough, leading through the lonely ranges. He had one packhorse — carrying a blanket, a small quantity of food and a tent — a spare horse, and the one he was riding. His only weapon of defence was a tomahawk. His nerves became strained from facing the loneliness of the six hundred and fifty mile journey alone.

He had gone about halfway, when one night, after he had settled into bed, he saw two balls of fire shining through the opening of his tent. Thinking they were the eyes of a wild native, he seized his tomahawk, jumped to his feet, rushed towards the balls of fire and threw the tomahawk with full force at the apparition. He said that he yelled as he had never done before. He then heard something scuttle through the grass and was relieved when a dingo gave a long howl a short distance away. He started off again at daylight, or at least when he found his tomahawk, thankful to be alive.

After many more miles of weary travelling he came to a wayside inn on the Upper Burdekin River at five in the afternoon. He was very thankful to see the face of a white man and to obtain a night's accommodation, as his mind would be at rest from the fear of being murdered by the natives. He felt he would enjoy a comfortable bed and a well-cooked meal, as for days he had been existing on stale, sour-cooked corned beef and flour mixed with baking powder and water, which he cooked on the hot ashes after he had boiled the water for his tea.

After watering his horses and turning them into a small paddock he saw two white men in the distance coming towards the inn. They were drovers seeking a night's rest also.

The three of them, after exchanging a few words and having a good wash, had a large glass of beer — draught — the only drink available. They all enjoyed their meal together, talking mostly of their narrow escapes from being murdered by the blacks.

The two men returned to the bar to have more beer, while Tom went to his bedroom. He could not sleep because of the creepy-crawly things that kept biting him and which raised lumps all over his face and hands. His head ached so that at times it felt like bursting and with the taste of the stale beer still in his mouth, he left his bedroom, unrolled his own blanket on the verandah and tried to sleep.

The two men were seasoned beer drinkers. They talked of their droving and experiences with the wild natives until the early hours of the morning, quenching their dry throats with many more glasses of beer.

Tom, who had just dropped off to sleep, was awakened by the publican running about in a long white nightshirt, carrying a lighted candle and calling excitedly, "A man dead in his bed!"

Tom jumped up, looked into the room and was horrified to see one of the men with whom he had had a glass of beer the previous night, sitting upright in his bed, his eyes wide open and his face a ghastly colour. He was never positive as to whether he was actually dead or not.

It took him no time, however, to catch his horses and get away from this place of horror, and glad he was to be again facing the fear of wild natives.

FIRST YEAR AT MIDLOTHIAN STATION

Mackay harbour circa 1878. This is much as the harbour would have appeared late in 1886 when the Bardsleys sailed north from Rockhampton to Normanton. The harbour is very shallow, and cargo boats loaded and unloaded at Flat Top, some distance away.

He overtook a man walking along the road to Townsville, who gladly accepted the ride offered, although it was on a horse without a saddle. But to Tom's annoyance, his headache was getting worse and worse and at last he had to tell the stranger that he could not travel further as his eyesight was failing him and that he would have to lie down under a tree to die — as he thought — by the roadside.

The traveller, to whom he had related the story of the dead man and the beer, evidently thought that he was another victim and passed on leaving him lying on the lonely roadside, and in a few minutes he had disappeared.

Although we have been in bed most of the day on account of the mosquitoes, it is now sleep time so I shall close.

I am terribly lonely today and Tom's yarns have not been too cheery.

Love from,

JANE

My Dear,

Tom is still going strong and the rain is too. It pelts down on our iron roof so that at times I can hardly hear him telling me of his adventures.

His tale now is about the time when he and his father started off with another mob of seven hundred breeders for the Gulf.

The drought had broken and the country was a pasture of green, the waterholes were overflowing, and the pleura had disappeared. Once again the land settlers had forgotten the drought and were in excellent spirits, dreaming of the prices of cattle going up to balance the losses of the drought.

They gathered only twenty-five of the cattle left at Pentlands and then journeyed on to the Einasleigh to get the two hundred and fifty they had left in charge of the white man and the two Mackay black boys.

He started now with nine hundred and seventy-five head, not including the young calves born after the breeders had left Mackay. On this trip a dray was used to carry the new-born calves — which were many — to the Gulf property, Midlothian station.

His father returned to Mackay after living a few months on the newly formed station, leaving Tom completely in charge. I must here tell you a funny story about his father running out of tobacco during his stay and Tom, who at the age of nineteen was not supposed to be smoking, had some in a chest in his room and dared not offer any for fear of a reprimand.

Tom lived in a tent for weeks, watching the cattle all day. At night they were let loose, then at dawn they were mustered up and a rough count made. This went on for many weeks and the cattle had settled down to the new country before he even thought of building a strong hut to afford some protection from the constant fear of the spears of the wild blacks who were there in hundreds, judging by the number of footprints around the many lagoons.

Since they had to work all day, they cooked their corned beef at night. It was arranged that whoever was awake in the night should take it off and put it away in the pack bags. Tom always kept these at his head, just outside the mosquito net, in order to protect his head from the spears of prowling blacks.

On this particular night Tom's nerves were unhinged because of what had been happening lately. The day before, in the early morning, he had heard the bellowing of cattle and hurrying to the spot had found the blacks amongst them, frightening and separating them. There were two beasts freshly speared, one in the neck, and blood was streaming out from the wound. When cattle see or smell blood they bellow and nearly go mad.

On counting up, the herd was found to be two hundred short. This meant that their tracks had to be followed. They were not found until the next day, heading in a direct line for Mackay. It was then discovered that the natives had been breaking the freshly erected wire fences to use to point their spears.

Peter, the abo boy, was the one to wake this night to take off the corned beef. Tom, feeling something near his head, looked out and saw a naked nigger — aboriginals always sleep in the buff — standing erect with what he thought was a spear in his hand. He jumped out, tearing his net to pieces, and with a yell grabbed his rifle, the only one he possessed. It was an old Snider, manipulated with caps, and he always slept with it under his head, carrying it during the day wherever he went.

After the first year the blacks in the immediate vicinity of the homestead became a little more friendly, making it safe at times to go about unarmed within a mile of so of the camp.

He then built a slab hut in which they all slept, and as Tom says, at this time they all slept well allthought the hut was still without a roof; the iron was still to come.

It has not rained for the last three hours and we are looking forward to perhaps a week's fine weather. But as this is only February, and the wet season usually goes to the end of March, Tom says we shall have to eat, sleep and be merry for another month. I shall just have to stop now.

With love from,

JANE

My Dear,

The rain has set in again, and as there is nothing else to do but eat, sleep, and watch the rain coming across the plain in flying sheets of mist, and it is almost dark, although it is only three o'clock, I shall continue with Tom's life story.

Most of the natives were by now harmless and understood that they would be shot by the Government patrol if they interfered with or killed the cattle.

One day Tom and Peter were having a look through the cattle a few miles from the homestead, when suddenly Peter exclaimed, "I see Devil-devil, he sit down longa big mob of cattle over there," pointing with his finger at the same time. He then said, "My Chri Boss me thinkit, me and you get up longa that big fellow tree, that fellow he Devil-devil alright. He been jump up ghost longa some dead blackfellow from nother tribe. By Chri me plenty frightened, no plurry fear me won't go close up longa him. Supposen you no get up tree I get up me self."

Tying his horse to a nearby tree, he climbed it in a few seconds and from the top kept calling, "Come up Boss, quickly I see that fellow Devil-devil get ready koulla (kill) you. Suppose he catch you he take your fat out." This is a belief that exists and is the fear of all the Gulf natives. So much so indeed, that when they get sick they declare a dead native has taken their fat out while they were sleeping, and until they believe it to have been put back, they will remain ill and oft times fret and die.

On turning his attention to the Devil-devil, Tom saw a beast resembling a bull with tremendous horns coming at full speed towards him, and before he realised it, the animal was only a few feet from the horse on which he was mounted. He then dug his spurs almost out of sight into his horse's flank, to get every ounce of speed out of it. He said that a most terrible sensation came over him. His eyes seemed to leave their sockets and a cold chill crept down his spine, leaving him in a state of trembling nerves. He felt the breath of the infuriated animal on his neck and shoulders and could hear it breathing as if thunder was coming from its nostrils. He expected that at any moment the horse and the Devil-devil would stumble in a matted heap together and that he would be gored to death.

The ground over which he travelled was full of melon holes caused by some condition of the soil some eight to twelve inches below the surface, but he took a chance and made for a deep swamp. He thought this would stop the chase or at least give him time to climb a tree before the beast could catch him. He was too frightened to look round until a few feet in the water. Then, missing the breath of the animal and the roar of its nostrils, he turned and saw the beast standing on the edge of the swamp, tongue out and saliva and foam pouring from its mouth, as though debating whether it should follow him or go back to the herd of cattle with which it had been grazing. It decided to return, so with head thrown back and horns lying flat on its shoulders, it slowly trotted off to where the herd had moved about a quarter of a mile further away.

After a space of time Tom went back to the sapling where Peter had tethered his horse, thinking he would have to plead with him to get down from the tree and come home. To his amazement he found that Peter and the horse were nowhere to be seen.

It took him no time to get back to the homestead, there to find Peter sitting on a box crying and almost white from fear. Upon seeing Tom he put his arms round him and with tears rolling down his black face said, "Me thinkit you dead alright, boss. Horse he been break bridle and gallop away, him plenty fright longa that Devil-devil too."

The Devil-devil was a huge male buffalo which had come from the Northern Territory, and a few weeks later it was speared by the natives on Meranda station.

Securing his rifle, Tom went back to the scene alone, for although he threatened to shoot Peter if he would not come out to find the horse and to help to shoot the animal, he found to his astonishment that the boy preferred death to facing the Devil-devil.

Another day has gone by. Do you know, dear, that if I had known what it is to be so isolated in the bush during the torrential rains of the four-month wet season, no matter how I loved a man, I would have thought twice before venturing forth to face the loneliness of the bush. I really have a fit of the blues today, and have started to fret and cry which annoys Tom, who of course has been living this life for ten years. I think he loves the wet season as it gives him a rest from the natives, for they too just live in their gunyas and would sooner die from starvation than face the heavy rain that comes at times in torrents, smarting their naked shoulders.

FIRST YEAR AT MIDLOTHIAN STATION

I cannot write any more today, but perhaps in a day or so I shall be able to look on the life here through brighter glasses.

Love from your lonely old friend,

JANE ATHERTON

My Dear,

I have a budget of letters addressed to you to post when our mailman arrives. We have not seen or heard of him for weeks, so perhaps he has died from the effects of that appetite of his. Anyway, we keep a supply of beef and bread ready for him, as he might turn up at any moment now that the rain seems to be easing off.

I shall go on again with Tom's life. Oh! I nearly forgot to tell you I have learnt to play crib, a game of cards, so that gives me something to do besides listening to Tom's stories, which of course give me great pleasure.

Tom's first experience of the Gulf's wet season was a particularly heavy and long one. The rations and ammunition were very scanty and the flour was almost finished, so in desperation he sent his only white man and Charlie to Normanton to bring a small supply of food out on packhorses. He could not get the dray in for a good load until the roads were dry.

Three weeks passed without a sign of the men's return, and fearing that they had been killed by the natives, and with no flour left and only two caps left for his rifle, Tom started out with Peter, on horseback to search for them, leaving the station and cattle to the mercy of the natives.

The roads were in a deplorable state from the excessive and constant rains. Before they had gone many miles they had to abandon the idea of travelling by horse. Taking off the saddles and hanging them up on a tree well away from the reach of floodwaters, they started off on foot, with only the rifle, two caps and a tomahawk. Trudging along through water and bogs up to their thighs and sometimes swimming creeks, they made for a sand ridge near a lagoon where they intended sleeping the night, without even a tent fly to protect them from the rain.

It was five o'clock and they could hardly drag their legs along, so tired were they after their long and strenuous walk of fifteen miles. Suddenly Peter whispered, "Boss I see big mob blackfellow," pointing in the direction of the camp. Tom could see them, only a couple of

ACROSS THE YEARS

hundred yards away, all standing around a fire and looking in their direction. He no longer felt tired and asked Peter how he felt. He replied, "Me plenty fright inside more better me and you hurry." Tom says that he could have run the next three miles to the slab hut built as a halfway house towards Maggieville station. Here a little flour had been hidden, so that if it ever became necessary to get away from the blacks it would be possible to remain there until help arrived.

Looking back as they paced along, they could see a small party of blacks following, and could hear them calling "bacca". From their size they surmised that they were females. It was a trick of the natives for the men to send the gins as decoys while they manoeuvred and carried out their plan of attack.

They reached the hut almost in the dark and it took no time to get inside and barricade the door. They then prepared for the attack of spears which they expected at any moment to shower upon the hut. They listened well into the night before Tom suggested that Peter should have a sleep while he kept watch. He said he was too frightened to strike a match to have a smoke to steady his trembling nerves.

The blacks now knew what a rifle meant. Tom made me laugh, he said that he held it well out from his body when they were within sight of the tribe, and he is sure it was that which prevented them from attacking the hut.

They were ready at dawn to start on their twelve-mile journey to Maggieville, through water and bog almost up to their waists, as this country was very much lower than that through which they had travelled.

They reached their destination at five in the afternoon and found the white servant sitting on his bed enjoying a good smoke. He had been there five days waiting for the rain to cease. Tom, though glad to find him alive, gave him a piece of his mind and did not take him back again. Charlie the abo, who was old and weak in character, came along whining, "No my fault Boss, that white man says we can't go too much rain, I think let Boss and Peter die."

They waited a week at Maggieville to recover from heavy colds caused by the long exposure. They then borrowed horses and saddles to return to Midlothian, as the rain had cleared making the roads fit for travel.

They found their slab hut, with its slabbed walls in order, but the cattle were scattered everywhere. The natives had become very cunning. At every opportunity, they would kill a beast instead of

FIRST YEAR AT MIDLOTHIAN STATION

hunting for their daily meat diet of kangaroo and wallaby.

Tom had reported their doings to the Normanton police and expected the patrol to arrive any day. Thinking it best to locate the camp of the main body of natives before Mr Poindestre arrived, he took Peter out on the run with him to search for them.

They followed a watercourse where fresh footprints could be seen in hundreds. Suddenly they came upon two natives laden with spears, nullas and woomeras, a contrivance to fit the spears to enable them to strike hard and give a sure aim. The men were trying to get near enough to a mob of cattle drinking at the creek to spear a beast.

When Tom galloped up to them, one dived into a waterhole and crawled out on the other side on his stomach, but the other was nowhere to be seen, although his spears and woomeras were on the ground near a huge log. There was long grass up to the waist every-where, and after hunting in vain for a while Tom decided to get off his horse and break up the spears. As I said before the spears they use to kill animals are pointed with sharp wire, stolen as a rule from the fences. The ones they use to kill a human enemy however, have something like fish hooks attached to them so that they cannot be pulled out, and in addition are poisoned with deadly herbs or snake virus. Just as Tom got one foot on the ground, with the other still in the stirrup iron, and holding the rifle with one hand, Peter, who had caught sight of the native's eye peeping out of a hole in the hollow log near the spears, called loudly "me see him, he up log". Tom's horse took fright and began to whirl round and round with him hanging to the saddle. The hidden native, who could see plainly the plight Tom was in, jumped out and poised his spear in its woomera ready to put it right through Tom's body. Tom fired the rifle haphazardly at him and more from good luck than good management struck him in the leg. He watched him swim the creek and crawl out at almost the same spot as his mate had done previously. He found out years after, when the blacks were civilised enough to tell their story, that the black's mate had hidden on the opposite bank and had taken him on his shoulder to the camp to be treated for a broken leg.

Luckily the horse's jump at the report of the rifle freed Tom, because the sole of his old boot came off, otherwise he would have met his death from being dragged and kicked to death by his horse instead of being killed by the nigger's spear.

The horse bolted off and so did Peter, but when Tom arrived home on foot there was Peter, who met him with a smile and said, "My word Boss, I thinket you dead."

It is characteristic of the aboriginals that, if ever their help is needed they will run away until the coast is clear again.

We are now having a sight of blue sky the size of a Dutchman's pants so we are hoping for fine weather as this is an indication.

My gins informed me today why it rains so much. Some enemy blackfellow has found the bone of the other tribe and has thrown it into a waterhole and until it is taken out the rain will come. So dear, I am hoping he will soon lift it out and throw it away where it will never be found again.

I shall close now,

With love from,

JANE

My Dear,

The rain is easing off and we only get heavy showers now and again. It is a great relief not to hear the constant roar on the roof.

I shall continue with Tom's story which I think will soon be finished. It was some years before his father returned, bringing with him a thousand head of breeders from Cliftonville. He helped Tom to build a neat little two-roomed house of horizontal slabs with a verandah back and front. It was built on two-foot blocks without stump caps.

I shall enclose a photo of the first home with its nice garden of citrus and other fruit trees almost in bearing.

His father was so well pleased with the part the two abos had played in the building of the place that he offered them a free trip by boat to Mackay.

Charlie, the elder, said, "More better me stay here yet, catch young gin, clear out, take her poui-poui (long way) close up Cloncurry long way from her tribe." He was about thirty-eight years of age when he succeeded in running in a young lubra of about sixteen years and cleared off as quickly as possible to Clonagh station, two hundred miles from here on the opposite side of the river to her own "touri" — country.

Peter, the other boy, took the opportunity and travelled by boat to Mackay, expecting to find the wife who had been allotted to him at her birth. He was sadly disappointed to find that during his long stay in the Gulf, she had been stolen away by an abo from another tribe.

Twelve months later he returned by boat to Normanton and walked the forty-five miles to Midlothian to wait the chance to steal a young lubra and to take her back to Mackay as soon as possible, but he had to wait nearly a year before he succeeded.

FIRST YEAR AT MIDLOTHIAN STATION

Midlothian Homestead, 1886. Tom Atherton arrived at Midlothian in 1885 and erected the house soon afterwards.

He was a very intelligent nigger, for when Tom asked him how he liked travelling by the boat he replied, "My word Boss, he good fellow cook longa boat, he come outside make a big corroboree (noise), he hit tin (gong) with hammer. He says come on young man dinner time. Me and altogether white man sit down longa table. Plenty knives plenty forks, full up jam, pickles, bread, butter, cake. Me look when that white man pick up knife, me pick up knife, he pick up fork, me pick up fork, he eat, me eat. Cook say what you want, curry and rice, stew, mince? Man sit close longa me, he say curry and rice please, me say curry and rice please. Chinaman come longa door altogether white man say we don't want that yellow b------ in here. He like me all right. He say eat plenty my boy."

I shall stop now. The gins keep the fire going night and day to save matches, and even though it is one hundred in the shade they still love to sit round the fire.

Yours nearly a bush wacker,

JANE

My Dear,

When Peter caught his lubra, they had to remain two days to catch the triweekly boat to Mackay. They boarded in the Chinese quarter of the town. He was a very proud man the day he landed back in

Mackay to show his beautiful young wife to the other old men of his tribe, who had to be content with their haggard old wives, and he was prouder still when his firstborn, a son, arrived, even though it turned out to be a half-caste Chinese.

It is almost fine but now I hope it rains a little longer until Tom has finished telling me his stories. Then I can start to tell you of my own experiences.

Tom had just received his half share in Midlothian, when he noticed a sickness among the herd which he knew from experience was not pleura. He reported it to the Gulf stock inspector, who immediately sent for Mr Pound the Government veterinary surgeon in Brisbane to come out, for the cattle were dying of it in hundreds.

After he had made an inspection and taken tests, Mr Pound declared the disease to be redwater, caused by the ticks dropped from the buffalo that had chased Tom some years previous. It was on Midlothian that the ticks made their first appearance in Queensland.

Oh! I had almost forgotten to tell you, there is a nigger in the blacks' camp who has a hole right through his right hand. The accident occurred when he was a young man. Tom was rounding the niggers up in their camp, of about eight hundred, when he caught sight of one man at the back end of the camp with a spear poised in the air ready to kill him. You may guess it didn't take long to take aim, hence the hole in the nigger's hand.

This ends my story of Tom's bachelor days. I hope you have not found this too tedious.

Love from,

JANE

My Dear,

The rain has gone for nine weeks. Tom says I shall be wishing it back after a few months, especially when everything has that dried-up look.

I am frightened, because five hundred wild natives have been made to camp near our front gate, a bare mile away, so that an eye can be kept on them.

On a still night sometimes I can hear a mournful sobbing sound, which means they have not brought in enough food and are hungry, or a gay corroboree with screams of yelling and laughter. They sing in their singsong tune, their dogs barking to the rhythm of their gaiety,

FIRST YEAR AT MIDLOTHIAN STATION

which all indicates they have an abundance of food, such as kangaroo and wallaby caught by the men, and lizards, wild duck eggs, possum and lily bulbs brought in by the gins.

The lily bulbs — crushed between two flat stones, worked into small cakes and baked on hot coals — are eaten as bread.

When I hear that mournful throb from their camp, I get scared stiff. So much so, that if Tom does not go to bed when I am ready and I have to go from the dining room, which is a verandah connecting the two main buildings, and then round two verandahs to our bedroom, I simply bolt, for I fancy I can see wild eyes glaring at me from all directions and their white shining teeth ready to eat me up. I am glad to get inside the room and bolt the door, look under the bed, behind a cretonne curtain and jump into bed, sometimes even before I have said my prayers.

Even my gins are frightened when they hear that mournful sound and they tell me the wild blacks are so hungry they might come in the night and take their caul fat out and make them die.

When the moaning continues for days Tom goes to their camp and finds out the reason for it and if it is caused by a death in the camp he threatens them with a rifle, but if it is that they are hungry he has a beast killed for them.

I have great pity for them although I am frightened; as they are not allowed to camp anywhere but at the gates and although they walk miles in search of food, it must run out at times. Tom tells me that when they get a little more civilised, he will allow them to shift out on the run where there will be more hunting ground. I shall be glad when it happens as that moan has entered my brain and at times I feel like tying a piece of string tightly around my head as the gins do when they have a headache.

Good night, I hope to write you a more cheery letter soon.

Love from,

JANE

My Dear,

We have got Sim the cook back again. He had been so long with Tom that he just could not keep away. He helped to build my home which is very nice. making verandah squatter chairs, little rustic tables, bookshelves and a linen press, but Oh dear! he is so jealous of me and looks on me as an intruder.

I had never managed a washing day before, nor had the gins

ACROSS THE YEARS

washed in any other way than sitting straddle-legged on a log at the edge of the water with the clothes spread out on the log and rubbed with very little soap. So I shall tell you about my first washing day. I knew that one does not boil everything, of course we have no flannels here, but for the life of me I could not think how to make starch. So I decided to appeal to Sim, which I hated doing for I could picture his eyebrows going up and his saying or yelling "you no savvie make starch".

He gave me careful instructions, with his eyebrows up, but omitted to say the quantity required. I thought he meant the whole packet so put it into a small-sized tub, moistened it with cold water, then Kitty poured the boiling water while I stirred until we had got the tub half full. I could have burst out crying, not about the starch, but at having to face Sim again. I mustered up courage however and to my horror he said, "Poor Boss, he married a big fool alright, when I tell him he plenty growl, he not got much money to buy plenty starch."

The gins are still interested in my clothes and on a washing day I have to sit and watch them pin my clothes on the line. We haven't any clothes pegs on the station, so poor Tom's clothes still have to be strung on to a barbed-wire fence.

When the gins come to an article of clothing they do not understand they will take a good look at it, shake it out, and almost try it on, then call to me "what this fellow". One happened to be a nightdress, buttoned well up to the neck, with long sleeves. When I told them I slept in it, they looked surprised and said, "More better you give it to me altogether. Mary-mary sleep longa buff, more better you sleep that way too." Personally I cannot see why my nightdresses should have high necks and long sleeves seeing that I do not parade around in front of anyone but my own husband.

I am getting along much better. Sim has promised not to tell the boss this time about the starch and the gins do not know that it was a mistake.

Love from,

JANE

My Dear,

I wish you were here, I am sure you would enjoy every moment. I am having a wonderful time with the wild gins, they are screamingly funny. I hope I shall not become like them before I get away from here.

There are all kinds in the wild camps. Some are old and have reared a family of three or four. They never have large families. My gins say, "Suppose too many come, hit him on the head more better." I do hope I shall not come to that should I have a dozen.

The natives have their own religious laws which prevent inbreeding. They arrange their tribes into different sets, such as possum, wallaby, goanna, snake and so on. A lubra may not marry any man in her own set, that is a snake cannot marry a snake or a possum a possum. Some beautiful lubras are allotted to their husbands at birth and if possible are prevented from seeing any white man as they grow up. These allotted husbands are called Benjamins. Now and again the gins will say to me when speaking of Tom, "Benjamin he belonga you."

The wild gins, upon learning that I was interested in gathering birds' eggs, were most anxious to gather them for me, and would call to me from the boundary fence of a small house paddock, about a mile square, "Missus, Missus gib it munda (bread)." I always gave bread in exchange for eggs.

These gins were always in the nude. At first they were very shy and frightened and would try to hide their nakedness. After a week or so, when offering the eggs they would look me over, touch my pretty dress and hat with their beautiful tapering fingers, with nails of delicate pink which no manicuring could improve, and they would smile, showing a perfect set of clean white teeth, which I could not understand as they had no toothbrushes. Tom tells me, however, they keep them clean by using a sort of brush made from pandanus tree roots, and by chewing bones. They would look into my face and say "Budgeree?"

After a couple of months the collection of eggs began to run out. They had gathered all sorts and sizes for me, from the large emu's to the tiny finch's and still they would come to offer the same old whistling duck eggs — whistling ducks are very prevalent in the Gulf country — and almost whine "munda please".

I tried to explain, or at least got Annie who was from the same tribe to do so, but whether they liked the munda or an odd chew of tobacco I do not know, for they persisted in bringing the old duck eggs.

In the laying season they would bring in dozens and dozens, but not all at once. They knew too much for that, as each gin would receive a slice of munda for about a dozen eggs. We used the eggs for scrambling and boiling, but not for cakes as the whites were too hard to beat.

ACROSS THE YEARS

I was awfully tired of the call for munda, and there was Sim to face, who would exclaim every time, "Me tell him Boss what for you give my bread longa gins, Bossie, he no got plenty money." So dear, I had to stop the annoyance to myself and Sim to say nothing of Bossie. I hid a leather holster of a revolver behind my back — I forgot to tell you Tom won a Colt revolver at a picnic race meeting with an exceptionally well-bred mare by The Scud — and when within a few feet of half a dozen gins, I pointed it at them. They knew what a revolver was for; often it was fired to let them know what it could do. Eggs were scattered everywhere and the poor gins ran at full speed along the track worn by the egg trade to the opposite side of the fence. They were screaming for mercy while I flashed the holster which they thought to be a revolver, and pretended to take aim.

From laughing so much and puffing from the speed at which I was running, I lost sight of them after the first fifty yards. I did not see or hear of them for weeks — I was sorry then as it made the life here so lonely — or at least it did until they found out from my gins that the gun was leather and could not shoot.

When I returned to the kitchen after the chase, Sim, who is almost my Godfather now, was horrified and said, "I tell Bossie, longa you chase wild gins." He certainly did tell, judging by the continual lectures I get daily about not playing with the wild gins. I do get so tired of lectures, I thought when I married they would cease. It must be that Tom is eleven years older than I am, he has lost all the silly ways of youth. Another thing I am not allowed to do is to give my sick lubra friends medicine, no matter how sick they are, for if they should die I would be classed as a Devil-devil and the tribes would kill me at the first chance.

It was sad yesterday, a little gin, about seventeen years of age, was moaning from the paddock fence, "Missus missus come." I could see it was not eggs she wanted to exchange, for she was carrying a piccaninny. I looked at the poor little naked mite, a few weeks old, wrapped only in a sheet of bark. I felt it and found it was hot and shivering. I knew it was very ill and taking it into my arms I carried it to my bedroom, wrapped it in a blanket and then took it out to the kitchen fire.

The poor little gin mother was hot and feverish and overcome with grief. No doubt they do love their babies, that is if they turn out black; but if a half-caste should arrive it is knocked on the head. There are no half-castes in this camp, but whether it is the gins are true to their husbands or the hit on the head is a very effective method I do not know. So I gave the little gin a nip of whisky to warm her up.

They know whisky is not medicine. She lay on the flour sack in front of the fire and went off to sleep, while her little child was breathing and moaning.

I thought I would chance a hot bath and a dose of oil for the baby, while the mother slept, but my Godfather Sim grabbed the bottle of oil and threw out the water saying "what for, tribe might kill you I tell Bossie". I shall be glad when the wretched chinaman goes away for another holiday.

I spent the afternoon crying about the dying piccaninny. The little soul only lived a day longer. I cannot write any more, my eyes are filled with tears.

Yours lovingly,

JANE

My Dear,

I know you think I am writing a diary, but when you realise that I twiddle my fingers from peep of day, which is about four-thirty, to sundown at well past seven you will understand it takes something to put in the long day.

Now that the wet season is over Tom is up with the birds and away all day long; there is no resting after he gets up. From what I can see all bushmen are alike. There are no neighbours to annoy, so consequently when you want anybody you just bellow out their names, and wait for the word "Yes" and give your orders. The funny thing about the natives is that they speak so softly you have to get quite close up to them and say "wallow woolko", meaning ear no good. I cannot even talk to Sim for if I should go near the door, before I even have time to enter, he will say "what you want" in a most stern voice. I feel my legs tremble and then I think he knows I am lonely, so perhaps he thinks I want sympathy or affection.

I had almost forgotten to tell you what happened in February. There was a lull in the wet season, so Tom took the opportunity to go into Normanton to see the local butcher. He always gives him first preference with our early fat bullocks. We received one pound ten shillings per head for them.

Fat cattle are plentiful in the Gulf. Tom and Major Collis are the only owners. The banks have taken over all the others and their managers are not interested enough to travel boggy roads and swim swollen creeks to make a sale.

Tom started off with our only white stockman, leaving me with

Sim, two gins and five black boys. He was to be away only one night and two days, but as I have learnt to shoot with a revolver I was not afraid. Heavy rain set in that night and I was half expecting to see them back at any moment as I did not think they would reach Normanton.

Two days passed, a third, then a fourth and still there was no sign of their return. In desperation I would go to Sim and say, "What you think keep Boss?" He would put on such a wise look and think for quite a minute, so that I would feel so sure he knew something about the ways of men, but dear, when he replied "perhaps he dead, perhaps he not", I felt like running along the road to get away from his yellow face.

At times, although I was distracted with worry, I would have a laugh, for when I cried and wiped my eyes, out would come the gins with red handkerchiefs to put up to their tearless eyes to imitate me. Their crying was between a corroboree and a wail.

I had been watching since daylight on the fifth morning when the gins, whose eyes were never off the road, yelled out, "Boss come up, see, big mob blackfellow come up too," and they danced with joy.

The natives have wonderful sight and they can see for miles. I suppose it is because they do not abuse the eyes by reading or sewing. The gins would certainly never mend a stitch if I did not watch them. Well, it was Tom and the white man and they had walked the forty-five miles, in places, with water up to their waists and had swum all the swollen creeks.

The big mob of blackfellows were coming for tobacco, for when they saw Tom in difficulty in the last deep creek, battling against the strong current and trying to catch on to a tree, almost exhausted, they swam to him, talking in their own language and slapping their backs, meaning him to get on. He was too frightened to trust them, so only held on to their shoulders, while he and they drifted quickly, until they reached a tree in midstream where they could rest before they tackled another swim.

Love from,

JANE

My Dear,

I hate the very sight of Sim. However, he has been with Tom ten years, ever since the forming of Midlothian, and he has been a wonderful help. He is exceptionally good at woodwork and built almost all the stockyards on the station, as well as the home and all the nice odds and ends, such as the rustic tables and chairs, little ones for the verandahs and large ones to serve afternoon tea under the shade of the poinciana trees when in full bloom. He even sent to China for matting to spread under the trees, so that I can lie there during the hot days. He does the cooking, gardening and Tom's mending. When I arrived he had oranges, hard-boiled eggs from China — wrapped in mud — and salted water melon seed from China prepared in readiness for me. He gave Tom a huge bottle of preserved ginger the afternoon we arrived at Midlothian, saying, in my absence of course, "You give Missus plenty bye and bye fine big son come up."

The vegetable garden where we grow sweet potatoes is about half a mile away, so when Sim works one day a week in it, I feel monarch of all I survey and have a grand time learning to cook. I tried pastry today, but really dear, it turned out like hardboard. Tom says he would need a tomahawk to serve it. I took good care that Sim did not see it, by dipping it in milk and covering it with sugar and giving it to the gins saying "budgeree sugar bag". They smelt it, turned it over several times and began to lick the sugar before they were game to eat it.

We set the milk in large flat tins to gather the cream, to make our butter. Then the cream is placed into large fruit bottles, which after securely corking are buried in wet sand at the waterhole edge for at least twenty-four hours. Then at daylight the gins begin the process of shaking until the butter gathers. It is so funny to see them. When first they start they corroboree in a whisper with a very bored tune. They have only the one tune in their songs. It goes something like this, with a tremolo, yar, yar, yar, yahh. But oh my! When the butter has gathered it is like a yell, for it has taken from four in the morning to nine at night to procure a cup of butter.

Tom says our cows are not a milking strain, but someday when times improve he will work up a good herd of milkers. The roads are now dry enough to get our six months' rations out from the little town of Normanton. I am looking forward to a fresh supply of flour, raisins and currants. Anything we have left in the storeroom has grubs about half an inch in length.

ACROSS THE YEARS

I do not like telling you how stupid I am but if I do not I shall be short of news. Tom called me, when he was writing out the store order for flour, tea, sugar, kerosene, rice and so on, and asked what I needed. "Well!" said I, "we want clothes pegs and spice for flavouring cakes." "How do you order clothes pegs?" asked Tom. "By the case I suppose as everything else is ordered that way," I replied. "Well," said Tom, "I shall order twenty-eight pounds of spice as we never order anything under that figure and I know how you like cakes."

The greatest day of all for me and in fact for the whole station was when the store order arrived and we inspected the load. A huge case amongst the order was inspected thoroughly before opening and was found to contain clothes pegs by the hundreds. No more hanging clothes on a barbed-wire fence. There will be no shortage of pegs for years and years.

Tom was reading the letter that came with the order. I noticed a look of annoyance on his face and when he said "you should have known something about cakes, they are in your line", I was horrified. I read the letter from Burns, Philp & Co. immediately. They said twenty-two and a half half-pound tins of spice was all they had in stock and that they would forward the balance when a fresh shipment arrived. I knew why Tom was annoyed with me. Needless to say he wrote back to say that we were well satisfied and had enough spice to last a lifetime.

Good night dear. I do enjoy eating bread without the fear that a grub has got through the sifter.

Love from,

JANE

P.S.   We have passed the grubby flour to the camp natives as they do not mind grubs. I have seen them bring them in by the hundreds from the trunks of the Acacia trees. When they are cooked they look like the marrow from a joint of roast beef. All the hands on the station eat the big grubs — not the little hairy flour grubs — in fact I have tasted them myself but I cannot get away from the idea of their being grubs.

My Dear,

Our annual picnic races, which take place at different stations each year, are being held this year in May at Delta Downs, a station fourteen miles further from the town than Midlothian.

Great preparations are made for these events, bough sheds, tents and tent flys are erected to accommodate the two hundred visitors; men and women holding prominent positions in Normanton, Croydon and Burketown, station managers, stockmen, bookies, jockeys, black boys, gins and piccaninnies.

The gins dress in men's moleskin riding breeches, elastic side boots, coloured shirts and felt hats, so with their cropped heads it is impossible to say whether they are boys or Mary-marys. The stock-men, jockeys, black boys, gins and piccaninnies have just an ordinary cook to look after their meals, while the other visitors are entertained at the manager's residence.

The Delta homestead is a large fourteen-roomed dwelling with very low walls and an ant bed floor covered with Chinese matting. The dining room is very large and the whole house is covered with a strong vine. Luckily the rooms are ceiled with hessian otherwise I would not have been able to sleep for fear of an odd snake or two falling into the mosquito nets. The house is built so near to a deep waterhole that there is only a narrow track and a wire netting fence to stop one falling into the water. I shall continue this letter in a few days' time.

Well! The preparations for the races have begun. Waggons filled with foodstuffs, tinned luxuries, beer and spirits have been passing our gates for a whole week now, causing great excitement amongst the gins to say nothing of myself. I am not doing any more work than I can help nor are the gins, but it is lovely to see some signs of civilis-ation.

The gins' eyes are never off the road and when they see a waggon, dray or buggy, they clap their hands on their thighs and start their corroboree "yar, yar, yahh", exclaiming "wheelbarrow come up". When horses are seen the same performance goes on except that they cry, "Big fellow smoke (dust) longa road Yarraman (horse) come up too, you find (see) him Missus."

I must away now as I am all behind with my housework. I have to fill vases with gum tips and branches of wild berries as, strange to say, there are no wild flowers in the Gulf country.

Love from,

JANE

P.S. I forgot to tell you we have adopted a little black child. Do you remember Charlie who stole a lubra and carried her off to Clonagh in the Cloncurry district? He arrived with a two and a half year old baby girl on his shoulders. The mother had cleared off and left him with the child and he had brought her to give to me. The poor little thing, whom I called Pigeon, was almost dead from exposure. She was hot and delirious from being wet so long. Luckily we have a doctor's book which Mother gave me. It took a lot of studying as her symptoms fitted so many ailments. However, after a lot of argument we treated her for pneumonia and she gradually got well.

Since we have no child of our own we are treating her as our adopted one. She is such a tiny little mite and is so grateful for our care. Tom has made her a wooden cot and she sleeps on the verandah near our door. When she was very ill she slept in our bedroom and Tom took his share of watching while I slept.

I am much happier now that I have little Pigeon. She is a darling and will stretch out her little frail arms when either Tom or I go near her cot and whisper Missus or Boss with a loving light in her eyes.

J.A.

My Dear,

I received your letter today and was pleased to hear that your mother has quite recovered from her illness. It must have been a worrying time for you so I shall try to make this letter a cheery one.

I must tell you about something funny which happened during Tom's absence. The boys and the men of the wild tribes used to be allowed to come up to the kitchen in the nude to sell their wares; fish, duck, crabs etc. Now they are compelled by the Government to wear some covering round their loins. They find it hard at times to obtain even a dirty piece of rag and will tear a piece off the blanket supplied to each native yearly, by the Government. I have rescued serviettes taken from my own clothes line. You cannot leave anything on the line overnight as the poor wretches see no harm in stealing and they really love handkerchiefs. A while back I saw a gin with a handkerchief and said to her "that fellow belonga me" and after a lot of persuasion she gave it to me and I saw that it bore the name of the proprietor of the leading hotel in Normanton, C. B. Healy, and it was a perfectly good serviette.

Well one day I heard screams of laughter coming from the kitchen and shrieks of "yecco" which means something unusual in the native language. I ran out and peeped through a crack in the slab walls to see what was causing the excitement, and I had to laugh also, in fact I nearly yelled "yecco" myself.

I saw a huge native holding up a fish for sale, while two of our own boys, from whom the laughter was coming, were kneeling to see how he had arranged a black openwork stocking. He had stolen it from our clothes line and was using it to serve the purpose of Eve's fig leaf. The foot of the stocking formed a bag while the leg, torn in two strips was carried round his loins and fastened with string at the back.

I then noticed that my gins, who are always so modest were also peering through cracks in the wall. I really do not know what my Mother would say if she knew that I had been guilty of deliberately witnessing such a scene.

This is only a short letter this time, but I shall make my next one much longer, and tell you something about our doings at the picnic races.

Goodbye for the present,

Love from,

JANE

My Dear,

We arrived early to join the party for the Delta Picnic Amateur Races.

First I must tell you about the cooking for the house guests. This was not on the usual station living scale but was quite extraordinary. A chef was brought from Croydon, who had French names for stews, mince and hash and so on, and waiters were procured for the event. For a few days we were living at the best hotel in Sydney or at least we fancied we were, judging from the wines and beer that flowed at meal times. All was so gay with laughter and jokes and the wine made me forget our Midlothian diet.

Many pedigree horses were brought from the other stations and good prize money was offered for the principal events. Each stockman brought his fancy horse so many a race was run off before the advertised programme began. A visitors' race was arranged for the last day's sport.

Quiet horses were run into a yard and auctioned. The buyers, who bought for the day only, had to ride their own purchase, to win a case of whisky.

Some of the visitors — police magistrates, lawyers, bankers, parsons — only knew their horses by the numbers on the saddlecloths and were surprised after winning their race to find they were dis-qualified for having ridden the wrong horse. It had been arranged while refreshments were being served, immediately before the race, to change the saddles and cloths of several of the horses.

The last race of each day was a black boys' race which added much fun to the day's outing. Thirty horses started off at the drop of a flag amidst the screams from their gins and piccaninnies of "go it Homer, Pompy, Percy, Cyril" etc. It was seldom you heard the names Jack, Bill, Tom or Harry.

In the evenings it seemed as though a huge bazaar was in progress at the station. The manager's guests were entertained with dancing to the music of a piano, which stood on a small stage of bricks so that the white ants would not eat the wood, card playing, singing and *no naughty yarns*.

The stockmen squatted on their heels, or leant against a tree or a post and discussed the possibilities of their horses for the next day's races. Some related and re-enacted at the same time how they rode a buckjumping horse to a standstill; or told of their past droving days, when they started a thousand head of cattle travelling from the Gulf to South Australia without losing a hoof even though the cattle rushed several times. I myself think they must have picked up many strays. While telling their yarns, there was plenty of swearing, spitting and standing up to give their pants a hitch as they were dropping well under their belts.

It was not cold but they would assemble around a camp fire at night to tell their yarns, because otherwise they would have only the flicker of a fat lamp, which is the only lighting used on all stations in the men's and blacks' quarters. The managers are allowed a couple of cases of kerosene a year.

I shall have to explain about the fat lamps as you might think they are something special. It is a jam tin filled with fat, standing on a tin plate, with a piece of moleskin stuck in the middle to form a wick. This produces a small flame which smells, splutters and spits out a stray bubble of boiling fat every few minutes.

Peals of laughter came from the station and the visiting blacks' camps — bark humpies. The noise from the abos was caused mostly by their mimicking of the doings of the white men on the race during the day. They are really wonderful mimics. We could also hear in the distance the rejoicing corroboree of the wild blacks. This was on account of the killing of a bullock each day, from which they were allowed to carry the bones and offal to their camps. All these sounds added to the festivity of the occasion.

I'll write to you again soon. I am not quite myself yet, but Oh dear! it was lovely to see other white women.

Amateur Picnic Races, Delta Downs, 1896. Jane is seated at centre, flanked by the clergyman and the gentleman seated on the ground. Tom (bearded) stands behind her.

ACROSS THE YEARS

Do you know that now I can speak the blacks' language, I have to watch my p's and q's. I was frightened that while I was at Delta, when talking about eyes I would say "tilly" instead, or call ears "wallous", a nose "nindy" and a foot a "mundoe".

I'll enclose a photo of the races taken at the side of the Delta homestead. I wonder whether you will be able to pick me out. I know you won't because it is years since we have seen each other, and now I am a grownup woman. Anyway, I am sitting on a chair between the parson and the only man lying down. Tom is leaning over my chair. He wears a clipped beard which to me is much better than a week's growth of bristly hair, which is taken off on Sundays.

Love from,

JANE

My Dear,

It is so good of you to answer my letters so promptly. Letters are the only pleasure I get apart from frolicking from the gins.

I pass my time now sitting on the top rail of the stockyard, watching Tom breaking in horses.

The horse which is to be broken in is driven into a round yard and lassoed with rope made from plaited strands of bullock hide. When it is caught, it careers round and round the yard with Tom holding on to the rope, until the animal is nearly choked. It then remains still with a lather of sweat pouring from its body. Next it is made fast to a stockyard post, and rears and rears with its eyes nearly popping out from being nearly choked.

Then the fun really begins. Tom gets a long stick with a piece of bag tied to it, which he uses to rub — I say tickle — the animal all over, until it stops kicking and moving. Now the rope is let loose from the post with Tom still holding on. The horse will rear again and even try to strike with its front feet as well as kick with the hind feet.

Tom uses a small whip to make it lead and come up to him before he places the bit in its mouth.

After a lot of coaxing, a saddle and cloth are put on its back, and the front and back legs are tied together with an easily loosened half-hitch rope. When it is complete with a saddle and a rope halter it is set free.

One time I was over at the yard when Sim sounded the dinner bell, which is really a bullock bell, just after the horse had been saddled. I would have liked to stay a little while longer to see the horse

ACROSS THE YEARS

bucking, but I dared not for I have learnt from the severe scowl on Sim's face to bolt almost to the table. He will say to me, "What for you no hurry up me want to work longa vegetable garden." But no matter how long Tom takes to get to the table he will politely say, "No matter Boss, you no hurry up, plenty time." The best joke is that Tom will say to me, "Sim does not like you to be late for meals." Dear, if Sim was not a man I would be jealous but I am really amused, perhaps he thinks I am too ignorant or too young to look after myself and is waiting until I am twenty-one. I still have to wait two years. It was, as you know, my birthday on 7th March.

If I do not get to a town soon I shall be finding myself saying "this fellow belonga you", or again if I think I am not being understood I shall say "you savvie". Tom has warned me to watch my step and not make slips in my English.

The wrangling and argument amongst the black boys as to who shall ride the handled horse is most amusing. To me, it looks like sudden death.

One of the horse's eyes is blindfolded while the rider gets into the saddle. It is then removed and the horse starts to buck again. The nigger's back looks at times as though it would break in two from the swaying backwards and forwards, to the call of "kick him" coming from the other niggers sitting on the rails a few yards away.

If, by any chance, the nigger is bucked off, the audience will scream with laughter and then commence to jeer and hoot, for it is considered by them a dreadful disgrace to be bucked off. The crestfallen nigger will mount again, with set teeth and with a vice grip on his legs that no horse on the station could move, and will ride the horse to a finish amid loud applause from his mates.

The gates of the stockyards are kept in place by what is called a cap. This is a piece of stout wood fitted above the gate from one post to the other. When one of these boys was riding his mastered horse out to the paddock, the beast bucked just as he was under the cap and it almost took the scalp off the top of his head. His mates screamed with laughter although they could see the blood running down his face.

It is a good thing God took mercy in the making of these unfortunates by giving them such thick skulls. I have often wondered why, if they require punishment, they are never hit over the head, but get their shins tapped instead.

I shall stop now, as I am almost out of news.

Love from,

JANE

My Dear,

Your letter arrived a few days ago, I have been waiting for something special to turn up, but everything here is humdrum, so I shall tell you about the lives of the wild natives.

At the first sign of a thunderstorm they will get busy with house building, selecting a fresh well-drained spot near a waterhole. They are not able to build near their last camp as fleas, lice and other vermin have multiplied in billions and after they have lived nine months on the same spot it becomes too filthy.

They mark out several circles about fourteen feet in diameter, with about a foot between each circle, which is the foundation for their wet-weather homes. When the wet season is over they discard these homes and live and sleep in the open air.

The gins of the tribes gather soft pliable green sticks, fifteen or more feet long and point them at each end with a stone tomahawk, which is a flat piece of stone sharpened on one side by rubbing two stones together. I have seen them cut down large trees with them. They place these sticks in bundles for the men to carry to the camp. They force them some inches into the ground at each end to form a hoop. The tops of the hoops are tied with strong rope which the gins gather from the young centre leaf of the cabbage tree palm. They work this after the same manner as they do in making the twine for the dillybags.

The men of the tribes make their womenfolk do most of the work while they sleep, showing no mercy even to expectant mothers. The poor old gins gather bundles and bundles of grass, always keeping the bundle neat. It is then handed to the men who do the thatching of the house — *gunyah*. A hole is left just large enough for them to crawl in on their stomachs. After the houses are finished, a smouldering fire is lit by the gins at sundown, to drive out the mosquitoes that infest the place at all times of the year.

After all the men, gins, piccaninnies and their dogs — which are skinny, half starved, mangy and diseased — have crawled inside, the hole will be stuffed tight with grass to keep out the rain.

You can imagine what the heat in these gunyahs would be like in midsummer. It is no wonder that I have to hold my nose when they come to the kitchen to sell their wares. I am sure it is the melted fat inside the natives that keeps them so skinny. You never see a fat native.

The branding of all the calves is finished. It has taken nearly three weeks. Our neighbouring stations have sent one stockman and several niggers to attend the muster to gather their stray stock. They are camped on a creek some distance away. Before I came they all camped at the homestead but Sim tells me that they do not like white women.

I could easily see the men and niggers walking about together but was horrified when Kitty said, "He no boy he Mary-mary, white stockman Benjamin (husband) belonga him." The natives never use the feminine gender. To them everything and everybody is "he". The stockmen look such nice men, too. I could not believe the gins until I asked Tom. Do you know dear, I am sure Tom was not like these men before I came to stay. He declares he knew nothing about Mary-mary gins and I do believe him.

My piano which Mother had given me amongst other lovely things arrived this afternoon. When I struck the first chord, the two gins, who were standing on the verandah and who only knew the music of the jew's-harp, ran off screaming, "Devil-devil sit down inside he make big corroboree."

I shall stop now,

with love from

JANE

The Normanton Races
June 1896

My Dear,

Tom left a few days ago to attend the Stirling station muster, some forty miles from here.

I am alone with Sim, two gins and Pigeon. Last night I was terrified, so pulled the wardrobe against the door and left the window open slightly, about two inches, on account of the heat.

I had a loaded revolver under my pillow, but now and again my heart would stop beating and my ear drums would ring from fear, as I could distinctly hear footsteps creeping round my room and stopping at my window. I had the tiny bedroom lamp turned very low as I was frightened of the dark. I thought it was the wild natives looting the storeroom and I imagined I could hear the bags of flour being carried away.

They had broken into the store immediately after our first load arrived and although their footprints were traced to their camps we never found the bag of flour and sugar that was taken. You can imagine how loyal they are to one another, especially as there is a chance of the patrol coming out to investigate. Even the quiet employed blacks of their tribes will not give them away, in fact they will steal bread or save it from their meals to give to their wild mates. They did not take spice or clothes pegs.

I did not sleep a wink until daylight. You have no idea how helpless I felt. To be alone with Sim was bad enough without the fear of the blacks.

When Kitty came to my room the next morning carrying my breakfast — I always have breakfast in bed when Tom is away — I remarked to her, "Me plenty frightened last night, I could hear wild blackfellow walk about, I think he might kill me." She screamed laughing and said, "It been me, me sneak up plenty times, look in window, me thinket some one might sit down in room longa you."

Dear, I was horrified and cried and cried to think she was insinuating that I was flirting with Sim, since he was the only male on the place, but when I told Tom what she had said he roared with laughter. He told me not to be a goose as that was her way of telling me she was watching over me in my loneliness.

She was very indignant at the idea of me thinking a blackfellow might kill me and said, "Blackfellow he no kill you, he alright, white man he no good. When you and Boss go sleep, he, that white man, come up to door longa my room, he knock, he say, me got plenty lollies, you come out I give you some. Me say, me no want lollie, supposen you no clear out me yabber (talk) missus. My word me plenty laugh when me gammon (pretend) call out. He run quick. Me plenty laugh good joke."

You would never believe after all the years of church and Sunday school I would not know when it is Sunday but for the gins, who count off the days by knowing a big plum pudding is made for them on those days. On other days they get the puddings and cake left from our table. Kitty was always complaining that she only got a little pudding and cake from Sim while Annie got plenty.

On one occasion she came to me saying, "That chinaman he no give me cake, he say old gin no want cake." Not thinking what I was saying I replied, "You koula (hit) him next time."

A day or so later, after my midday meal, when all the men were out on the run and I was having my usual nap, I was awakened by a noise of flap, flap, coming from the direction of the kitchen. It was Kitty, with the long heavy stick Sim uses to lift the lids off the camp ovens, chasing Sim in and out of the kitchen doors. His pigtail was hanging loose and he had lost one of his straw slippers, causing the flap-flap noise that had drawn my attention. He was almost white from fear in trying to escape the death blow and very glad to see me. He ran behind me calling loudly, "What for that gin kill me." Kitty nearly mad with rage yelled, "What for you call me old gin."

I shall close once again. I do hope you are not shocked by anything I have written. I had no idea of what goes on in the bush, I had learnt so little in town, but now I feel my innocence has all gone.

Love from,

JANE

My Dear,

I do love your letters, they are so very different to the life I am leading. You can look over my rude things and be sure to tear them up as soon as you have read them. I know your mother is so prim and proper.

THE NORMANTON RACES

I must tell you that last week I made up my mind only to write about the tinted leaves falling in spring, I mean in winter, or about birds floating in the air but somehow I am unable to stretch my imagination so shall have to drift back to writing of realities.

I have to write you about this incident because it is so screamingly funny. Jim and a couple of white men came out from town to have a duck shoot and at the same time to see Jean Currie who has been paying me a visit.

We arranged a camping out picnic. I had no idea what camping out meant but learnt during the night. The ground was hard and a lump of something was under the small of my back. All the others in the party said it was imagination as loads of grass had been cut for use as mattresses.

Jim and his two friends rode with Jean, cantering ahead of the buggy through the long grass to make a clear track and to watch out for logs and stumps. There was not even a track to follow and the grass came up to the horses' backs.

We arrived at the duck holes in time for lunch. By the time our tents were pitched, grass cut for the beds and the beds made it was six o'clock and time to send the niggers out to frighten the ducks up. Immediately, the air became thick and black with wild fowl, so the shooting party went off with their guns.

I remained at the camp alone, to gather the fruit of the wild grape, which was hanging in bunches along the edge of the scrub. They are a very delicious fruit but leave the tongue swollen and sore for quite an hour after eating. While gathering the fruit a bird fell at my feet, which I thought had been wounded by the party. It was flapping its wings and calling as if in pain and as I stooped to pick it up, it floundered a few feet further into the scrub. I suddenly realised I was out of sight of the camp and lost in a dense scrub. I knew the camp was not far off, so sat down to wait until the party returned to hear their cooees for me. The bird was a pheasant, which had its nest near the camp and had decoyed me away from its young ones.

Two flour sacks of black duck were shot and cleaned before we left the next afternoon for home. We were laden also with fish, crab and grapes and started home in the greatest excitement.

Several races were run on the way home when a clear piece of country was entered. My two gins asked if they could join in the race. They rode astride and were only clad in calico dresses, which on mounting their horses came well up to their thighs.

A race started to see who would be the first home. The two gins got to the front, their dresses after they had gone a few yards slipping

ACROSS THE YEARS

up to their waists, and as the race grew faster, so their dresses moved up to their armpits, leaving the rest of their bodies naked.

The white party gave up the race either from laughing too much or from being too embarrassed, with Jean there, to catch up with the naked gins who, of course, easily won. They said to me, "Cripes me hurry up, plenty frightened, me been forget my trousers."

This is all for the present,

love from,

JANE

My Dear,

I seem to be always doing the wrong thing. Sometimes I wish I had never come to the bush. I busied myself, much against Tom's will, to get Joe O'Reilly from Mentana — where the niggers are very savage — to catch a little Mary-mary about ten years of age for a friend in Normanton to break in for housework. I do not mean she would use a rope as in breaking in a horse. Joe arrived with a child, however, who was more like a wild cat than a human. She would claw and bite when I tried to touch her. We kept her tied to Kitty — who was a Mentana gin also — for a few days, until she was quiet enough to take to town.

Ross, the previous manager of Maggieville, who now lives in the stockman's quarters, and Tom took her to town and they both declare that if I want any more gins sent in I shall have to take them myself. Poor old Ross was clawed and bitten in several places while holding her, for at every chance she would try to jump out of the buggy. They were glad to deliver the cat to my friend, who locked her in the bathroom.

It was two o'clock the following afternoon when they started back home. Looking back as they were crossing the punt, they saw the little child swimming the crocodile-infested river. She had escaped by breaking a window. They waited to give her a drive back to her own country, but as soon as she reached the bank she fled through the mangroves and did not call at a station until she got back to her own *touri* (country).

We are off to Normanton at daylight. I am so excited I am sure I shall not sleep tonight. It will be the first time I have seen Mother for five months. I am taking her a bunch of flowers — cosmos, balsams, cockscombs, zinnias and marigolds — which I am very proud of as I have grown them myself. I shall finish this letter later as I still have to pack Tom's clothes.

THE NORMANTON RACES

Later: I am sorry to have kept you waiting so long for a letter but it has taken me some time to settle down and get the house in order. Well dear, we did not get to Normanton the day we started after all. In many places on the road, water was still lying in pools. When turning round the watercourse near Maggieville, our horses fell suddenly into a waterhole and the point of the buggy pole struck the opposite bank and splintered to pieces.

Landsborough Street, Normanton 1892. This was the main street of the town and has been decorated in festive spirit, probably for the Annual Races. The appearance would have been essentially the same in 1896 at the Annual Races described by Jane.

ACROSS THE YEARS

There we were with our front wheels in the hole, while the back ones rested on the bank. I was thrown against the hood, cutting my lip and blackening one of my eyes. We had to walk back to Maggieville station and remain the night while a makeshift pole was cut from a ti-tree and fitted to the buggy.

I feel so awful, making my debut into civilisation with my black eye, especially as I know all eyes will be on me to see how I am standing the rough bush life. I hope their decision is not that Tom gave it to me or I got it from the niggers. Anyhow, I shall have to be brave about it. But dear, I am crying even now about it and wish I was back on the station.

I have a beautiful green dress and toque from Finney's of Brisbane. It is Tom's choice. He says I must dress differently now I am a married woman and buy materials one cannot see through. The choice is a bottle green, almost as thick as a billiard table cloth, trimmed with black velvet, and a very severe toque.

Looking in the mirror, I certainly do look married. There will be no hope of getting admiration elsewhere as I could be easily taken for a grandmother. It is a good thing it pleases Tom.

Our annual races interest whites and blacks from Croydon, Burketown and every station for miles around Normanton. The ladies are all in their best winter frocks. An occasional fur might be noticed in the crowd on someone who had lived at some time in a cooler climate.

The men from the bush are dressed in full suits. It is lucky bushmen do not become corpulent until they are well past forty, otherwise I do not know how most of them would manage, for by the look of some suits worn, they were their first long trousers.

We have a nice mare, Lobelia. She has been trained on Midlothian and her gallop reveals a wonderful time on the stopwatch. We are keeping the secret with the hope of winning a few hundred pounds to pay for her feed, my frock and toque, and still have a few pounds in the bank.

I shall stop and will give you a full description of our gay doings later on when we return to Midlothian, which I hope won't be "to whip the cat"! I have a feeling Lobelia will pay for it all.

Love from,

JANE

My Dear,

We are back home again to the simple diet of corned beef, bread and jam, a far different menu from angels on horseback, chicken in aspic and so on.

Our annual gaiety was a great success and I shall start off at the beginning, but do forgive me if I wander a little for I had such fun.

Lobelia, whom we knew did excellent time on our home track, encouraged Tom, although he could ill afford it, to back her heavily in the different races for which she was entered. The day before the races she showed an appalling result, so you can imagine how our hearts sank and I fretted at the idea of losing about one hundred pounds, especially with fat bullocks at thirty shillings a head and no chance of receiving help from elsewhere. We only sell our fat bullocks to the local butcher and there one has to use a great deal of tact.

Donald McIntyre of Dalgonelly station erected a boiling down works, which was thought a great boom to the cattle man; but when Tom had to pay two shillings and sixpence per head after three hundred fat cattle had been treated, to defray expenses, all hope of the meatworks was gone, so we have to hobnob to the butcher again.

Mr Peter Macarthy, an elderly gentleman, took me to the meatworks to break a bottle of champagne, to declare them open. Donald McIntyre did not like women, so none were asked but myself. My brother Jim had been at school with his son and I was only nineteen so that made it different. The head man of the works there said, "I would like to boil you down to make glycerine." I suppose he thought me terribly fat.

On the first day of the races, even the black boy trainer had completely lost interest in Lobelia, and although I was wearing the smartest of outfits I felt very depressed.

I could feel the perspiration dripping from my neck down my spine to be collected at the number eighteen waistline of the tight corset, and again down my legs and into my shoes. My dress was almost touching the ground in front and had a swooping train at the back which gathered up dust as well as heat.

Poor Lobelia looked so neglected when she came on to the racetrack. Some of my women friends were very cheery while others were very sarcastic and half rude. One exclaimed, "You should have called her feathers!"

Our neighbour from Delta Downs was a naturally sarcastic man and so he said, "I cannot see my neighbour's horse go out without a ticket on her so I had better go over to the totalisator before it is too

ACROSS THE YEARS

late." His friendship or perhaps his sarcasm brought him a dividend of seventy-seven pounds nine shillings.

I blamed Tom and he blamed me for being such a fool as to go back on her known form, but nevertheless from that moment onwards I never noticed the hot day, the billiard-table cloth dress, or the perspiration.

Lobelia was then treated with great respect by our neighbours from Maggieville, Stirling, Delta Downs and Meranda, who all felt ashamed and were sorry that after knowing her time they had let her race without their support.

She won every race that she started in, and we went home with a little over four hundred pounds in our pockets, after all expenses. Even my green dress had been settled.

I must describe the race. Although looking uncared for Lobelia was full of spirit as she gave her "preliminary" past the grandstand. There were many cheers from our niggers who called, "Good O Belia by cripes she win alright."

The race was eight furlongs, and all horses were at the starting post ready to go at the drop of the flag. Off they started with our mare in front, and she kept that position all through the race, winning by five lengths. The excitement was so great that one could only hear "Lobelia, Lobelia". It was so funny to see Tom being carried shoulder high, leading his horse after she had been weighed in.

My nasty lady friend apologised for calling the horse "feathers" and took great pains to congratulate me, saying that she really did not mean it, knowing what a beautiful beast Lobelia was. I felt like saying "Buthue", which is a very dreadful swearword in the blacks' language.

Mr Epworth, manager of Delta station, offered Tom half of the tote win but Tom was too well satisfied to accept any of it.

I cried with excitement and forgot all about looking like a married woman as I flung my arms round the man who happened to be standing next to me, and cried on his shoulder. Can you imagine how I felt when I discovered that he was an old half-sweetheart whom I had flirted with and of whom Tom was frightfully jealous. So again my feelings dropped. When I saw what mood Tom was in, I knew I could have kept my head on my friend's shoulder for an hour and he would never have noticed. It did not take me long to remember who I was and I now felt so important in my billiard cloth dress and severe toque.

The race days were beautiful although a little warmish. The men

THE NORMANTON RACES

*Leichhardt Hotel, Normanton, 1890. This may have been the hotel
in which Tom and Jane stayed during the Annual Races of 1892.
Alternatively it may have been the unnamed hotel opposite.*

of the town and bush had arranged everything for the ladies' comfort.
There was a marquee with tables and chairs, and morning and
afternoon teas were served free to invited guests. The men, mostly
bachelors, were very attentive to the ladies and often presented
totalisator tickets in repayment for the hospitality given at our picnic
races.

The first night there was a ball, arranged by the town folk. It was
wonderful. The hall was decorated with gum tips and the hundreds of
chinese lanterns presented a very glamorous effect.

The men in full evening dress looked so different from how they
appear in the bush, with their white moleskin pants and coloured
shirts; but alas, after the opening dance — the lancers — which was
danced with vigour, they were left with a pulpy mess around their
necks instead of the nice stiff, highly polished collars. No lady cared
whether her feet touched the ground or not as she was held so firmly
by her strong bushman, and she could be sure that only a stray ankle
could be seen as our dresses were so long and we also wore starched
petticoats.

After the ball, which ended at three in the morning, a practical
joke was arranged by one of the bushmen to place a full bucket of
water over the door of the room occupied by the manager of Iffley
station. It was placed so that when the door was opened he received
the contents.

Seizing his own bedroom jug of water he threw it into the room
opposite to his. The attack was unexpected but before a few seconds
all of the hotel visitors were running about with jugs of water ready to

ACROSS THE YEARS

Unknown hotel, Normanton, circa 1890. This may have been the hotel owned by Jane Bardsley senior. If so, it would be likely that Tom and Jane stayed there during the Annual Races of 1892.

throw over the first person who came their way. Some were clad in evening dress, others in pants only, and others in their pyjamas. All were running from corridor to corridor with Mr Healy, the hotel proprietor, soaking wet — for he had gathered many a bucket of water — and screaming for the riot to stop or he would call the police, who I think were enjoying the fun.

The women, who were all huddled in one corner of a room, were discussing the events of the ball when the waterfight started, and the fleeing men raced through the door which had been left wide open.

I know dear, you will be shocked at such proceedings but when you realise that some of the bushmen only see the town once a year, and then have to make most of their own amusement, you will not blame them. I am sure you too would have joined in the fun as we did.

After the waterfight everyone knew a huge account would have to be paid. They then hoisted the remaining crockery chamberpots up the flagpole, for poor old Healy the hotel keeper to pull down in the morning. The evening's frolic cost the twenty men thirty-five pounds before Mr Healy was satisfied.

The second evening after the races there were some theatricals of poor quality in the town, and as it was an annual event the hall was packed to the door long before starting time. Most of the women did not laugh at the naughty jokes. I did not even smile because Tom was sitting beside me and I am sure some of his ancestors were truly Scotch. Oh! My! most of the men from the bush simply roared and laughed until the tears ran down their cheeks.

THE NORMANTON RACES

Tom got very bored and left the hall with one of the bank managers and three other men who occupy prominent positions — they were Scotch — to procure a donkey he had purchased for stud purposes only that day from a man selling a mob in the town. Much to everyone's surprise they carried the donkey into the hall. This completely wrecked the end of the already poor entertainment. The men of the audience left in a body to follow the donkey, and to have a few hours' better entertainment.

Great was the surprise of Mr Healy on descending the main stairway the next morning to find a woebegone looking donkey tied to the foot of his staircase. He was rampant with rage and tried to push the donkey out, but the more he pushed the deeper the donkey sank his hooves into the polished floor. He at last had to plead to his boarders to lift him out. At the same time he threatened vengeance on all concerned in the joke, but the poor old chap had to shout drinks for the crowd before they would lift the animal out.

The next night the stockmen gave their ball. It was much the same as the previous one, except that the women had to dance with the men who asked them first. My first partner said, "You like dance with me?" I replied "Yes", so up we got to dance the polka. It really was so funny, between his puffing and blowing he would tell me I looked beautiful.

I shall stop now but shall write in a few days, when I have more time to spare as I have quite a lot to say about our doings.

Love from,

JANE

My Dear,

Well I must tell you some more about our trip to the races. Mr J. M. Macrossan, an MLA,[18] was expected to speak on parliamentary affairs in a few days, so of course our stay in town lasted well into the second week.

The Liberals arranged their supporters in the hall to stop interjections. Tom, who was one of them, saw his mate Barny Magee in holts with a big wharfie, who held him by his necktie and had him

[18] John Murtagh Macrossan (1833–1891) was the MLA for Kennedy (1873–1878) and for Townsville (1879–1891). Although politically a Conservative, as Secretary for Mines (1879–1883 and 1888–1890) he was responsible for much reformist legislation to do with mining in Queensland.

about strangled, when Tom came to his assistance.

In the scuffle to throw the man out through a side door, Tom was accidentally thrown out with him on to a railed porch, where he and the wharfie finished the fight. His mates, missing him from the hall, began to look for him. Luckily for Tom he threw the fellow over the railings, and thumped hard on the door. He was almost inside the door, when the man — who had jumped to his feet — made a wild rush at Tom, grabbed the back of his shirt and tore it off his back, leaving him standing in the hall with his collar and parts of his sleeves. I can imagine your saying what a lot of madcaps, but Tom says he is lucky to be alive.

I have a wonderful secret to tell you, but really dear, it has worried me so much at times I could almost wish it were not so, but the stork is to pay us a visit sometime in the first week of November.

Sim has ceased to be my Godfather and in fact looks the other way should I go near him. Sometimes however, I see him giving me a sly look, but by the frowning look on his face I wonder if I have done something wrong. Kitty has adopted me instead, and watches me constantly. If I go to jump a log or hop down from the verandah she will exclaim loudly, "No do that, you killem little fellow."

Tom reads the doctor's book from morning to night studying up my case and he will hardly let me move about freely, let alone run about at all. At times I feel I have turned to stone and then again I feel like a princess, with his care and attention.

Sim got the huff and left us suddenly this morning. Tom asked me if anything had happened and I said, "I do not know but I have not seen him since the day before yesterday. Perhaps he does not like my figure."

It is almost dark but the gins can see Mr Harvey, the manager of Milgarra station, coming. He is going to inspect a mob of bulls for the bank, so I must go and straighten my waistline and put a little prepared chalk on my face and pinch it to make the roses bloom.

It was five o'clock when Mr Harvey arrived at the house, and Tom was out attending to the cattle. He handed me a letter of introduction from the bank. While I was reading it, Kitty looked over my shoulder and said, "Where this fellow sit down inside or out." I coughed hard and said, "Kitty you wait awhile and go away," but she persisted with, "Sun go to bed me want to know where he sit down please."

Mr Harvey, knowing what the gin meant, started to apologise for his appearance saying, "It was a very dusty road that I travelled. No wonder the gin thinks I am an ordinary traveller, and wants to know if I am an inside man or meal in the kitchen."

THE NORMANTON RACES

We are without a cook and I am so tired. It has been brain worry all day here to get a meal ready on my own for Mr Harvey, without Tom's aid. I did not try to make pastry this time. It is boiled rice, dried apples, corned beef, potatoes and pumpkin, and tomorrow's breakfast is to be fried corned beef and eggs. I cannot make a curry without having Tom near me because I either fry the meat too much or too little, the pieces are either cut too large or too small, or I have put in too much curry powder or not enough. At times I feel like throwing the whole thing out, but I remember my mother's advice: "Give and take."

I shall go to bed now and let the men carry on the usual conversation of the bushmen; cattle, horses, dry spell, ticks, and so on and on.

Love from,

JANE

P.S.   Mother says it is necessary to be in town six weeks to prepare for the baby's advent and to get the clothes ready for the little fellow. Tom is busying himself running in the buggy horses and sending relays on, as the heat is almost unbearable for horses to travel any distance.

J.A.

First son
Frederick Arthur — 6 September 1896

My Dear,

I cannot wait for a reply to my last letter, because so many dreadful things have happened in the meantime.

After a stay of nine weeks in Normanton I am back at Midlothian. I'll start from where I left Mr Harvey and Tom talking about cattle etc.

Our home is looked upon as one of the nicest homes this side of the river, although it is only a two-roomed house of corrugated iron, with a ten-foot verandah on three sides, built in front of Tom's original two-roomed cottage. I have made the two main rooms so artistic by lining them and ceiling them with art muslin that has a greyish background with pink roses and green foliage, but alas! it is far from being soundproof. When we have visitors and want to talk, we have to do so in whispers.

Oh! I have forgotten to tell you that when I was looking through some of Tom's boxes, I came upon parcels of unopened linen. By the look of things his mother must have sent a big supply of all kinds of house linen at least once a year. When we were married she sent a huge parcel of double sheets as well as the usual lot, and dozens of yards of the muslin which I used to decorate the iron wall, so with the linen that Mother gave me I have enough to furnish a large hotel. I have cut up some of the sheets to make underclothing for the gins.

After leaving the men I went into my bedroom and then went out again and chased a mob of little pigs out of my garden, forgetting all about the little fellow. I was suddenly seized with cramps and did not enter my bed all night.

Mr Harvey, who was a married man with a family, could hear me crying and told Tom what he thought was wrong. I could scarcely believe him as Mother and the doctor both told me that it would be the first week in November that the stork would come. Mother is so shy about storks and the advice she gave me was in a whisper.

We had nothing in preparation either for the arrival of the little fellow or for the horses on the road, and it was ten in the morning before we started for Normanton, forty-five miles away. I shall never

FIRST SON

forget the first twenty-five miles. We both took a vow then and there that if the stork ever flew over our house again he would be shot dead.

We called into Maggieville station to borrow fresh horses and seek the aid of the white woman housekeeper, but she was an old maid and knew nothing about storks. So we continued our journey. I was desperate and fainted with each spasm of pain. Sometimes I clung to the hood of the buggy and called to the Almighty to know what I had done to deserve such suffering.

At Walker Creek, four miles from Maggieville, the shire council had men repairing the crossing. It was in such a bad state that while the buggy was being driven over by Tom, the foreman carried me over. I heard him say to Tom, "Put her in my tent, she is too ill to go any further."

However, we arrived in the town at half past eight, and I was quite delirious by this time. Doctor Roth, who was the only doctor in the town, was sought and he tried to receive the stork's message but quite failed and said, "I can do no more for her."

Tom Nevitt who was a wardsman at the General Hospital and his wife who had been a nurse, were an exceptionally clever pair, and knew exactly what to do in cases like mine. So at five in the morning on 6th September the stork arrived, and brought a tiny son weighing two and a half pounds into the world; so tiny that he could have fitted into a quart pot.[19]

I was just nine months and two days married. It was so sad to see our little fellow wrapped in cotton wool and carried round on a pillow and hot bricks for three weeks.

Oh dear! I shall always remember when I opened my eyes at midnight and saw Tom Nevitt leaning over my bed. My mind promptly registered the fact that it was wrong for a strange man to be in my room, but I was too weak to order him out. Then I saw my beautiful mother with her head of wonderful black curls. She was dressed in a black silk frock relieved with a point lace fichu — years old — which gave her a soft gentle look. Her eyes filled with tears when she looked at me and there was an expression on her face that I had never seen before, but it did not occur to me that I was dying.

It was ten o'clock when I again opened my eyes, and I tried to speak but my tongue would not move. Then I wondered whether I had had my baby, and tried to lift my hand to feel my body, but not a muscle could I move. When the old midwife, who was fourteen stone, came sideways through the door carrying in her arms what I thought

---

[19] Frederick Arthur Atherton was born on 6 September 1896. He died in 1955.

was a bundle of blankets, she said, "For God's sake don't try to talk, you have been through a lot, and you have a nice little son." I must have gone to sleep again then, because when I next awoke the house was in perfect stillness. Even then it did not dawn on me that I had nearly crossed the Great Divide.

I asked the nurse to show me the baby and she started to unwind the blankets and soft linen until at last its face was to be seen. It was the size of an afternoon tea teacup, all black and patched up with plaster.

Then the parson came into the room and I thought I must be dying and asked him if he thought so. He replied, "No, I think you have pulled through, but your little son is not out of danger and so I have come to christen him."

I asked to see the baby's body. It was awful, just skin and bone, and it was hardly breathing. I was too weak to cry outwardly but my eyes filled with tears. My ideals of a beautiful little fellow were shattered.

Poor Tom, when he saw his firstborn, put his head down and cried for a second and then said, "Take it away, I didn't think it would be possible for me to be the father of such a mite."

We did have one laughable happening whilst we were in Normanton. Kitty, who had travelled with me to town, declaring that she knew what to do if little fellow came up, was troubled at night by some man knocking on her window, and would bolt into my room saying "white man look longa my window".

Tom spoke to the sergeant of police who promised that he would send one of his men to look around the place during the night. We accordingly explained to Kitty that when she saw the man, she was to run out and grab him and call out until the midwife came to her. A man came that night, and she held him all right, there was no possible chance of his escaping. But alas! it was the policeman she was holding. Of course we all agreed that he was just doing his duty although Kitty declares that he was the man who came to her room every night.

My little fellow requires such a lot of attention and I am not strong myself. I have gone like a chinaman, all yellow. A friend says it is jaundice, but I am so afraid I have caught Sim's colour. I have gone from eight stone four pounds to six stone three. I have no shelf to rest my bosom on now.

We are so worried about our little fellow as he has a big lump on his head, and it will be necessary for us to take him south to a good doctor. These messages from the stork cost such a lot of money, but

FIRST SON

my parents are helping. I do not know whether my old clothes have stretched or not, but they will go round me twice. Mother says I shall need new clothes to be presented to my in-laws at Mackay.

We will leave here as soon as the wet weather is over. I shall not notice the rain so much with a delicate child to care for. Pigeon looks such a big thing beside him. She never leaves him for a minute and even when he sleeps, there is the faithful little thing fast asleep on her mat.

The baby is causing quite a stir amongst the wild gins who call from the fence "see piccaninny please". After looking at him they shake their heads, and with love and sympathy in their eyes, start that sad moan which is so often heard from their camps when something is wrong.

At first I began to shiver wondering who they were so sad about, me with my yellow skin all over my body or the tiny little baby. They never stopped talking nor did they take their eyes off my face.

I asked my gins what they were saying, and they said, "That piccaninny no good, more better you chuck it poui-poui (long way), catchem nother one."

I must end now,

With love from a little mother,

JANE ATHERTON

My Dear Althea,

I have been extra busy cleaning up before we leave for Mackay.

Tom has a room which he likes to call his own, but really it is most impossible. I can just squeeze in. I am sure he has never thrown anything away in the whole of the nine years that he has lived here. Amongst the rubbish were two large flour sacks filled with a collection of mail papers, envelopes, circulars and love letters.

Dear, we have had our first row, and at the moment are not speaking. I might tell you that we have many an argument, but of course that's nothing to married folk. I thought he would be so pleased about my tidying up, but to my amazement after he had questioned me carefully as to whether I had looked right through the sacks and filed all the Government receipts, and I had answered sweetly, "Yes, dear," he glared at me and roared like a bull. Not exactly at me, but at women in general. If I hadn't the little fellow I would go back to Mother straight away. Anyway I haven't gone so that's that. I should have thought that I ought to have been the one to become annoyed as I found out that I wasn't his first sweetheart. He certainly told me before we were married that I was.

The natives are very friendly towards me now and often call out "piccaninny". Sometimes I visit their camps and see the filthy lives they lead. I get Tom to make them clean them up every so often by burning off the old rags, bones, and dirty grass. When eating their food they squat anywhere, and after a mouthful or two they pitch a handful or so over their backs to be picked up by the dogs that always wait in this way to be fed. It is necessary to keep at this tidying all the time, otherwise the homestead would be overrun and little Fred's face covered with flies.

Pigeon is bathed every morning in the same water as Fred, and she says, "I like Baby's pretty water, nindy smell soap." I then have to powder her also. Then I put my black and my white child together inside a cheesecloth mosquito net on a piece of Chinese matting, under the poinciana trees. They are clad only in their shirts as the heat is terrific here in December. Sometimes I find both of them asleep.

If Pigeon wanders about with her eyes unprotected she will be stung by a poisonous fly and both her eyelids will swell up. Then she cannot see unless she pulls them apart with her fingers.

We expect to get away south at the end of March. Baby still has the lump on his head.

I don't think that I mentioned the fact that our baby has been named Frederick Arthur.

Love from,

JANE

My Dear,

You would simply love the birds of the Gulf. They are here in millions, of all sizes and colours. The painted finch resembles all the colours of the rainbow. There is the blood finch of the deepest red, black throats, double bars, diamonds and a great many more varieties.

In November each year people get permission from Tom to camp on the run in order to catch these beautiful birds. They sell them in the southern towns.

It is interesting to watch the birds being caught. At the end of each year the waterholes are nearly dry. The bird-catchers cover all but a couple with bushes and grass. On the other two a fine net mesh and the attached strings are pulled by a man hiding behind a bush. When the birds are all settled and having their evening's drink, they are captured.

Their buckboard buggies are converted into huge cages and the birds are taken away in them in thousands. Sometimes the young natives will climb a tree eighty or ninety feet high in order to catch a galah or corella parrot. They make nicks in the trees with their tomahawks. For this perilous job they receive only a plug of tobacco. They do not of course understand the use of money.

Tom made me a large cage for the birds that the fanciers gave me. I am sorry now that I bothered about them as birdseed has been added to our meagre store order. I am sure that they are underfed and I think that I shall let them go when the supply of birdseed runs out.

Hard times are on us now and we have to do without a cook and economise in every way. Oh dear! Sometimes I fancy a little ham, and then again my mouth will water for an apple or a piece of chocolate. Mother knows that we are very poor and that I am very delicate and often long for more tasty food, and so she pays the mailman a shilling to take dainties weighing about a pound. I would die otherwise, living only on corned beef, rice and eggs. It is too hot to grow vegetables or make butter. The cows give very little milk and will not improve until we get an early thunderstorm at the beginning of December.

The banks have taken over almost every station in the Gulf, in fact I think that there are only two left to their original owners, Midlothian and Magowra, and these are financed by other paying concerns. Some of the poor pioneers, after their years of hard and perilous toil, are turned out penniless.

From financial pressure, expenses would be curtailed by forfeiting small portions of their country to reduce the payments of Government and local rates, which are extremely high. Immediately the time for the resumption of their small lands was advertised in the Government *Gazette*, there would be a dozen or more applications lodged, and the lucky applicant settles in with perhaps a wife and large family, two milking cows, a team of working bullocks and perhaps, a little money.

Do you know dear, luck seems to favour these settlers with their twenty-five square miles or so of poor land, and though they have had very little experience they become expert buyers. Anyway, their herds certainly grow. They know many good points to remember when buying a cow, which the old pioneers did not. The new type of cows have anything up to seven calves at calving time, whereas in the old days "twins" were fairly unusual.

We have of course to combat the straight cattleduffer whom we all know and try to avoid. All calves are branded very young so that there will be no mistake about their identity.

At mustering time all cattle not bearing our brand are tailed — herded — and word is sent to the owners to remove them as quickly as possible.

I must tell you a joke concerning the word "tailed". I was tired of salt beef and longed for killing day to get fresh meat. I asked Tom what he meant by the word "tailing", and was overjoyed when he told me that it meant that the tails of the cattle were cut off and that we could have oxtail for months. Noticing that the salt beef was still just as much in evidence, I asked a stockman when it would be coming along. He roared with laughter and said, "The boss is pulling your leg."

I wish I had Sim back again. My first batch of bread was very good to look at but awful to eat. We only have camp ovens in which to bake our bread. The gins lift the heavy lids and red-hot ashes for the ovens. I do the bread making. I forgot to ask Sim before he left how long a batch of bread should be cooked.

My first batch, after I had had it in the oven for about three-quarters of an hour, looked a beautiful golden brown. After the gins had taken it off the fire, and turned the oven upside down on a clean flour sack, I covered it up carefully smiling to myself and thinking all the time that never did Sim make bread as well as I had just done. But alas! when I looked at it in an hour's time the middle had leaked out. It was only a golden crust with uncooked dough inside.

I did not explain about the cattleduffers, and I want to as I would like you to know what we have to endure in the midst of our poverty.

So many brands are found on the stray stock that it is necessary to refer to the Government Brands Book in order to find the owners. Some of the brands are so pretty, some blotched and faked. One brand I loved to hear an Irishman pronounce was one which sounded something like "take you too" (TQ2). Killing day is the day of all days as we live on salt beef for six weeks. Not that we do not have plenty to eat but we have to be careful not to use too much salt. Our house blacks eat the fresh meat until they are scarcely able to walk. They look like kewpies, and don't do much work while the fresh meat lasts.

We make our own soap, sandsoap and extract of beef. The extract, when cooked with vegetables, makes delicious soup.

FIRST SON

Luckily we have plenty of wild game and their eggs. The boys shot thirty-two whistling ducks yesterday, with one cartridge.

I shall have to close now as it is time to see to the meal tables. If I do not attend to this there will only be a terrible jumble of knives and forks spread all over the table. There is one thing however, that they never forget, and that is the sugar. I am sure they eat it on every occasion.

Love from,

JANE

My Dear,

A terrible, terrible thing has happened. We wondered why Sim left so suddenly without giving any reason, but we know now, because Annie is expecting a visit from the stork and Sim had a lot to do with it.

I have taken such care of the gins, too, locking them up every night at sunset, to look at their books, have their smoke and also be free from molestation. When I questioned them, I made both gins toe the line, and then I asked Annie how she got "So so", and was horrified when she replied, "Sim when I go gather eggs in fowl house, when you and boss eat dinner, he look longa egg too. I bin catchem piccaninny then." So you see we have not only chooks in our fowl house, but storks too.

Anyway, Kitty and Annie ran away last week leaving me with only Pigeon to help me. Tom has excelled himself as cook. He is something extra special at cakes, scones, curry and rice and pancakes. However the worst part of it is that I am his offsider and have all the washing-up to do after he has finished, and seeing that he uses dozens of pans to mix with I seem to be doing it all the time.

Neither Kitty nor Annie are married but on account of the latter's impending visit from the stork we have decided to let both gins marry. It would be terrible to have a little baby here without a name.

We sent Charlie, aged about forty years, and Homer, aged about twenty years, out with a gun to bring back the gins. Blacks often run away. The gun was not loaded with anything but blank cartridges.

Charlie and Homer both wanted to marry the young gin Annie, but neither wanted Kitty, who is classed as an old gin. Tom explained to the boys that whoever catches Annie can have her as his wife. This is all the marriage ceremony required. After searching for twenty-four hours they came across the two gins who, upon seeing them, climbed into a Leichhardt tree. Homer fired the first shot at Annie, thinking she would fall and be caught by him. However Kitty, all too anxious to get to Homer, whom she loved, fell about ten feet out of the tree right into his arms and clung to him so tightly that it was impossible for him to escape from her clutches. They arrived home at midnight married.

In the early morning Kitty came to my room and said, "Homer Benjamin longa me now, me wash and mend clothes longa him." Poor Annie was so disgusted at Charlie's age that we had the greatest difficulty in making her settle down.

Ned Atherton, a cousin of Tom's, has arrived from Emerald End. He is to manage Midlothian when we are away in Mackay with Fred. We should be leaving in two weeks' time. Time seems to drag while waiting to start off, and to make matters worse we might all have been killed if I had not learned to use a revolver.

We were having trouble in procuring sufficient milk for the house and for Fred's bottles. The white stockman had been told to look after the cows and see that they gave enough milk, otherwise he would go short of milk for his tea, and his pudding diet would cease. He found it was not the fault of the cows but of Homer, who liked his little draught of milk before leaving the yard.

The next morning Tom called him and accused him of drinking the milk. This was the result. I was awakened by a peculiar sound like a muffled distressed sound from a man. I ran out and found that it was Tom lying on his face, with Homer the nigger sitting straddle-legged on his back, bumping his nose on the ground. I screamed for help. My cries brought Ned Atherton, who had been sick the previous day and was therefore still in his pyjamas, the white stockman, Old Ross from Maggieville, four black boys and two gins to the scene in a few seconds.

The seven niggers began to attack the four white men, holding Tom and the old man down to the ground, and biting pieces of flesh out of their arms with heated excitement, yelling all the time. Ned Atherton, who is six feet two inches, was warding off the blows of two niggers at once calling for a revolver.

I quickly ran to my room, snatched my baby under one arm and grabbed a revolver from under Tom's pillow with my free hand and ran out again. We used always to keep the gun in a chest in the daytime and under Tom's pillow at night.

I pointed the thing at one of the niggers and when he saw it, he let out a scream of fright and bolted for the humpies, followed by his mates.

Kitty, who did not belong to the same tribe as any of the boys, ran to me saying, "I hold little fellow, you shoot boys." However I was too frightened to trust her.

In a few minutes the niggers were all recalled one by one while I stood a few yards off with the revolver in my hand. The old man of seventy held the baby. His face was in a terrible state, hardly a bit of skin remaining. Tom too, had his nose broken, two black eyes and pieces of flesh torn off his arms. The stockman was very badly bitten on the hands and arms.

The blacks were strung up onto the rafters for an hour or so, with their toes just touching the ground. Their shins were tapped now and again. This treatment is better than whipping.

I am shuddering even now at the remembrance of it all even though it happened days ago, in fact I have been in bed with swollen breasts. Kitty who has had some experience of this in the wild tribes tells me to "keep him two fellow hot, rub longa goanna fat". So we understand to use hot foments and olive oil. As a matter of fact our doctor's book suggests the same treatment. I lie awake at night thinking and wondering whether the time will ever come when we shall be free of the fear of being murdered. Toms tells me that I was a brave little woman for not running away and putting my head under the pillow, which I always do when I see a boy riding a buckjumping horse in the house paddock.

There has not been a sound in the blacks' quarters since the row and Kitty says "altogether boy sorry want to kill Homer".

Goodnight dear,

Love from,

JANE

My Dear,

The blacks have forgotten the fighting episode and try to show us that they are sorry. Poor things, they are very hasty and "kill" is the motto when in a temper.

Our citrus trees are loaded, and we have sold the crop to fruiterers in Normanton for thirty pounds. They expect to make quite a profit themselves by selling the oranges and lemons at six shillings per dozen.

Some of the unripe fruit is falling off, so much so that we cannot eat it all ourselves or persuade the blacks to eat more in order to save bread. So Tom, who is a good cook, and I, the offsider, have decided to make marmalade. I hope it will be a success because we cannot afford to waste sugar.

It will be lovely when the fruit is riper and we have thirty pounds in our pockets. That will help to pay the doctor's account for removing the lump on Fred's head.

I have to wait a few days longer in order to gather some more news to finish this letter.

A week later: I hope you will not say that I am a moaner, but dear, I have no one to tell them to but you and Mother, who tells me that she cries when she receives my weekly letters, and advises other mothers not to be too anxious to get their daughters married and started in life in the bush.

A fly has got into our fruit and it is falling in tubfulls every day. The camp blacks are lucky as they come to the homestead to gather the fallen fruit. What I cannot bear to hear is their joyful corroboree concerning our loss, which is their gain.

The only good we got out of the whole thing was a clothes boiler full of badly made jam. I shall have to tell you about the jam making. It will be such a nice change from my usual moans.

It took half a day for the gins to cut the fruit into shreds. The next day we boiled it with water, then let it stand overnight, and started to boil it with sugar the following morning. We boiled it all day with no signs of its going to jam. It was nearly sundown when we gave up the idea of its ever going to jam, so we strained the liquor from the peel and stored each separately in earthernware jars. It appears that the fault lay in the fact that we boiled it for eight hours instead of thirty minutes. However, we have candied peel in one jar and jelly, or I should say toffee that sticks to your jaws, in the other. The peel is so hard that we use a broken file to chip it out with. The niggers call it sugar bag, which means delicious in their own language. We also call it sugar bag because we used half a bag of sugar to make it.

We are still having a great deal of trouble with Annie, who intensely dislikes her old man husband. She runs away from him at night and returns to work in the morning, her face sour and miserable.

The camp blacks have learnt the use of opium or at least the charcoal which remains after it has been smoked. From this the natives make an intoxicating drink after it has been soaked in water.

Opium is obtained by all the chinamen on stations, and after being smoked the residue is sold to the black boys mostly for the loan of their Mary-mary gins.

FIRST SON

I have watched Sim smoke the opium in a small stone ink bottle attached to a hollow bamboo cane which is held over a flame.

I am almost ashamed to tell you that I have peeped into the kitchen through a crack in the wall — he always has his afternoon nap there — and I envy him the peaceful look which gradually creeps over his face until he is fast asleep. He has no troubles, he is master of every situation. He can, like all Chinese cooks, come and go as he wishes. They all receive thirty shillings a week for cooking curry and rice, mince, stew, an odd pudding, with an odd plum one on Sundays.

Please do not think me too dreadful but I have to do something to keep me alive. When I thought Sim was fast asleep I sent Kitty in to ask him for hot water for Missis. He woke up in such a stupid state and abused her by saying, "Old gin, your Missis, she mad, what for she want hot water. Too b —---- hot weather now."

Goodbye dear, I will write from Mackay after I have met my in-laws. I am not looking forward to it one scrap but it is necessary to get medical aid for Fred's head. I have made up my mind to behave just as I did before I made the acquaintance of the Mary-mary gins. Tom says that on no account must I use "buthue" or "dilbry", as his sister knows the meaning of these naughty swearwords of the blacks' language. It is no use asking me the meaning of them in your letters. I shall just have to whisper them into your ear.

Love from,

JANE

Second son
Edmund — 17 October 1898

My Dear Althea,

I have been six months in Mackay and I think that you will be interested in our doings since we left Midlothian. It was the middle of March when we started on our journey and March in the Gulf country is a particularly hot month. The boat cabins were too hot to sleep in so the captain ordered berths to be made in the smoking room which opened onto the deck. One was for Mrs Yaldwin and her two children — her husband was manager of Milgarra station — and the other was for me with my delicate baby. We were the only females in the saloon.

I became seasick as soon as I entered the Gulf, or rather as soon as the boat entered I should say. I became weaker and weaker and could not satisfy my baby. Luckily there was a woman in the steerage who offered to nurse my baby as well as her own. When we reached Townsville Tom's brother insisted that I should stay with them for a few weeks while Fred's head was being treated, and until the chinaman look disappeared from my skin. He ordered me to drink a

Plane-Creek Sugar Mill, Sarina, circa 1908. This sugar refining mill was founded by Edmund Atherton II, Richard Atherton, Henry Bell and a small number of other local landowners.

small bottle of Porter daily. It has done its work well for I am now eight stone four pounds instead of six stone one.

Oh! I must tell you what the chinaman cook said to me today — "Mrs Tom you too fat now, you got plum pudding face, when you come here first, you pretty girl." So the chinamen in Mackay are no more polite than Sim was.

Tom had to go back to Midlothian to muster and drove the eight hundred bullocks to Townsville for sale. He heard before he left that fats were selling well, but when he arrived there, there was a slump in the market and he only got two pounds a head for all his hard work and five months droving. This was just enough to pay expenses. The eight hundred bullocks were practically given away.

I went to the first meeting of the Plane Creek Sugar Mill, and was very interested in seeing the sugar made. The mill was built almost entirely by Tom's father, his uncles Dick and Henry, and other land-owners who mortgaged their land to the Government for the loan of sixty-five thousand pounds.

We are to leave Mackay in a few days as Fred has lost the lump on his head and the doctor says that there is no fear of the child being silly. We are not allowed to teach him to talk or force his development in any way, as he is really too advanced for his age.

We have gathered ferns, orchids and slips of the rose tree the Athertons brought from England, and a sweet little hyacinth plant which grows in water. It will take something like this to brighten our outlook. Our future is so black. The meatworks have been scrapped, Croydon goldfields have almost petered out, local butchers do not require many cattle, the Townsville works are paying prices that are not enough to pay droving expenses, and last but not least we have been advised to curtail our own expenses. I tell Tom that I do not know how we are going to do it as our store order now only consists of flour, tea, sugar, cream of tartar, hops and a case of kerosene. Perhaps we will not be able to employ so many blacks in future as they work for their food and clothes. Their food consists principally of corned beef, which is made into stews or mince flavoured with shallots grown by ourselves, a little bread and dripping and the tea left over from our meals which is sweetened with a little sugar. Their clothing consists of three calico dresses and a couple of pairs of drawers which they wear only on special occasions.

Love from,

JANE

My Dear,

Time flies with me now as I am kept busy looking after the baby and the cooking is a big job. The gins do a fair amount of the rough work but at times I could cheerfully slaughter them as I spend all day driving them. They take turns about doing the washing-up. Annie really is the limit. I left her in the kitchen while I attended to something else and was away easily twenty minutes. When I returned she was still washing the same plate. Now do you wonder that I say "buthue" instead of the ordinary b— ?

Fred, who is eighteen months old, is a lovely child with fair curls, and he is running about everywhere now. He is always pretending to be out mustering.

I was having my usual afternoon rest and had left Fred in Annie's charge. From my bed I looked on to a clear level plain of short grass. I became interested in what I took to be a red flower waving to and fro, so I called the gins. I was horrified to learn that it was Fred who had wandered a mile with a bridle on his shoulder. He was dressed in red and was looking for horses. You may guess that Annie had her shins tapped.

The wet season is on us again and we are so distressed. Our little hyacinth plant has almost covered the lagoon. It is a wonderful sight when in full bloom as it has the loveliest shades of pale blue and mauve. It has been admired to such an extent that all the station owners have asked for some to decorate their waterholes with. Now that the floodwaters are so high we are afraid of the garden floating out to sea, so at the present moment there are fifty camp blacks waist-deep in the water holding some of it back.

We had another row at the yard this morning, and I was again forced to gather up Fred and the revolver. After the fight with the blacks it was arranged that Ross would go to the yard to watch the milking.

Kitty gets the fresh morning milk from the same cow each morning. This morning she was dressed in red and entered the yard where a young fresh cow and calf were in for the first time. She was charged, but instead of jumping the rail of the yard to get away she ran behind Ross who had a long stick in his hands which he used to drive the cows into the bails. When the cow charged she hauled him round the waist and dragged the old man round to protect herself from the infuriated animal. Hearing screams and yells all hands rushed to the yard to find Old Ross, breathless with rage and fear, trying to free himself from Kitty's vice-like grip.

It still rains for days and days on end. Sometimes it clears up for a day or so and, should this day be a Sunday, it would still be a day of perfect rest for the whole station, even if it has rained every day of the previous week.

The station blacks do as they please. The boys sleep mostly while the two gins, Pigeon and myself go hunting and swimming. Kitty carries Fred in the native fashion. He sits on her shoulders with his legs around her neck, holding onto her hair. Sometimes she pretends to be a bucking horse, and it looks as though Fred would be able to stick to anything. With his free hand he hits her to make her buck more. The other gin carries the afternoon tea and a tomahawk, while Pigeon runs at my side.

The afternoon's pleasure hunt starts off with a bogey in the nude in the sandy-bottomed lagoon some miles from the homestead. At first I felt shy at being naked but after a few Sunday hunts the gins found out that I was made the same as they were and stopped staring at me, and so I did not mind.

Kitty takes Fred into the deep water and he splashes with his free hand while he stands erect without touching the bottom. In fact the pool is almost bottomless and so she just treads water. She walks along in the same way with ease.

The gins gather seeds and roots from the white and blue lilies which simply cover the waterholes in the Gulf. They have a wonderful time catching crayfish by feeling the logs at the water's edge, bringing up fish sometimes twelve inches long which they hold in such a way that they cannot nip.

I enjoy watching the gins catching the green climbing snakes by hauling them off the trees by their tails. They give a certain twist to their wrists, crack it in midair and off comes the head.

Yams very like dahlia buds, which only spring up in the wet season, are dug up, also the climbing ones which are ten to twelve inches long.

Possums are caught by climbing a tree with a hole many feet from the ground, and there is great rejoicing. They feel it all over and if it is a Mary-mary they corroboree for a few seconds and yell "budgeree". A fire is made in a few seconds by rubbing two pieces of stick together with grass immediately under the friction to catch the spark. When our matches do not strike our morning's fire is lit in this way, but this seldom happens as the fires are mostly kept going night and day as the blacks like to keep the mosquitoes away and to light their pipes with the coal from the fire.

No preparation is needed for native cooking. The animal is just thrown onto the hot coals, fur and all organs intact. In fact the insides of animals and fish are considered the greatest delicacies.

The gins love to gather the native bee honey from hollow trees, and they serve it on white ti-tree bark which they obtain by peeling off layers of bark till they come to the one desired. I enjoy the speech they make to me when they hand it over: "Budgeree fellow he maket bingy good altogether blackfellow he take it. It may make him go g----(lavatory) supposen it make you big fellow sore more better eat nunda bark."

If dysentery gets into the natives' camps they chew this bark until they are cured, and for constipation they eat honey. Sometimes they eat charcoal and tie a tight band of cabbage tree twine around the head to stop it aching.

The native bees do not sting but crawl into your hair and eyes by the dozen, all over your clothes and down your back, and seem to have the art of sticking on to your skin.

Once when out hunting we came upon four naked gins holding onto the tail of a huge snake which was halfway out of a hole in the ground. They were trying with all their might to pull it out and suggested that I should lend a hand. My gins would not let me try and said, "That snake he saucy (venomous) suppose he bite you you die."

They taught me to crack the heads off the harmless green tree snakes, and would scream laughing when I missed the right twist of the wrist and the thing wound itself around my arm. From a good distance I watched with interest the pulling out and killing of a fifteen foot venomous reptile. The four naked gins and my own two, who had lent a hand with the digging out of the snake, cooked it and ate it with great relish about half an hour later. They were never satisfied unless I tasted their native food. Snake tastes very like the breast of a young fowl.

At times I feel black and I'm sure the natives think that I am some dead relative who has jumped up as a white fellow. They wanted to tattoo my arms and legs by just cutting the first skin and inserting a white mud, and also put a pattern of dots on by burning a pointed stick and making the dots with this. I was afraid of the sharp glass and the burning stick otherwise I should have been branded for life. Another thing they suggested was that I should knock one of my front teeth out so that everyone would know that I was married. This did not appeal to me either.

Pigeon, who has never been in a blacks' camp, has no desire to eat their tasteless saltless foods.

Tom tells me that people who live in the Gulf for a long time become like the natives and that is one reason why we must get away.

SECOND SON

I can certainly corroboree as well as any gin already.

Goodnight,

Love from,

JANE

My Dear Althea,

I seem to have no news apart from the doings of the gins. I supose it is all so new to me still that I notice every little thing. We are still waiting until we are a little better off for our chinaman cook. We never see a soul except the mailman. That reminds me I must tell you about the wretched man, who arrived during the week. The mail of course is not the wretched part but the man is awful. He has diabetes, and a stomach which laps over his belt and ends goodness knows where. When he hands me the mail he looks at me in a supercilious way and blows and puffs so much that he makes me shiver. He had to remain a couple of days while he looked for a fresh set of horses for the run.

The gins tell me that he comes to their kitchen window when they are washing-up and says to them "you come longa my room I want to talk longa you". I explained to the gins that if they go near him they will get big fellow bingy (stomach) like him and that next time he came to the window making love they were to throw a dipper of fairly hot water over his sit-down. One night they did this and we heard a yell. Then there was silence.

The next morning the gins told me what had happened, and although Joe the mailman walked straight enough, he left almost immediately with his mail from the yard. I suppose he did not want me to know that he had blisters.

We are so poor that it is necessary that we should make a little money apart from the breeding of the cattle, so we are keeping a few fowls. Already I have made quite a fair amount in turkeys and roosters. When Tom was passing the Leap Hotel in Mackay, after nearly giving his cattle away in Townsville, he purchased a pair of peacocks, for luck, two guineafowl, turkeys, geese and Muscovy ducks.

The young ducklings live in the waterhole at the foot of the garden, and were disappearing rapidly until we discovered that the catfish were the cause. Knowing that the natives catch freshwater fish by poisoning the pools with bloodwood leaves, we sent them to poison ours. It took some time to lay the leaves around the water's edge. The next day the fish came to the surface in dozens in a dazed condition, and were gathered by the camp blacks and eaten in the midst of a joyful corroboree. Luckily for us we had most of the fowls in pens, but most of the ducks died from the stagnant water. So I shall have to start all over again with the ducks. The galah parrots are most annoying at this time of the year. It is their mating season and they screech and scream and flock to the ground in front of the house just at Fred's sleeping time, so it is Pigeon's job to keep them from settling there.

I must stop now as I have written you a long letter and the funny part of it is that when I sit down to write I feel as though there is nothing to say.

Love from,

JANE

My Dear,

We have nearly all been killed again. Frank Bowman brought us a little nigger boy about eight years of age. The gins had got afternoon tea ready, which they do very nicely now. They set the meal tables and wait on it exceptionally well, although it took quite a while to make them understand the knives go to the right; they are inclined to be left-handed. They have forgotten they ever wore men's shirts, and look so smart in navy-blue dresses trimmed with red.

We were sitting in the dining room, some distance from the kitchen, when we heard the report of a gun and the spattering of shot on the roof over our heads. So near was the report that we bounced out of our chairs. I felt I had been shot. Tom and Frank dashed out to the kitchen, from where the sound came, and found the little new lad petrified and almost white from fright. He had lifted a gun, which had been accidentally left loaded in the kitchen after some duck had been shot.

We called the little nigger Frank, not that he resembled Frank for he was jet black, but so we would always remember the incident.

The white stockmen still steal the young lubras from their allotted husbands, so I know now why the blacks have such a grudge against the white men. A year before I was married, two white stockmen from Delta Downs, our nearest neighbours, were arrested and tried for the murder of a poor unfortunate nigger who was trying to recover his young lubra from Delta. The nigger had previously been a member of

Queensland National Bank, Normanton, circa 1890. This building, and a similar one belonging to the Bank of New South Wales, were those where Tom had to go to secure a loan.

the gin's tribe. His burnt bones were found at the bottom of a waterhole and the wild natives knew they had been thrown in. Of course there were no means of identification as he was in the nude. One of the stockmen was the manager's brother-in-law. A good solicitor got them both off and a ball was given to celebrate. So that's that, as the saying goes.

Tom as you know owns a half share in Midlothian. He has been asked again to reduce expenses by his people. In fact, every letter is the same. We really cannot do this unless we go without everything and live on the air, so he has decided to try to buy the other half share, valued at two thousand pounds.

I feel so worried, but still I feel we are doing right. I shall end now,

with love from,

JANE

ACROSS THE YEARS

My Dear,

We have had nothing but business worries at present, and in fact since I last wrote. The cattle industry is in such an appalling state, it is impossible to get the two thousand on the whole mortgage on the station, even though it included ten thousand cattle, two hundred horses and improvements.

After we had tried several banks for accommodation, the Bank of New South Wales came forward with fifteen hundred pounds and Tom made arrangements with his father for the other five hundred, free of interest. We completed the purchase of Midlothian on 4th August 1898.

For months we have merely existed. We never think of going to town and all the racehorses are turned out. Burns Philp have given us credit for our very simple store account. We are even burning fat lamps in the house. Luckily I have learnt from the natives that their fruit and yams make excellent food. Duck eggs and kangaroo tail is included in our diet. But, Oh dear! on top of all our poverty I am expecting another child in November. It is lucky for me that Mother lives so near, otherwise I would have to go to the general hospital. I am the only station-owner's wife in the Gulf, since Major Collis died and Milgarra has become a bank property.

We have a new doctor in the town, but nevertheless I shall try to do without one as that will save five pounds. Old Tom Nevitt has given up his job and is now a member of parliament for the Gulf of Carpentaria. I do wish I was near him again. We are leaving the station very early this time, and everything is prepared. All the clothes for the little fellow are ready — just leftovers from Fred's babyhood — and the horses are in and the buggy greased.

This is a short letter as I have a real fit of the blues. It is so distressing to be bearing another child, when we already have so many expenses and "not a bean with which to bless ourselves".

Love from,

JANE

My Dear,

We started off in good style this time with no pains or groans except those occasioned by the effort to economise. I am hoping this baby will be a daughter, as this is the last time for many a day, or until we get rich, that we shall want the stork to look our way.

SECOND SON

114

*Burns Philp & Co., Normanton, 1890. This store, the first built by
Burns Philp & Co., is a typical example of the chain of general
merchandising stores run by the company in country towns throughout
Queensland. In hard times the company provided credit for the
purchase of essential supplies and in good times it made great profits
from the suddenly acquired spending power of its country customers. In
its own way, the Burns Philp store was as much an institution in
Normanton as the post office.*

Owing to the intense heat it was necessary to do the journey in
small stages. So it was five o'clock in the afternoon before we reached
the town, although we started at six in the morning. This time I had
to bath Fred and Pigeon before starting on our journey.

We all had the usual shower-bath after we arrived in town. This
was necessary after travelling forty-five miles through a cloud of dust.
Rain as a rule does not fall for at least eight months of the year, after
the wet season ends in the middle of March. We wore cheesecloth
veils over our faces to protect our noses and ears from the dust.

After a good tea — far away from corned beef and laments concerning our poverty and the hardships of the bush — we talked to
Kate, my elder sister,[20] who is well satisfied with her lot in life, and
then decided to walk out a short distance to see Mother.

I do not think I have mentioned Kate in my previous letters. I suppose that is because she went away to live with an aunt in Warwick[21]

[20] Catherine (Kate) Bardsley (1873–1948), later Catherine Davies.

[21] This should be Annie Smith (b. ca. 1855 d. 1891), who emigrated to Queensland with her
elder sister, Jane, and their mother, Caroline Smith (née Finley) in the *Warren Hastings* in
1864.

when she was only seven years of age, and I would have been just four. She was delicate and was ordered to live in a better climate. She was eighteen when our aunt died and came home to live until she was twenty, when she married Moses Llewellyn Davies, an accountant in Burns Philp.

We had just opened the front gate when one of Kate's babies stirred, and she said, "You sit on the step while I go back and hush him off to sleep, the little nurse-girl cannot manage him if he wakens."

While I was sitting on the front step envying the comfort of the town folk, I felt something sting me on the pit of my stomach and grabbed the place where I was stung. I discovered it was a thing inches long, clinging on and stinging at the same time. I became panicky and rushed into the house, tearing my maternity wrapper and combinations off, and stood there with a huge centipede, seven inches long, on my shoulder.

I was so badly bitten and in such agony that the doctor, who was a single man and the only doctor in the town, was sought, in vain. Not a soul in the town knew where he was, so it was decided to organise a hunt. He was found dining with the protector of aboriginals, three miles out of the town.

When it had been explained to him that I had been bitten by a centipede and was expecting an infant in a month's time, he said he had heard those tales many times, and that I was lucky that this is the second child.

On 7th October, after a day of agony and anxiety, I gave birth to a premature son, weighing four pounds.[22] And to make matters more difficult for me, he was a breech birth baby.

He is very like Tom, with his dark olive skin, and the poor little chap had a great many bruises. When I showed him to Kitty, whom we had in town as nurse girl, she said, "Missus me thinket you been catchem half-caste more better hit him on head."

Good night dear, I am so tired, I have two babies to look after now, though I am glad to say Pigeon is a great help.

Love from,

JANE

---

[22] Edmund Atherton III was born on 17 October 1898. He died in 1978.

SECOND SON

Third son
Thomas James — 18 June 1900

My Dear,

It is a long time since I have written to you. We have called our second boy Edmund, after his great-grandfather and grandfather.

When he was nine months old, a lovely child, olive-skinned, dark-eyed, with fairish curly hair and almost walking, he was seized with a bowel complaint. We gave him the dose of oil that bush folk believe in for babies, and which at other times cures, but this time we had to rush in to see a doctor. He was very ill for weeks, when my old midwife suggested packing him in hot bran and douching his bowels out with very strong tea. After a short time he began to mend and we are back on the station, but our lovely fat darling is just skin and bone.

We are expecting a cattle buyer from Cardwell, to inspect a mob of one thousand store bullocks at two pounds ten shillings a head. I lie awake at night building castles in the air. First, the bank can be paid off, no more high interest and troublesome letters from them; and second, Burns Philp's store and drapery account can be settled. This has accumulated to one hundred pounds for the year, and includes the food and clothing for all hands on the station, their pipes and tobacco and so on. We have not employed a white stockman since we bought the place. The children have not tasted any sweets, except the toffee made with sugar and lemon juice.

There are such a lot of things I want, I do believe I shall hug the buyer if he takes the cattle. Oh! if he turns them down how will I endure it. I am crying now for fear he might do so.

Disease amongst the blacks is getting worse and worse. The poor wretches are not allowed near the homestead and their camps have been shifted much farther away. All I can hear now of the fun and frolic I used to listen to, is the sound of a muffled drum. This noise is made by the healthier gins who bathe at midday in the waterhole near their camp, and strike the water with one hand and keep time with the other. This hitting the water at the same moment produces a muffled drum sound that travels for miles.

ACROSS THE YEARS

It is heart-rending to see the little children, some only a few years of age, afflicted with a filthy disease, mostly centred in the groin, hunting for the seeds and roots of the lilies, with their poor mothers, who can just crawl along with their legs far apart.

The poor Mary-marys look the same age, with weary eyes and drawn faces. The men of the tribe, by their walk, do not seem to suffer the agony the gins do. Tom says they are dying as fast as the gins for now we have about two hundred left from a camp of five hundred warriors who hunted with straight backs and keen eyes only three and a half years ago, when I first made friends with them. They now drag one foot after the other, almost too ill to hunt at all. You have no idea how pitiable they are.

My gins tell me some of the whites have it too. I do not know how they find out, but sometimes when a nice clean white man from up the Peninsula calls in for the night, they will whisper, "He got him, no you touch it towel, sheet, more better me get stick put it in boiler water." The natives evidently know the use of hot water to kill germs. I said to Kitty, "More better altogether gin and boy go to doctor." She replied, "Doctor he no good medicine he no good altogether die. White man been go longa camp, he been put Devil-devil there." Germs I presume. "Some fellow gins, make it more sore, he been put mud, Devil-devil shuttem mouth." I think she meant lockjaw. I have seen some of their spearheads coated with a black mud, which my gins tell me, "He plenty saucy (venomous) supposen he hit he make it shut mouth." So they evidently know the tetanus germ.

Only yesterday a nigger came from the camp pleading for whisky. He had been fighting. They never fight with their fists only with sticks, nullas or anything they can pick up with the intention of killing. He was in a dreadful state with gashes about the face and with his head all plastered over with a white mud. There was not a bit of hair on his head. It had been burnt off a day or so previously by singe-ing with a burning stick, the native mode of hairdressing. I do not know what they used to get rid of their beards and moustaches before they learnt the use of broken glass for shaving, but you never see a man with hair on his face.

I do miss the days of fun with the poor Mary-marys. My life is just spent swishing flies away. I do hope we can sell our cattle as that will bring us a step nearer to leaving this dreadful life.

Love from,

JANE

THIRD SON

My Dear,

We sold the cattle, a whole thousand, for two thousand five hundred lovely pounds. We have paid off the bank and the Burns Philp account.

You should see our store order! It is no longer plain flour, tea, sugar etc. There are cases of dried apples, peaches, currants, plums, jam, pickles, biscuits, scented soap and a bottle of lavender water. Burns Philp sent out a whole tin of boiled lollies for the children and a gallon of whisky for Tom as a present. I wonder why they did not send a present when we were so poor? It seems to me so silly to wait until we have the money to buy ourselves anything we want. Tom says "it is a mackerel to catch a whale".

We have decided to keep a cook once again. The aboriginals have to be watched and the peculiar thing about them is that, when you are in a desperate hurry, they do their work more slowly, so it often means that I have to do the cleaning as well as the cooking.

All the stations are out to secure the services of Sec Donimo, a New Caledonian, who is an excellent cook and waiter, and is always spotless in his white Eton jacket and white shoes when waiting on the table.

After being a bachelor for years Sec decided to buy a young lubra gin, who was amongst the natives at Delta. It is remarkable what the natives will do since they have learnt the use of opium. They even sell their gins.

Sec was allowd a fortnight to spend his honeymoon in Croydon. He was a very important man when his pretty young bride clung to his arm to face the Clerk of Petty Sessions in the Normanton Court House.

The visiting white men at the court house were in a gay mood, for Sec had made them, and in fact the whole town, drink his health ever since daylight. So lots were drawn to see who would kiss Sec's bride. It unfortunately fell to a quiet young Englishman, who was a prosperous commission agent. Afterwards the ladies of the town cut him dead and gave him such a bad time that he was glad to sell out and make to where there would be no lubras to kiss.

The bride was frocked in white silk, with a slight train, a veil of soft tulle, a wreath of orange blossoms, laced up boots and no stockings.

A few months later a son was born bearing the features of Chinese, Maltese, kanaka etc. it certainly lacked any resemblance to Sec. Nevertheless he loved his only child dearly, and spoilt him so much

ACROSS THE YEARS

that after working at Delta for years he lost his job on account of his unmanageable five-year-old.

I shall close now, so far we have not found a suitable cook. They come and go after a week's trial.

Love from,

JANE

My Dear,

We engaged Sec with the understanding that Sweeny, the child, and his mother keep to their own quarters.

All went well for three months. It was lovely to rest and sit back and enjoy a well-cooked meal and the after dinner conversation without the thought that the washing-up has still to be done. The comfort did not last long. Of all the children in the world, Sweeny is the worst. He is an absolute devil let loose. He will watch my children looking out through the paling fence, then wait his chance to poke their eyes out with sticks and then laugh and chatter like a maniac. Perhaps it is because there are so many breeds mixed in him.

We have lost our cook again. He gave notice, and it was all Sweeny's fault. The gins had taken the children for a walk to get away from Sweeny and I was lying down on my bed, tired and worn out from watching him, for that morning he had almost bitten Fred's ear off. I fancied I could hear what I though was a native cat — a dear little animal with gray fur spotted with white, but a terribly furious thing which eats all the young chickens and eggs — in the dining room, so I hurried to call the dogs to kill it. I was horrified to see the medicine chest, Burkley and Taylors fever mixture, castor oil, Epsom salts, quinine, Beechams pills etc, all emptied into a half kerosene tin by Sweeny. I grabbed hold of him and ran him through the division fence of the house and kitchen, saying at the same time "you half-caste chinaman".

Sec was within hearing and sight of all this, and gave notice to Tom saying, "It fair broke my heart to hear my only child called a half-caste chinaman."

We are offering thirty-five shillings instead of the usual thirty, but still we are without a cook. Somehow I am not feeling it hard, the endurance of Sweeny had nearly got me down. We have vowed that until we can get a chinaman we shall not bother with any cook. We have vowed so many things I hope we shall not put Sec on again.

Sometimes I feel I do not know whether I am here or there. Babies

THIRD SON

are all right but when it comes to getting up and down to attend to them in the night, I often wish I was single. So dear, take a fool's advice and simply don't marry.

I am unable to write any more, my poor brain is distracted.

Love from,

JANE

My Dear,

We have had cooks and we have been without cooks. This is mainly because Tom has gone modern in his ideas since we have become rich.

He purchased a garden plough, thinking it would be much better than digging with a spade. He first tried the ploughing on the natives. At times by the sound you would think murder was being committed. I would hear a yell — perhaps he tapped their shins — and then I would see them running at full speed, without looking back, to their camps.

The first chinaman, second and third were tried out before we got one interested. Now we have a garden of cauliflower, cabbage, peas, beans and onions, which grow profusely during the winter months. All the watering is done by the natives, who carry kerosene tins of water arranged as a bullock yolk across their shoulders.

I have a very dear friend, a Mrs Dalby, who is ten years older than I am. She has lived most of her life in the bush and loves the blacks too. She is a wonderful musician, but has no piano, so she often pays us a visit, bringing her two children along with her.

Each time she arrives I am sure a Marconi message is sent over the air, as we get songsters from far and near. A pure bred Irishman, Joe O'Reilly, who lives fifty miles up the Peninsula, always arrives, dressed in the same suit of clothes shirt and necktie, and with always the same excuse of having forgotten his pyjamas. He says, "I wish you can lend me a pair of pyjamas, I have forgotten mine." For the four years I have been here I have never seen a pair. I am sure he has learnt to sleep in the buff, but he never forgets to bring his seven Scotch songs. He is quite willing to sing the lot straight off and if you are not careful, you will get the lot over again. He always starts with "Annie Laurie" and ends with "Bonny Dundee". He has a shivery shake in his voice, and an Irish accent. We always have a pair of pyjamas put aside for him now.

ACROSS THE YEARS

It was winter when Joe arrived this time and he looked as if a good bath would take that crusty look away. My friend said, "I'll take Joe out this morning with Doris (her daughter) to run in a quiet horse for you to learn to ride, and at the same time I'll see Joe takes a bath."

The pink lotus lilies were out in full bloom, but to gather them meant going out into five feet of cold still water. My friend said to Joe, whose teeth were already chattering from the cold westerly wind, "I want to take Mrs Atherton a bunch of lilies, you know how she loves flowers and I really think it a duty, so while Doris and I ride on, would you mind gathering some."

I am sure he never felt a bath so awful. He had to strip off all his clothes to enter the water; but, when they returned with a beautiful bunch of fresh lilies Joe was fresh too. In fact he looked so clean even his moustache turned a different colour.

I mentioned that a quiet horse was being run in for me. I must tell you about my first ride. Tom took me out to a mob of cattle, where calves were being drafted from the herd. I was riding a very old camp horse, Paddy, who had been pensioned off on account of his age. I was enjoying it very much, until we came to the cattle, when Tom said, "You wait here while I give a hand with the drafting." Unfortunately, a calf broke away from the mob, near where I was waiting. Off went Paddy after it. He was so well trained to the job he knew the work. It was dreadful for me. I clenched the horn of the side-saddle with my leg and hand and screamed for help. Luckily I did not fall off but really I would sooner be dead than go through it again. I did not receive even a little bit of sympathy and as for Tom, you would have thought he was riding the runaway horse. His face was deadly white, but nevertheless all he said was: "I'll be damned if I teach you to ride, you can get Mrs Dalby to do it."

I shall stop now and hurry under the blankets. It has been a cold, drizzly wet day. We get a lot of this weather in winter every year in the Gulf. It is just wet enough to be uncomfortable all the time.

Love from,

JANE

My Dear,

I am most upset. I am going to have my third child in June. It really is hard on us having another one. Neither of us wanted another child so soon, but now the baby is coming I hope it is the little daughter I have always longed for.

THIRD SON

It makes a difference having money. This little fellow has all new clothes in readiness, I have even got a baby's basket, decked with pink satin, white hailstone muslin and plenty of lace trimmings. I feel sure the Lord will not give us another son, so our little girlie must start off with pretty things.

Kitty was ill with earache so I have Annie in with me. There is something about her which attracts all the visitors, and even the camp blacks. Perhaps they are sorry for her being married to an old man. All the niggers call him Old Charlie. Perhaps they do not like him because he does not belong to their tribe.

I left Pigeon behind. She is a dear little mite but is becoming very spoilt. It was funny to hear her teaching Fred to swear. She appeared to be saying nursery rhymes at first, but presently I was amazed to hear "bug, bug". At first I thought she must have heard someone speaking about bugs, as we have a lot of them around our lamps in summer. I asked her what she meant by "bug, bug, bug", and she replied that Old Ross always said bugger when plaiting a rope.

I am very careful to see that she speaks correct English as it would be dreadful for the children if she did not. I have to watch myself too as it is so easy to slip back. Often I catch myself saying "this fellow belonga you" or "you like kiki (food)?".

I shall stop now as it is late. Please excuse the small letter.

With love from,

JANE

My Dear,

I waited nearly four months before the stork came. This time instead of being before time I was behind. Between the long wait and the annoyance from the blacks I was nearly driven mad.

Jim, who came to see me every night before he retired, said that he would be glad to see the last of me and the stork. It so happened that he was just nicely settled in bed after his birthday party on 18th June, when I had to get him to go a-hunting for the stork's messenger.

Well, he brought another little son.[23] I was so disgusted but could not waste the trimmed-up basket so am leaving it on the off-chance that we may have a little daughter sometime. No doubt you think I am either very optimistic or very brave. So do I. We called this son Jim, after his uncle, who was so sweet tempered when called out of bed at three in the morning.

[23] Thomas James (Jim) Atherton was born on 18 June 1900. He died in 1903.

ACROSS THE YEARS

I had two dreadful experiences while waiting for the wretched stork. This night Jim called as usual — he says that he feels like a policeman doing duty — to find me frantic with fear. Annie, who slept at my bedside, whispered, "Missis, someone knock floor underneath house."

I could hear the knocking plainly but was too frightened to investigate its cause. Only the day before, a neighbouring station friend who was also expecting a baby, had a nigger walk into her room in the middle of the night, calmly lift the sleeping gin in his arms and walk out with her, with the idea of taking her away to another tribe. The black boys love to steal other gins as by doing this they can have more wives, only having one allotted to them at birth.

I told Jim how frightened I was and he went to get a tomahawk which we keep in the next room for chopping the wood in the morning. He walked two steps down towards where the knocking was heard and then threw the tomahawk with full force. A nigger hopped out ready to fight but when he saw that he had a man to deal with he ran out into the street with Jim following close at his heels. The chase was not a long one because on rounding a corner the nigger sailed right into a policeman who shortly afterwards handed him over to a hospital for treatment to his hurt ankle.

On another occasion I had closed up the cottage and taken the children and Annie out visiting for the afternoon, returning at five o'clock. I pushed open the bedroom door to find a nigger, half-covered with blood, under my bed. He had become stupid with drink and then started fighting with the other boys. To escape his assailant he ran into my room. Jim tapped his shins to wake him up. It was really quite laughable to see him rubbing his eyes as he scrambled out from under the bed.

Poor Kitty was brought from the station to town for treatment. She had earache very badly and one ear was so bad that it was discharging terribly. Two weeks passed and she was no better so she then ran away to get back to her native treatment. When I arrived home she was still very ill. She had abandoned all the doctor's treatment and had a thick mud plaster over her ear.

She used to lie alongside the fire with her ear as near as possible to the flame without burning it. It was heart-rending to hear her moans and groans all day and night. She had wasted to a shadow as she had not eaten anything stronger than milk and very weak tea for weeks and weeks.

The mud plaster was removed every four days and the discharge simply poured out of her ear. After weeks of torture she ceased

THIRD SON

moaning and began to take a little nourishment, but the illness left her permanently deaf in one ear. She used to say to me "wallow woolko"; wallow means ear and woolko means no good in their language.

I am very glad to be home again. It is July and a very cold winter, so I will away now and snuggle into the blankets.

Love from,

JANE

My Dear,

The good Lord is smiling on us at last. The station hands are busy mustering a second mob of one thousand store bullocks which Tom sold at two pounds twelve shillings and sixpence per head.

Although we have so many disadvantages in the Gulf, the country is the very best with its Flinders and Blue Mitchell grasses and edible shrubs. Although we are without rain for about nine months of the year, there is no shortage of water. Every five miles you come to lagoons covered with beautiful lilies. Around our house we have four separate waterholes. One we keep for household use, another we bathe in, while the house blacks have the third and the camp niggers the fourth.

The waterhole hear the house is my greatest pleasure. I never miss fishing for sweet little perch or rock cod. The perch will bite almost as soon as the pin hook is thrown in, and then the little fish are usually put through the mincing machine and form our principal meal of the day.

We were expecting the buyer to lift the cattle in a day or so. To muster a big mob and hold them means a lot of extra work. Each morning all hands had had breakfast by sunrise and were away to work at the first peep of day to take and tail the mustered cattle from the yard. They would return at night tired and worn out from their fourteen hours work.

They had all washed and dressed for their evening meal. The tables were all brightness and laughter, for the hard work was over for a while and soon all would go back to the easy life of the station. Stockmen get thirty shillings a week with board and lodging. They save on this, which is a blessing for they never grumble or complain at their food.

The tinkling of the bell on the night horse, which is hobbled in the night paddock near the house, could be plainly heard. Our meal, after much talking and laughing, was almost over — we had the managers of Delta, Maggieville and Stirling stations dining with us — when a muffled peal of thunder rent the air. Everyone jumped up from the table and ran madly into the saddle room, leaving the meal unfinished.

I thought that they had all gone mad from the drinking of beer to celebrate the end of the muster. Or perhaps someone has been struck dead, although I did not see lightning but heard the thunder distinctly.

I gained enough courage to go out to the men's quarters to see men and niggers catching horses and riding off at a fast gallop without saddles. At last the chinaman came to me saying "bullock, break yard, all clear out".

The gins kept about a foot away from me and were saying "all the white Devil-devil sit down longa yard". It was their first experience of a cattle rush too.

It had turned into a half-drizzling wet night, which we do get sometimes in July, enough to fill the tubs and kerosene tins. No station homes have tanks to catch the water. They all dip their household water from the lagoon on which the home is built.

Something had frightened the cattle — perhaps a leaf falling, or the snapping of a dead twig — and made them rush to the side of the strong yard, flattening it down and carrying some of the huge rails with them as they careered madly on.

I could hear in the distance "whoo, whoo" from the men who were trying to settle down the frightened cattle. This went on all night. At daybreak they found ten head either with broken legs or hurt so badly that they had to be shot, and many others which had to be taken out of the herd before the buyer arrived. We used some of the meat, and the balance was taken away by the natives.

Love from,

JANE

My Dear Althea,

Tom often went to Croydon and Normanton to sell spayed cows to the butchers. It is a funny thing but one is never satisfied. We are well off now and want for nothing. I will take the children and Pigeon to Normanton to stay with Mother and Kate while he is away.

We will soon have to get a drag as the family is getting so big. Our little family buggy is quite packed. We take our clothes in on packhorses, and Pigeon rides.

During one of these trips a party of four leading citizens from the

THIRD SON

town called at Midlothian for their midday meal. They had been on a shooting expedition further up the Peninsula.

Kitty, who is a clean-living gin, came to me on our arrival home to tell me that Annie had half-a-crown, so of course I wanted to know who had given it to her.

She said, "When you been longa town, four men came eat dinner, chinaman he say two gins get clean towel fill up jug that man he big boss, he want wash face before he eat. Annie and me go longa waterhole when that men he eat dinner. My word missus! he cheeky fellow, when he finish dinner he come down to waterhole to go bogey. Me sing out you bogey longa waterhole over there. One fellow he take it off clothes, he come into waterhole longa me and Annie he plenty try catch Annie, me get out and hid behind tree. Annie get out too, that big man boss he get out too, he call Annie."

I asked Annie what he wanted and how she had come by the half-crown. She shuffled her feet, looked down at her toes and replied, "I don't know."

Post Office, Normanton, circa 1904. This building was probably not in existence when Tom and Jane first lived at Midlothian — the architecture suggests a date in the late 1890s. It, or its predecessor, however, would have been a focus in the town for all those dwelling on the outlying stations.

ACROSS THE YEARS

I then turned to Kitty and asked her if Annie had washed clothes for him — they often get a shilling from the stockmen for washing their clothes — and she replied, "No, she no wash clothes." I said, "Well, what did he give you the money for?" She said, "I no know, me think it you know alright."

I hope that you will understand the previous paragraph. Some of the men are simply dreadful. Many of them have wives and children, but of course must go for their annual shooting up the Peninsula.

I feel so angry with this man, my blood is up. I would like to shoot some of these men or tell their boss. But of course I cannot for one of them is the boss. Tom says, "Open your eyes and keep your mouth closed."

This is a short letter this time,

With love from,

JANE

My Dear,

We have not seen our mailman for weeks. Perhaps he is dead and then perhaps he is not.

All the creeks are flooded between here and the town so we have sent two niggers with a note to the postmaster for our mail.

We are without a cook again. The gins who do the washing-up eat any sugar that is left over from the tea tables, consequently we are without this too, and now have to use native bee honey which tastes to me like frogs. Besides bringing our mail the two poor beggars are carrying four pounds of sugar, which they have to carry on their heads to keep dry, while they battle along, at times waist-deep in water, or swimming in flooded creeks.

They are given half-a-crown when starting out on their journey, with which they procure charcoal opium to warm their stomachs. On their return home they are given bread and tobacco.

We decided to employ a white woman as cook instead of a chinaman, and got one about forty-five years of age. She is a German, and amuses the gins with her accent. She says "tings" instead of "things". They come to me and say, "What tribe this white Mary-mary?"

She nearly drove me mad. She couldn't cook and forgot to look after the oven when I had put in my cooking. She was always playing with the babies or the little chickens saying, "De dear little tings, dey are lufley."

THIRD SON

This got on my nerves so much that I found myself saying "tings", so I thought it was about time to let her go.

I now have the daughter of the housekeeper from Maggieville. She is sixteen years of age, is clean, looks well, and is something white and English to have about the house, so just now life is worth living.

Mrs Dalby and her two children came here again. She brought her lubra maid of seventeen with her. She is a nice looking girl and gets admiration from everybody. She knows that she is good-looking and keeps herself clean and tidy, always wearing flowers in her hair. She has been taught to read and write and considers herself far superior to my girl.

While they were with us the new manager from Maggieville came to pay us his first visit. He had just arrived from Sydney and was a particularly courteous young gentleman, and was very nice to the children. As Tom says, "Of course, this pleases the mother."

He was entertaining us with tales of his doings amongst civilised people while he was drinking his afternoon tea.

I could see my baby being wheeled round and round the house in his pram, and I could hear Nellie, the good looking young lubra, laughing and crooning as I thought to amuse the child. She kept coming to the front of the dining room which was behind my back.

Imagine my surprise when my gins told me, "That fellow Crawford, he no good, he gammon talk longa you, all time he wink eye longa Nellie, she laugh and wink eye longa him too." Needless to say, it was Mr Crawford's last visit inside the homestead.

Kitty loves all my children and loves me too. She watches me and understands if I feel sad. Sometimes I do for I miss the companionship of other white women, and I worry about the children growing up in such surroundings. She will come to me and say, "Me think it you sad, me make it you laugh more better." She will then disappear and come back with flowers and leaves arranged in her hair. She will then do her native corroboree before me. With graceful movements, almost dancing with her hands and arms, she sways her body from the waist with supple movements. She curtsies almost as one does in the minuet, but always spoils it at the end by stamping her feet, with her legs far apart and with her tongue out as far as it will go, making nasty guttural noises, clapping her thighs to make the sound rebound.

My little white girl, Jessie O'Sullivan, is a treasure and is causing a stir amongst the white stockmen, who no longer bring their little Mary-marys along with them when attending a muster. I don't know whether it is so when they go to other stations, but one thing I am sure of is that the gins have made her wise because she keeps all the men at a distance.

I'll stop now.

With love from,

J<small>ANE</small>

My Dear,

The gins rise at dawn to water the flower and citrus gardens by carrying two kerosene tins of water arranged at the end of a stick. This they carry on their shoulders.

They run along, doing a corroboree all the while, to dip the water from the hole at the bottom of the garden before eight o'clock.

Then they enjoy their breakfast of curry and rice, bread and jam and very sweet tea. Then comes their morning sleep and smoke. In fact they sleep and smoke after each meal. They are not allowed to bring their clay pipes near the house.

All the blacks smoke, even the very young children. We buy pipes and tobacco by the case for the niggers. The boys and men are allowed two sticks of tobacco, and the gins one per week. Since we have become rich we have given them each a blanket in addition to the one provided by the Government. We have also given the men pipes, shirts, felt hats, trousers, elastic-sided boots, handkerchiefs, jew's-harps, mouth organs, and pocket-money. To the women we give dresses, underclothing, handkerchiefs, blankets, jew's-harps, mouth organs, coloured wool, beads, scented soap and hair oil, which is nicer smelling than the fat from goannas.

Under this system the station blacks were always very happy and well-clothed, but when the Government brought the *Native Labourers' Protection Act* into force it was one continual grumble from them. The men would come to Tom and say, "What for that plurry Government take our money? He never give us plenty clothes."

After the *Act* was passed we had to sign on all men and women at the local police office, and their wages were placed to their credit at the bank.

The local police sergeant gave them clothes and pocket-money which he thought would be sufficient for them, while the balance of the money would remain to the credit of say, Bill, Tom, Nellie or Maggie and so on. I could never understand where the balance of the money went to when a nigger died or in fact why it was kept away from them in their lifetime, or how the Government knew one nigger's account from another's as only a cross was made by each

THIRD SON

individual in the presence of the sergeant when withdrawing from their account for clothes and pocket-money. I guess the sergeant had a worrying time trying to balance the accounts.

The wet season is the time for the white ants in the Gulf. Tom did not put stump caps on the cottage he lived in before the addition was built for my coming.

I use the cottage now for spare rooms, and after each wet season two or three boards have to be replaced with hardwood. If I should forget during the rainy period to have my daily inspection of the rooms, or if by any chance the mosquito nets are left touching the floor, the white ants will make great progress and the nets will be ruined.

Frank Bowman left a pair of really good boots under his bed. They were not noticed for a week and when I was tidying up the room prior to his return I was ashamed to find that they were full of white ant nests, and even the leather was destroyed.

On one occasion I remember we had a hole about one and a half feet long and as there was no hardwood, or time to mend it for that matter, I tacked a mat over the spot as I thought that this looked better than the hole. The doctor's brother-in-law was coming to pay us a very short visit on his way to Delta Downs.

After he had retired I heard a groan coming from the direction of his room and nearly fainted when I thought of the hole. I suppose the poor man had wondered at the mat being in the corner though personally I wondered why he should be bothered going over to the corner. Anyway, one of his legs had dropped through the hole which was about a foot deep. It was very fortunate that the cottage was built on such low blocks otherwise he might have done some serious damage to himself. As it was he got off with only a barked shin.

Oh dear! I always seem to be doing something. Tom says that I should have told him about the hole. So next time the ants eat anything I'll put up a notice "Beware of ants and holes".

Goodbye,

with love from,

JANE

My Dear,

The wet season was almost finished when little Jim was stricken down with malaria fever. He lay for days delirious, panting for breath, and like a hot coal. Tom was away at Stirling attending a muster, so I sent one of the gins twenty miles to fetch him back as I hated being alone, and I was so certain Jim was going to die.

Mr Epworth, the manager of Delta, offered to give us a hand with getting to town to a doctor. Some of the roads were very bad and so we had to take all the niggers with us and get them to walk in front of us in order to settle the mud down, and incidentally, to lift us out of the bog at times.

The horses floundered over the squashy mushy roads at times up to their girths in floodwater and mud, and when we reached Walker Creek — which is twenty miles from Normanton — at four in the afternoon, we were still in heavy floods.

The shire council kept a boat there so we were able to row across. There was no time to lose as night was drawing on. Mr Epworth and Tom drove the buggy across, sitting one at each end of the seat in order to balance it. The creek was fifty yards wide. Unfortunately a bag of lemons which was left in the buggy floated downstream.

The deep cutting on the other side of the creek where the road followed was misjudged, and consequently the place where the horses found their feet was ten yards downstream, and they were faced by a fifteen foot wall of creek bank, naturally impossible for the horses to climb. All hands unharnessed the horses, then the buggy was lifted, with Maggieville branding ropes tied to the top, and away we went, this time over a dry claypan.

Jim was ill for weeks so the doctor advised us to take him south for a change. Then word came that Tom's father was dying and that he was wanted at once. Bad luck was with us still, for after leaving Thursday Island I noticed a lot of drinking going on amongst the passengers, captain and the crew. The other woman in my cabin and I were afraid to go to bed the first night. We could hear wrangling and swearing at the steerage end of the ship, and could distinctly hear the captain sooling the sailors onto the saloon passengers who mainly comprised our husbands.

The next day every man had either a black eye or a cut face, including the captain, officers, sailors and unfortunately, our husbands. The following night I was very afraid but our husbands. assured us that the captain had slept all day and was now perfectly sober, and that there would be no more fights.

At twelve midnight I could hear something under our ship, just as though she was scraping rock. Then she would shudder and creak as though about to break in two. I had not gone to sleep, I suppose it was my nerves keeping me awake, and I was envying Tom and the children being asleep. Then I heard men running about on the deck

THIRD SON

above my head and calling out loudly. Suddenly the chief steward flung open the cabin door and said, "Get into your lifebelts as soon as possible. We are sinking."

Tom jumped out of bed hastily, thinking that the blacks were attacking the homestead, but nevertheless lost no time in helping me into my lifebelt.

Fred, who was old enough to know that we were in great danger, was screaming with fear. Edmund, three and a half years old, clung to my legs almost in convulsions as he too knew there was something wrong. Our sick baby who was too weak to cry loudly was left to Tom's care when our boat went down.

I shall never forget the scene — women and children from the other cabins could be seen running around; they were screaming loudly and crying to God for help.

We were all gathered on deck massed in a heap, and some of the women fainted. We could still hear the crunching of the rock underneath us, and we remembered how a vessel called the *Quetta* had gone down in this vicinity some years previously.

I suppose you remember the wreck. A Miss Lacey from Mackay floated for hours and hours, and was so sunburnt that she was ill for many months and quite lost her reason for a time. Do you remember also the aliens who tried to keep the little child which they saved when they seized a boat full of women and children? Of course the authorities would not allow this so she was adopted by a nice family of the name of Brown and was always called Quetta Brown, and although she was too young to give the name of her parents she grew up to be a very charming society girl.

We expected any moment to be lowered into the lifeboats. There was no sign of land but the sea was very calm so that was one blessing. I was thankful that I had Tom and our three little sons and that we would all go down together. It was so terrible that I am sure that whenever I hear of any shipwrecks I shall remember what I went through and offer up a prayer for them.

We were twenty-five miles off our course and well and truly on the edge of the Barrier Reef. When daylight broke the commotion settled down. We were still wearing our lifebelts, but by this time we could take an interest in our plight which I shall attempt to describe. On one side a coral structure could be seen towering up from the bottom of the sea. It was composed of innumerable small reefs, with beautiful gardens of coral seaweed and sponges. There were bright little fishes of every colour, shape and size, providing a fascinating pageant with the sunlight flashing back from their silvery livery as they raced away to hide in their beautiful coral homes, or to escape from the creeping crabs, sea-urchins, spiders and other foes. So eager were they to escape that they literally fell over one another, and within a few seconds the pools would be deserted. In fact the white sandy bottom of the pool looked quite bare for there was only the sluggish bêche-de-mer, who is too indolent to notice even the approach or the noise from the passengers on the boat.

On the other side of the ship we looked into tiny deep lakes, bejewelled by beautiful sea-snakes and monsters who swam backwards and forwards, waiting to see whether our boat would float off the reef when it was high tide.

You may guess the excitement when we felt our ship gradually floating into deep clear blue water, and we were allowed to take off our lifebelts.

Tom's father has passed away after a long and painful illness.[24] He had his fifty-ninth birthday the day before we arrived.

While at Cliftonville a travelling Church of England clergyman held a service for the many people who had settled — growing sugar — round the homestead. We let him christen two of our children, Edmund and Jim. Fred was christened when only a few hours' old.

Edmund watched his baby brother going through the ceremony and when the clergyman sprinkled water on him it was too much for him and he yelled and screamed, "Mummie don't let that naughty man chuck water on me too." We simply had to hold him down to make him go through with it.

What hurt me was that the good parson said, "You have a very naughty spoilt child." My blood was up in a moment and I should have liked to reply that he was an extra good child but was frightened of his clerical attire. I also remembered that I was in church and Tom's advice to keep my eyes open and my mouth closed. However, I had an opportunity of telling what I thought about the matter a little later on.

We did not stay at Cliftonville long as cattle were bringing big prices and it was worthwhile looking after every little calf. We have good neighbours in Delta, Stirling and Maggieville, but three small selectors have taken up lands nearby and they are always worth watching.

I forgot to mention what became of Annie's visit from the stork. Well, I do not know as we were at Cliftonville for many months. So

---

[24] Edmund Atherton II died on 8 February 1899, at Cliftonville.

THIRD SON

whether it arrived and was knocked on the head, or simply never came at all, is a mystery as they are so secretive about these things.

Well, I shall say goodbye now.

Love from,

JANE

My Dear Althea,

I have always forgotten to tell you that we have bought a separator so we now have fresh cream with our fruit pies. The poor gins have almost forgotten the songs they used to sing while shaking the cream in bottles as we now have a nice little churn. Oh! and we also have a nice big tank now to catch rainwater, so there is no more muddy water to drink.

On our return to the Gulf we remained three days at Cooktown while waiting for a much smaller vessel to take us the remainder of the trip. We really did enjoy our stay, and while there we hired a cab and saw a number of fruit farms, mostly worked by chinamen. We amused ourselves throwing pennies into the deep clear water, to be caught by the small native children who would dive and scramble for them. Sometimes there would be a brawl underwater if more than one reached the prize at the same time.

A peculiar headdress was worn by the lubras there. It comprised hundreds of black beads, made from beeswax and formed into small cocoons, and attached to a few strands of hair which forms a heavy fringe to their shoulders. There too the children were all in the nude.

It was also a wonderful sight watching the natives in their canoes leaving the town in hundreds to cross the wide shallow Endeavour River at sundown. They are not allowed to remain in the town after dark. We noticed a big percentage of half-castes amongst them, too.

Life in the Gulf is much pleasanter now and we no longer envy the business folk their comfortable life. We have our storeroom filled with luxuries, small lamps for each bedroom, and a beautiful one with dilly-dangles for the sitting room. In the kitchen and men's rooms there are bracket ones hanging on the walls. Sometimes I think that the chinamen cooks would rather have the old-time fat lamps as there are no breakages with these. They have to replace all breakages, that is if you can find the culprit. We have a proper bathroom without cracks, so dear, when you pay us the promised visit, you will not have to worry about gins looking through cracks to see what you are like.

Our neighbours who manage for the banks have a pleasanter look about them now. I suppose they are not bothered by letters to reduce expenses. They seem to have a freer hand and quite a lot of entertaining is being carried on.

At last I have a second-hand sewing machine. It is a funny thing but Tom thinks that sewing is a waste of time. He says that it would be much better if I had them made, so it does not look as though I shall be getting a new machine in a hurry. Alas! when the dray was crossing the Norman River the machine fell in. After being hauled out it became a third-hand machine, as I cannot move the treadle. Luckily Kitty, being a big strong gin, can do the sewing of straight large seams. You would laugh to see her at the job. She looks for all the world as though she is winning the last laps of a bicycle race. Amusement is so scarce on this station that when she first began to sew it brought all hands to the spot to enjoy the performance. I still have to make the little boys' clothes by hand.

We often had a visit from a young man who is a clerk in Burns, Philp & Co., and he and Jim are very good friends. He arrived unexpectedly one day and during the course of the conversation he said to Tom, "What price do you put on Midlothian?" After a little consideration Tom stated his price and within an hour we had sold out for ten thousand pounds, on a walk-in walk-out basis. All our wedding presents and the beautiful piano that Mother gave me were to be forwarded to us when we settled down again.

I sent for my lubra friends to come to the fence to say goodbye. Eighteen arrived and my eyes filled with tears when I saw the hollow-eyed lubras with the sad expression on their faces. When I said "me go poui-poui no more come back", they tried to catch my hand, but I dared not let them do so as I could detect the disease in their bodies. And then they started their mournful wail saying "no missus please no go". I broke down and wept and turned for home, never looking back. I could still hear them crying "no go, no go, no go".

My faith in the Almighty was almost shaken when I saw these poor women in such a sorry state through no fault of their own. We were both sorry to leave them behind. Tom had always been a thoughtful master although at times he had had to check them harshly. Then again we were sorry to have to leave our first little home which we had beautified together. But our children come first so we had to move into civilisation.

We tried to get permission to take Kitty and Homer with us but

THIRD SON

*Thomas Arthur Atherton I, circa 1901.
Tom was born on 8 February 1866, at
Mt Hedlow, near Rockhampton, while
his father, Edmund Atherton II, was
away in the Mackay district, setting up
Cliftonville Station, on which the family
was to settle. He lived most of his life in
North Queensland and this
photograph was probably taken in
Sydney in 1901. In later life he lived
at Taronga, near Bli Bli in the Maroochy
district, where he died on 10 February 1935.*

they were not allowed to break the *Aboriginals' Protection Act.* I was allowed to take Pigeon as the Government looked upon me as her foster-mother.

I remained a few days in Normanton while Tom handed over our racing stud. He was also eager to have a last ride on his favourite mare, Lobelia, so Mr Underwood, who purchased Midlothian, arranged a wild pig hunt. I forgot to tell you that Tom brought a prize white sow with six suckers to Midlothian in 1894. I hated the sight of them for they were allowed to run wild and consequently they stirred up all the waterholes in search of lily roots. This is especially annoying in the dry season when there is not much water. These pigs increased in great numbers.

A mob of pigs were seen feeding on the plain and Tom and his friend gave chase. Suddenly a huge boar ran across the path, got tangled up in the legs of Tom's horse, throwing him, his horse and the pig into a tangled heap on the ground.

Watching the road for his return I could not understand why a buckboard was coming instead of the usual mob of riders. It turned out to be Tom lying in the back of the buggy badly bruised and shaken, with a broken collarbone.

So we left the Gulf, the land of peril, on 13th August 1901.

Our boat remained anchored at Thursday Island for six hours so we explored the whole island, and had a look at the garrison from a distance. A number of soldiers were stationed there to look after our shores and to keep the New Guinea natives in order. The South Sea

Islanders were also engaged in great numbers by white men for the pearl shell trade.

The New Guinea natives roamed the streets in their native costumes of grass skirts. They did a great trade apart from diving, by selling to the travelling public beautifully carved shells, pearl and others, worked and carved into many shapes. We bought one which represented a rickshaw, with the seat padded in royal-blue plush.

We called into Mackay and of course had to be slung over the side of the ship in a basket as the sea was too rough to walk the gangway. I liked it this time and it was certainly much easier for me with three children and Pigeon. After visiting friends and relations we left for Sydney.

Oh I did feel so shy facing civilised people again, especially when one of my sisters-in-law said I looked like a clucky hen with her chicks around her. I then woke up to the fact that I was only twenty-four years of age, yet had three children and a little black child following me.

I will away now,

With love from,

JANE

My Dear,

I was really very shy and strange in Sydney, as I had never seen much of city life. In all the time that I was at school I only went shopping three times, and then it was with a woman whose business it was to take the girls shopping or to the dentist. When we went to church we walked in file, the Protestants went to All Saints', while the Catholic girls went to Saint Stephen's. Although I lived with the nuns for seven years[25] I was never asked to change my religion, so I am still a Protestant.

I had never seen a telephone and it took me a while to pluck up enough courage to lift the receiver. I imagined it might burst and kill me and I did not want to die as life had become very sweet. I am sure Tom must have felt the same way, as he always called me to do the speaking and would say "don't go such a way back". After two or three times I got over my fear.

We stayed at Petty's Hotel for a week, but found it too cooped up

---

[25] See footnote 6.

THIRD SON

for the children, so moved out to Ranelagh where there were large grounds for the family to play. Tom's mother and sister were staying there also.

We met several people and a number of relations while in Sydney. Staying at Petty's was Mr Frank Cobbald, whom fortune had smiled on, for he was no longer a station manager but an owner of several large properties. Tom met him on his first trip to stock Midlothian, in 1885. His sister Clara and her husband George Audley-Coote were also in Sydney on their honeymoon, before departing for their home in Western Australia. Poll Atherton and her sister Essie, daughters of John Atherton of Emerald End, were also there.

Did I mention in one of my previous letters that Frank and Arthur Bowman, of Mount Brisbane station, bought a mob of cheap cattle, twelve hundred head from J. Harris at seven and sixpence with calves thrown in, to form a station up the Peninsula, seventy miles from Normanton.

Frank married a Miss Tremble and took her out there, shortly

Jane Atherton and her three eldest sons, August 1901. Fred is standing (right), Edmund is seated (left) and Jane holds Jim, then 14 months old. The photograph was taken soon after the family had left Midlothian but before they had taken up residence at Woonon.

ACROSS THE YEARS

after we left the Gulf. She was a sister of Mrs Dubois, whose husband managed the Bank of New South Wales. We often saw the Bowman brothers and liked Frank very much, he was so manly and gentle. We were horrified to learn that he had been speared by the mission blacks, who attacked the homestead. Frank was speared in the eye. His wife broke the spear and pulled it out, then douched the cavity with permanganate of potash, diluted with water.

Their white man ran away, taking food with him, while the blacks were attacking the homestead. He remained in hiding for a whole week, before he ventured forth to find Mrs Bowman frantic for Frank was ill and delirious. He assisted her with her two children and helped her to take her husband to Normanton to see a doctor. Frank died the next day from tetanus, caused by the poisoned spear.

Arthur was in Brisbane at the time and Mrs Bowman could not return to the station, so she sold her share of the property for a mere pittance. I did hear that she went to South Africa and became a very rich woman.

I have got away from our experiences of Sydney, which were not pleasant. Poor Pigeon was such a novelty to many, that we were forced to leave her at home. When she entered the street, we would be followed by a crowd of men, women and children, all of whom had never seen an aboriginal child before. The annoyance became so dreadful, that the poor child was only at ease in a nearby park. Sometimes there too, she would cause screams from the children, who would run off to their nurses, while others would stand at arm's length and offer her sweets and nuts as though she was a monkey.

The clothes fashions are beautiful and so are the hairstyles. I have had mine dressed several times, but the worst part of it was I had to sleep in a sort of veil for a week and dare not brush and comb it. It is arranged over a round hair pad which in the heat becomes irritable. I have several dresses from David Jones and Farmers and have lost that old Gulf look, especially when I wear hats perched on the top of my head, all covered with flowers, and held on with a pair of silver hatpins.

We are leaving for Mackay in a few days. I shall close now,

with love from,

JANE

P.S.   I would love to be back in my own little home in the Gulf, it is an awful feeling to be homeless.

THIRD SON

Woonon
First daughter — Leila May
15 May 1902

My Dear,

We have purchased Woonon from Tom's Uncle Richard, who took it up in 1865. It is not a station like Midlothian, but has two thousand mixed cattle and we are well pleased to be settled once again. We have built a nice house, and Plane Creek sugar mill, the post office, school, baker and butcher and also a store, are only four miles away on the opposite side of the creek from us.

We arrived at Woonon, which means big waterhole in the blacks' language, last October, 1901. We have a very light wet season here, so different from the Gulf. In fact it never seems to rain heavily at all, and in a few months we found ourselves without water. The large waterhole at the house was almost dry, our cattle were dying in hundreds, and the water tanks were empty. Luckily there was a little water in Plane Creek, which we had to cart for household wants, a distance of two miles.

Plane Creek station is owned by Henry Bell, who had married Tom's Aunt Alice in 1861. He was annoyed so much by the travelling public on the Rockhampton coaches asking for accommodation, that he built and leased out a fair-sized hotel about two miles from the homestead. A general store, blacksmith's shop and a few residences soon clustered around the hotel.

The Plane Creek sugar mill was built by the Athertons and others in the vicinity. It was no time at all before a police barracks, State school, two stores, a post office, baker and butcher's shop had sprung up near the mill.

The people around the mill wanted a township formed, but Henry Bell wanted it near his hotel. Tom, however, who is a member of the shire council, got busy and formed the township, Sarina, near the mill, and in no time four more hotels had sprung up.

Soon after Henry Bell had built the first hotel, his wife Alice died and he lived on there with his youngest daughter Lily. She had a nasty experience one day which could have been more serious if it had not been for the speedy help given her by her two well-trained fox terriers. She was alone on the station when she heard a man's voice,

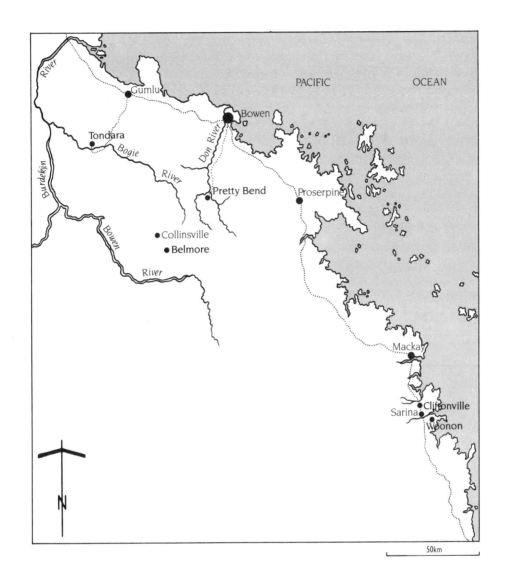

Map of the Bowen and Mackay districts showing the location of
Tondara, Pretty Bend, Cliftonville and Woonon stations. The dotted
lines show the modern access roads, which follow the direction of the
original trails. It should be noted that there was no direct road from
Pretty Bend to Tondara — access was via Gumlu. The area covered by
this map is indicated on the general map of Queensland shown on
p. xiii.

somewhere near the kitchen, so calling her dogs she went out to interview him. He was a dirty-looking fellow asking for food. She told him she could only give him some cooked corned beef as this was the day they got their order from the store near the hotel he had passed. He immediately caught her by the shoulder and said that he wanted more than corned beef. She tried to free herself from his grip, but being unable to do so, called "sullim" to her dogs.

They certainly did so, first ripping the shirt from his back. By the time he had run a few yards, he had no part of the back of his pants left and would have had nothing at all if she had not called the dogs off.

The drought still continues. One kerosene tin of water is all we dare use for the daily bath of the children and myself. First I bathe the children, then myself and lastly Pigeon, all in the same water. As you can guess our few pot-plants are not exactly thriving. Troubles never come singly dear, I am again pregnant. I hope it will be the little girlie I have longed to receive. Everyone tells me I waste a lot of energy in the making of pretty trimmed blouses for the baby boy. They all say if I had a daughter they are sure it would be dressed like a doll, as I sew so well and do ever so much fancywork.

* * * *

I am sorry I could not finish this letter and have let five months go by before doing so. Somehow, I had not the heart to settle down to letter writing. The drought was terrible and other circumstances have been upsetting, too.

We have a baby daugher at last.[26] Needless to say we are overjoyed, in fact, we have even had telegrams from the Gulf congratulating us on our achievement. We have called her Leila May. Oh dear! I was so angry and hurt when I found out why Tom loved the name Leila, it was because his first sweetheart was Leila S—. Anyway, after I had threatened to go back to Mother with my family of four, we made up the quarrel and he showered presents on me, in the way of an emerald and diamond ring, a chiming clock and many household requirements.

Last week we had a visit from a nigger, called English John, who remembered Tom when he was a lad. He offered to bring us oysters and crabs in return for some tobacco. Tom drew his plug of tobacco from his pocket, placed it on the verandah step and with the nigger's tomahawk tried to cut off a piece. He missed and nearly cut his thumbnail off instead. He let out such a yell and jumped about a bit,

---

[26] Leila May Atherton, later Leila Shaw, was born on 15 May 1902. She died in 1975.

ACROSS THE YEARS

swearing at the same time that if another nigger came looking for tobacco, he would be glad to give him a whole plug or none at all. When he turned around however, to give the nigger the tobacco, he saw poor English John was a full quarter of a mile away and still running strongly.

The drought still goes on, I feel at times that life is not worth living, so I just must drift away from my woes and tell you of other things in my letters.

Years before we settled at Woonon, and long before the sugar mill was built, Nellie Mitchell — Madam Melba — came to Mackay on a visit and stayed as a music teacher. She met Charlie Armstrong, married him, and lived at the Marion sugar mill for a short time.

Charlie was a great favourite, especially with men of his own age. He was a grand boxer and taught Tom and W. Bell to defend themselves through life. He built a beautiful house for his bride on a selection adjoining Woonon, a portion of the old run, intending to go in for cattle raising, but Nellie never lived in it. She had a son and went back to Melbourne to her people. Charlie lived alone for sometime and then sold the home to Mr A. Innis, who moved it to his farm, Pratelina, near Louisa Creek, where all the Plane Creek sugar is shipped in lighters to the larger boats at Flat Top. We purchased fourteen hundred acres of land from the Armstrong estate, at five shillings an acre. We called the paddock on which the home once stood, Melba's paddock. I often go to see the remaining stumps, only a quarter of a mile away from our home.

I shall finish this letter now. We are still hoping for rain, we have to be so careful with the water still. I think Tom and the men bathe entirely in the Pacific Ocean.

Love from,

JANE

My Dear,

It is ages since I have written but the drought still goes on. This country needs big hearts and I am afraid I have no heart left. Everything is so famished from the heat and the men are out night and day beating the flames of the bushfires. I am sure the 1902 drought will be long remembered.

A short time ago I had a terrible experience with the bushfires. The men had beaten the flames out around the small house paddock and left, thinking we were quite safe from the flames. I was alone

Melba's house, circa 1913. This house was built originally on land adjoining Woonon. It was moved to a location nearer Mackay after Melba's husband, Charlie Armstrong, had sold it. Melba never lived in it, however, since she had already left her husband and returned to Melbourne before it was completed.

ACROSS THE YEARS

with a woman cook, Pigeon and the little ones, including Leila, a mere babe of six months. It was Pigeon who noticed a small fire spring up in the afternoon at our front gate, fifty yards from the house. There was nothing for it, but to hasten with wet bags to beat it out. I placed my four children in the centre of the road, near the house, surrounded them with wet bags and left Pigeon to care for them. The other white woman and myself worked unceasingly, beating the flames for two hours, battling and beating them with bushes when the bags were worn out. It was only after the fire had burnt our fowl house and one side of the paling fence that we finally mastered it.

When Tom got home the next morning to carry more food out to the fire beaters, I was in bed with a high fever and no chance of getting a doctor as all the available men from the farms and the township were beating the fire.

A week after the drought first broke I went to see a doctor and a hairdresser to find out why my hair was falling out in handfuls. The doctor said it was from being overheated and ordered my head to be shaved.

There has been a break in the drought dear, but everything is still terribly dry. You can have no conception of what the bushfires have been like, so I shall try to give you some idea of what they are to the country people.

They start so easily, when everything is so dry. A deserted camp fire was the cause of the last. Our men could see a small column of smoke rising from the beach, where some fishing party had carelessly neglected to put out their campfire properly before leaving on an expedition. Empty flour sacks were gathered and the horses caught immediately and in no time hardly, the men were riding at full gallop towards the fire. It was two o'clock in the afternoon when they rode off. All night long I watched the flames spread rapidly towards our homestead. It was really most spectacular, the flames climbed the tall trees as far as the small limbs and leaves which were not quite dry enough to burn. Then the burning and crackling twigs would be carried by the wind to the next giant and so on until only charred desolation and blinding smoke remained.

Our home was enveloped in smoke for days. Nerve-racking days when we feared all our work would be of no avail. The children were so afraid, clinging to my skirts continually and imploringly asking when their father would return. I was afraid myself that he would never outlive the heat and flames and get back to us.

The land has been burnt to a cinder, the very soil is so caked that cracks inches wide have opened. These are very dangerous to the horsemen, as the hooves of their horses can easily fall in one of these unexpected cracks and result in an ugly spill for both horse and rider.

Not a vestige of small plant life is left, not a sapling, and even the large trees have perished. We watch the storms work up, the black night is shot with blinding lightning and pealing rolls of thunder shake the house. It feels as though the end of the world is at hand. Finally the storm passes on without a drop of rain, only a terrific gale which carries away sheets of iron and in fact, anything we have failed to secure in advance.

I shall end this letter now, dear, I wonder if I shall ever see rain again.

Love from,

JANE

My Dear,

It seems years since I received your cheery letter. I have been thinking there is no cheer in this district for us and I am longing to be back in the uncivilised Gulf again, where droughts are not known.

We have experienced the hottest weather I have ever known. The Gulf heat was nothing to this. I find it very trying. The neighbours tell me it is because I am unused to moist heat. Moist, if you like; we are still in the drought.

The children are tired out and peevish. Poor little mites, they do feel the heat so and have to be encased in mosquito nets day and night. We have what are called mangrove mosquitoes, tiny black ones that bite savagely and swarm in billions. Tom has worked and worried himself to a shadow and my shaven head is no sight to cheer him up. I weep about my long golden tresses, so long I could sit on them, gone in the drought like everything else. Each night before going to bed the last thing we do is to look at the sky for lightning on the horizon which may bring us rain.

I must continue with this letter dear, I had to leave it as fresh disaster has overcome us. The much-wanted rain is to be blamed.

The other night we could see the flicker of a storm miles off and by ten o'clock it was upon us. First we heard the ironbark tree near the kitchen struck by lightning, then pieces of wood and splinters showering the house; leaving in fact huge lumps of wood on one of the

WOONON

verandahs. The children, governess, maid and Pigeon ran into our room for protection. The wind was blowing with hurricane force, tins and sheets of iron and limbs of trees were flying in all directions, then down came the rain in torrents. One thunderstorm followed another for hours. Our rain gauge had overflowed from the first storm.

Daylight revealed a changed landscape, instead of drought there was flood. The stockyards were under water. Looking from the house on the top of the hill all we could see was sheets of water. The poor weak cattle that had weathered the drought by being fed on molasses carted from the Plane Creek mill, died in numbers during the night from exposure to the long and heavy rain.

All the stock we could muster from the two thousand purchased was six hundred males, which we sold for seven pounds a head, and then restocked with breeders from Woodhouse station on the Burdekin, and Goorganga near Proserpine.

It is heart-rending even now to count the carcasses of the cattle lying on the top of the bank of the lagoon. It had been fenced-off leaving a stoned opening where the cattle had their drink of muddy dirty water, and the poor beasts had been too weak to climb the corduroy and stoned bank from the water's edge.

At peep of day the men began the work of pulling the fallen animals to the bank and lifting them on to their legs to give them another chance to live.

The children are much better since they can have a daily bath and clean water to drink; but I have not quite got over it all yet. The doctor says it is nerves. I never suffered that complaint in the Gulf, though of course we had no droughts to contend with there.

Goodbye, dear.

Love from,

JANE

My Dear,

Things look a little brighter now, though there is still room for improvement. You know after the drought we restocked with breeders and now we have little calves coming along in great numbers. They have, however, a great menace in the dingoes. Both the kangaroos and wallabies are almost extinct, as they perished in the drought, but the dingoes thrived on the carcasses of the cattle and consequently their numbers have increased and they have become a serious problem. Strychnine poison is being set everywhere to kill them.

Tom was away from home when the governess called me to have a shot at a dingo who was amongst the few milking cows we had managed to save through the drought. The dingo had a young calf down on the ground. They always prefer fresh meat. I fired a shot but only frightened him away, so knowing it would come back to the yard at night looking for prey, the governess and I set a large piece of fat pork poisoned with strychnine.

On second thoughts we were afraid to leave it, as the man who was breaking in some horses for us and lived in the quarters not far from the house, had a valuable cattle dog. We were afraid it might be off the chain, so sent Pigeon to get the bait and burn it at the woodheap.

With clear consciences we slept soundly, but in the morning Pigeon came to my bedroom and said in a distracted voice, "A nice-looking dog with a brass collar is dead near the kitchen." I felt shivery and shaky all over, in fact I felt a murderer. I woke the governess, who too, was greatly upset. It was no dingo but belonged to some person who valued it by the look of the polished collar. We got Pigeon to drag it down the gully, thinking how dreadful it would be if the horse-breaker saw it.

A few minutes later the man came to the kitchen door, and asked for me. I was shaking again and so was the governess, for we both knew something must be wrong for him to ask to speak to me so early in the morning. I had to be brave and went forth with an air of importance, but I nearly collapsed when I saw his ferocious face and was ready to burst out crying when he snarled, "Did you set poison near the house?" I explained to him what had happened and to my relief he laughed heartily and eventually told me that there were four dead dogs outside his door. So that made five dogs we had killed. The dogs had licked the spot where the fat had melted and the strychnine had killed them. They must have wandered at night from their farm homes.

Rupert Atherton called in to see us the following night. We were sitting on the verandah, which was moonlit, telling him of the dog episode, when suddenly he exclaimed, "There's another, where's the gun, we might as well put him out of his misery, he is sure to lick the bait." He fired a shot and we heard a yelp, but we never heard anything about a dead dog this time.

I must tell you what happened to Tom and his Uncle Richard, just after the drought broke. They went out to shoot dingoes and to poison freshly killed calves. They separated in a wallum scrub, which

WOONON

was literally covered with dingo pads along the narrow paths. Tom could hear shot after shot and was envying his uncle greatly his good fortune in finding the dingoes. When he came on the scene he found his uncle in great glee, shouting to him: "I have had the time of my life. I'll teach those kangaroo dogs to be chivvying a calf along a path, I've got rid of seven of the —, that will teach the owners to keep their dogs at home to keep wallabies out of their cane instead of killing calves."

A friend of ours, a neighbour in fact, kept a pack of these dogs. He has since remarked that he thinks a crocodile must have got his dogs as they have been missing for some time. He says he is not really sorry as he had great trouble in keeping them away from his calves. So then we told him what actually did happen.

We are prosperous again and so is the settlement around the mill. So prosperous is the district that a race meeting was run recently, which caused a big stir. A bough shed was built for the ladies, near a buckjumping show, within a huge enclosure of hessian. It was half-a-crown — every payment seems to be half-a-crown here — to go in to the buckjumping show. I told the children they could go in but on no account to try to ride the horses.

Our whole party of women decided not to waste so much money on a mere show. Suddenly we heard shouts of "Oh! he's on, no he's off! Oh, the naughty boy, he was told not to ride. Oh! Oh! Oh! Is he dead?" We rushed madly into the tent to find the horses had not even been saddled or a performance of any kind started. It was just a hoax and we were amazed to find it cost us a half-crown to get out again so we stayed. Anyhow we had a good laugh about it and our menfolk enjoyed it better.

I am not quite up to the ways of the men on a racecourse here. In the Gulf it was a fair run for your money and no sideshows or trickery.

Love from,

JANE

My Dear,

I must describe my recent visit to Cairns with Tom, who had business there. He persuaded me to take advantage of the trip to see the beauty of the Barron Falls. Tom's Uncle Richard, who lives in Mackay, came with us.

Tom bought the railway tickets to Mareeba, but after getting nicely settled in our compartment, he could not find them. He thought he had left them on the window, or perhaps the clerk had not handed them to him, so he went to the window to inquire. The clerk became abusive and so did Tom. We could hear the heated argument, as could all the other passengers on the train. The hand of the clock reached starting time and the train commenced to move out.

Uncle Richard looked worried and asked me if I had any money on me. I said that I had no money with me and felt like crying. Uncle Richard took this news badly and said, "Jane this is the last time I'll let that husband of yours buy my ticket. He is the banker too, I have not a penny on me. I don't know what in hell we are going to do in this strange locality." I had visions of us all being run in, Uncle, Pigeon, baby and myself.

Suddenly Tom burst into the compartment, hot in the face from the run to catch the train and swearing at the same time that he would fix that — clerk when he got back. I did feel ashamed. I became equally hot in the face myself and broke out into a bath of perspiration. I had dressed carefully so that I should not be criticised by my new relatives and now I had lost all my composure.

After the situation had become less strained I suggested to Tom that he look in all his pockets for the missing tickets. He felt in the breast pocket of his coat and we saw the expression on his face undergo a sudden change. I am sure if he had been by himself, he would have thrown the tickets out the window of the train. He certainly was not enjoying himself. I am sure he will never lose a ticket again.

We arrived at Mareeba at lunchtime and decided to have our meal in the township, before we left to give them all a surprise at Emerald End. Some person gave Uncle John, who had come to town on business, the news that we intended surprising them, so he promptly turned the tables on us.

I saw a man come to the dining-room door, glare around, then showing his teeth he let out a tremendous roar like an infuriated bull and made straight for us. Thinking it was a madman I grabbed up the baby, but to my great relief it was only Uncle John, whom everybody knows as the jovial king of the north.

Two commercial travellers seated near us were really funny. They jumped inches from their seats, one even spilling the soup on his suit. Uncle John did not even notice. He is the man in this little town, and the Atherton Tablelands have been called after him.

The sights were marvellous, I did enjoy myself. We walked to the bottom of the Barron Falls, a marvellous scene with palms, orchids and ferns of all sizes and kinds all around us. I shall long remember it as a perfect picture.

When we landed back in Cairns, I saw Tom slip the railway clerk a ten-shilling note, before he started to apologise. The clerk was all smiles and said, "Thank you, Sir."

Now that the drought is truly over, I have started a garden and a bush house. I am gathering a collection from everywhere. I have a wonderful tassel and Johnstone River fern, which is the envy of all at Sarina.

I shall close now, hoping to hear from you soon.

Love from,

JANE

My Dear,

My life has become a continuous round of social activities. At times I wish I had never left the peace and quiet of Midlothian. I go to church every Sunday, and dress my little flock to attend the Sarina Sunday school. Tom presented the piece of land to the Church of England, and now they have built the church we must go.

Tom is on the racing committee, both in Mackay and in Sarina, so between them both, I have a busy time attending the races. He is also on the show committee, which is held once a year. The show does not bother me but the children do. They get up so early to groom their ponies and have them ready for the different exhibits, before school time. You can have no idea of what it is to be a mother of sons and to have to referee easily twice a day, over the disputes about the owners of different brushes, and other things.

So many nice women have called to see me too. It takes a lot of courage on my part to return their calls after living so entirely alone for such a long time. I have been asked at times to sing at church socials and other events. I had the wind taken out of my sails at the last church social. The bishop asked me to sing again and said my voice was like one of the Westminster boys. I suppose from doing corroboree dances with the natives I have gathered a falsetto voice. I wonder what he would have likened it to if I had sung and danced the native corroboree?

The site for the suspension bridge — the first of its kind — over Sandy Creek, has at last been inspected by the members of the shire council. Mr Kidston, the Premier of Queensland, was present. I remained seated in my pony buggy some fifty yards distant, while Tom went with the men.

An elderly woman, Mrs Donald Beaton, who is noted for her eccentricity, came to me and asked if I minded her changing her riding skirt as she wanted to meet Mr Kidston. She changed and arranged her hat carefully and came back to ask me which was he. When I had pointed him out to her, the poor old soul, after staring at him a few seconds, remarked, "Why, he is no different to the other men, I'll be dashed if I am going down to see him."

I made a dreadful mistake later in the day. Tom asked a farm woman to give me a cup of tea and some hot scones for my lunch. Dear, I have never seen so many children in my life, they came from every door in the house. I knew there was a State school nearby, so asked the lady of the house if the school was out. You should have seen the look of pride when she replied, "They are all mine, fourteen and I hope to have many more, it is women like you, who should stop galavanting around and stay at home and have babies." I am not much good at defending myself, otherwise I would have told her I am the mother of four, and God knows how many more I shall find as I am only twenty-six. Also, I should much prefer the stork called on her more often and spared me.

I shall stop now as I am quite tired from the excitement.

Love from,

JANE

My Dear,

Tom is on the harbour board for Sarina and the district, and they have made plans to start a wonderful jetty, connecting Flat Top Island, near Mackay, to the mainland of Queensland. If successful, it will make Mackay one of the best cities in the north.

Well, the day dawned for the start of a wonderful era for Mackay. Everybody was in great glee. Businessmen from Mackay, mill managers, squatters and farmers, all left the town by steamer to witness the first pile being sunk and driven into position.

Unfortunately, their spirits sank, too. After the first blow had been struck for the pile, it began to sink slowly, until it disappeared completely from sight. I heard it has been picked up off the coast of Africa but that may be only a tale.

There is no doubt the members of the harbour board are very sore about the loss. Tom has received such a lot of chaffing about it and if he sees I have written about it to you, it will doubtless start a scrap.

We have had a lunatic working for us and what a time he has given us. I have been scared of my life of him. We got him from the Salvation Army, who said he was a good worker. He is about fifteen years of age. At every chance he would hang around the kitchen, talking sweethearts to the maid and Pigeon. The latter told me how rude he was.

I went to him on one of his sweetheart talks in the kitchen, where he dines, and told him if he did not stop the rudeness I would tell the boss.

He was the cowboy and was learning to ride. He got it into his head that he was a wonderful rider and plagues the life out of me, calling to me to come and have a look at his Tod Sloan style. I used to go just to humour him as he told Pigeon he would like to pith me. Tom used to say he is perfectly harmless and a good worker. I was sitting on the top of the kitchen steps watching him one day. He started off at a fast gallop towards the stockyards down the steep slope. Unfortunately the gates were shut and when the horse prop-

Mackay, Sydney Street, circa 1913. Mackay was the big town in the neighbourhood to which Jane would travel from Woonon.

ACROSS THE YEARS

ped, he was shot right over the top rail. We could see he was hurt and ran down with water and whisky to find he was stunned or I should say more stupid from the fall.

We gave the hands a few days off for the races in Mackay, except this boy Philip, whom we left in charge. When we all arrived back, we could not recognise the homestead; huge trees had been cut down and a road fifty yards wide had been cleared leading up to the house from the far gate, a full two hundred yards.

Many travellers had called, swaggies I should say, asking for food. We refuse most of them as they can get food from the police barracks in Sarina. Philip did not do so. He put them all on to work and paid them with rations from the storeroom.

We had to part with him, instead of pithing me he pithed my dog. It is a relief not to have him around. I am feeling better already. He certainly was getting me down.

Love from,

JANE

WOONON

Two more sons
Colin Bardsley — 27 December 1904
Henry Stuart — 19 January 1908

My Dear,

Our hearts are broken, we have had the first real sorrow in our lives. Our little Jim is dead.[27]

Tom, as you know, is a public man and has to be away from home three days a month to attend meetings. We had the carpenters and painters on the station enlarging and painting the homestead. Little Jim was three and a half years of age, just the age which appeals to all. He was a great favourite with the painter, who gave him an old paintbrush and a tin of water to paint with, while his brothers were in the schoolroom. He became suddenly ill. Tom was away at his meeting at the time. The men said it might be the smell of the paint and advised me to spread cut up onions through the house.

When Tom arrived in the afternoon, we immediately moved over to Eversleigh to his brother's home, seven miles distant from the smell of the paint. Two days passed and he was still restless at night. In fact he hardly closed his eyes, so we took him to Mackay to see a doctor, who assured us there was nothing wrong with him, but that I was the one requiring attention. So Tom left again in the afternoon, leaving me with little Jim and baby Leila at the Imperial Hotel, so that my nerves would settle down and I would stop thinking Jim was ill.

All Friday night he played on the floor, building houses with his set of blocks and coming to my bedside every half-hour or so for me to get up and play with him. Early Saturday morning I noticed a blue shadow round his mouth and was so worried I asked Mr Binney, the secretary of the general hospital who called to inquire how he was, how I could get a second doctor as I had no faith in the one I had. He told me there was a new doctor in the town, and to ring up my doctor to bring him along as soon as possible.

They arrived at ten o'clock and asked me to leave the room while they examined Jim. I was broken-hearted when the new doctor told me to send for my husband as there was very little hope. The child

---

[27] Thomas James (Jim) Atherton died in the Imperial Hotel, Mackay, on 14 December 1903, of acute nephritis.

was suffering from lead poisoning, gathered from the paintbrush.

I had to send a man out on horseback to find Tom. He was at the very end of the run, as he was delivering a mob of store cattle to a cattle buyer.

It was nine o'clock on Sunday night when he arrived. Jim, with the slight blue shadow round his mouth and his cheeks like roses, was playing on the floor with the toys the men from the hotel had given him. They all loved him and spent many hours entertaining the poor little fellow.

We put him in bed between us when he said, "Mummie, cover me over I can see snakes everywhere, they are all over Daddy too, but none on you, lie on top of me Mummie." I shall never forget my little chubby-faced Jim when the morning dawned, he was jet black round the mouth and the colour of death, but he still had a happy smile for all that. The doctors arrived and packed him in hot sheets. Oh!! I can still hear him crying, "I did nothing Mummie, I am a good boy."

Tom said he would hurry downstairs to send telegrams to our parents as it was evident we were to lose him. I was alone with him when I saw death creeping over his face. I lost my balance and grabbed my darling saying, "Don't die and leave Mummie." Tom arrived at that very second and our little Jim said, "I am not dying am I Daddy," to which Tom replied, "Sing me 'Sing a Song of Sixpence'." The poor brave little mite sat up with pillows at his back and started to sing in a voice so strong, but by the time he came to the end it was a bare whisper. He then said, "Kiss me Daddy, quick," and turning his face towards me he formed a kiss with his mouth and left us for his God.

I can write no more, my eyes are filled with tears.

Love from,

JANE

My Dear,

The death of our little son, the bushfires and the drought have been too much for me. The new doctor advised Tom to get me away south from the scene of remembrance for a while. Tom sent word to Woonon to have the home shut up, leaving only the men on the station. He then went out and collected the family and Pigeon, who had been staying with our relations to get away from the paint, and we all left for Sydney.

TWO MORE SONS

Mackay, Imperial Hotel, circa 1901. It was here that Jim Atherton died of lead nephropathy on 14 December 1903.

We were away six weeks and have now returned to Woonon. Dear, I could not stand it. There was his little cot with the imprint of his head still on the pillow, all his little toys, the paintbrush and old jam tin still lying around. It was most pathetic watching Leila toddling through the rooms calling "Dim, Dim", looking behind the doors and thinking he was playing with her still. We have decided to live at Tedlands, an outstation of Woonon, twelve miles distant, for a few weeks.

Tedlands is a comfortable cottage with five rooms and a detached kitchen. The stockyards almost touch the house. I love to watch the cattle going through the dip.

Tom left for Tedlands in a spring cart loaded with potatoes, onions and other groceries, and ten laying hens to supply us with eggs. I followed him in a small pony buggy, with Pigeon and Leila, while Fred and Edmund rode with the stockmen and drove the mustering horses some distance behind.

Within a few miles of Tedlands, we could see potatoes and onions scattered on the roadside, and fearing something was wrong I put my ponies into a canter and paced the distance out, wondering what had happened to Tom.

It was no time before we caught him up and were astounded to see eight of my laying hens dead and strung up by their necks to the side of the cart. It seems he struck a small stump on the side of the road, which overturned the cart, throwing him, the hens, potatoes, onions and groceries into the long grass. He was so badly hurt, he could not catch the remaining two live hens.

It is wonderful to me, to watch Fred and Edmund start off to muster on their ponies, and more remarkable that they can pick their own cattle from a herd of three or four hundred. Each child was given a cow and calf for his first birthday, after we settled at Woonon.

Well, dear, I must close now.

Love from,

JANE

My Dear Althea,

I did not tell you when we were expecting our last child. To tell you the truth I was almost ashamed to be telling so many yarns about the stork. Well this time he brought a dear delicate little mite who looked more like a transparent angel than a baby. He only lived for a year and ten months.[28] He was so pretty with his waxen skin and his head of fair hair, that people would stop in the street to admire him. We called him Colin Bardsley.

We did not seem to miss him as much as we did our little Jim. I suppose this was because he was always so delicate that we knew that if he lived to be a grown man he would still be delicate.

At the moment I am alone again and according to my letters you must think that I am always alone. The main yards are at Tedlands. At times I am rather glad to be alone as it gives me a great opportunity to make the children's clothes. Boys' clothes especially require such a lot of mending but still, being alone has its drawbacks. Only yesterday we had a frightful murder just four miles away on the opposite side of the creek. It was a woman murdered by a half-caste chinaman in her own home. The wretch, after killing her, waited for her four children to come home from school so that he could murder them, too.

One night Pigeon, who sleeps on the verandah, wakened me by screaming loudly. At first I wondered whether I had had a nightmare because ever since the death of my child my nerves have been so very bad, and I cry a lot in my sleep. I heard footsteps and immediately

[28] Colin Bardsley Atherton was born on 27 December 1904 at Rockhampton. He died on 8 November 1906 at Woonon, suffering from convulsions and pyrexia attributed to teething problems.

TWO MORE SONS

Colin Bardsley Atherton, circa 1906. Colin was born in Mackay on 27 December 1904. He died at Woonon on 8 November 1906. According to Jane's description, he had always been a sickly child, but his death certificate, which gives "dentition convulsions and pyrexia" as the cause of death, provides no real clue as to what malady he may have suffered from.

thought of the murder, and supposed that Pigeon would be the first to meet her doom.

I quickly clutched my revolver and held the trigger when a small voice said, "Missus let me in, an awful thing with shining eyes keeps looking at me through my net."

I was very thankful that it was not a chinaman and said, "Get in quickly when I open the door." My legs were literally shaking from fear and when Fred and Edmund heard the commotion they immediately came into my bedroom too.

When Pigeon was safely in my room she began to explain about the awful thing, but Oh dear! you have no idea of the number of fleas she brought with her in her blankets. I shall never forget them. I almost began to think that facing a chinaman with a revolver would be preferable to a night with the fleas.

Nobody had gone to sleep when we heard a noise and looking through a glass door we found a woolly dog that had strayed from Sarina. So you can imagine that it did not take long to get rid of Pigeon and her fleas and to move ourselves to another room.

We have purchased a small piece of country near Nebo — Thorndon — for fattening purposes. People say that it is the last place that God ever made, so do not think that it is an important town. We have shifted our bullocks — four hundred — there to fatten them up.

Another drought is on but I am getting used to them now. We have never had another like the 1902 one though.

Fred and Edmund, who are now boarding in town in order to get better schooling, have had to be taken away for a short time to help dip the cattle. The men on the station have been very busy attending to the waterholes which look as though they may give out on account of the drought.

Well, that is all I have to tell you just for the moment, so I'll close now.

With love from,

JANE

TWO MORE SONS

162

My Dear Althea,

Somehow or other I cannot get strong again and I do sorely miss my delicate baby. He took up so much of my attention for so long that now I am at a loose end. The loss of a child is very hard to bear. I wonder at times whether I have done something wrong, and then I think that that cannot be because I have always taught my children to say their prayers at my knee, although I am not so very good at praying myself, but have tried to do my duty to God and to man too, when I am dealing with the unfortunate blacks.

I am certainly not much good among the white women as I cannot understand their ways, but I shall always remember a Mrs Beresford who lived at Sarina, for when she heard that Colin was in convulsions she hurried to me at four o'clock in the morning, and knelt on her knees most of the time until he passed away at nine that night.

You may misunderstand me when I say that I do not understand the ways of the white women. I am sorry to have to say that Tom likes his night out and when he has it he usually takes a little too much drink. This usually happens about half a dozen times a year. Once when he did this a woman sent me a handkerchief which was accompanied by an anonymous letter. There was a little note to say "dry your tears".

Perhaps this has made me a little hard in my attitude towards the white women or perhaps they simply do not understand me, as I keep very much to myself and the children. They may think that as I am a station woman I am trying to laud it over them but really and truly it is just shyness with me, probably due to the fact that I was shut up in a school for so many years, and since then have lived so long with the natives.

The doctor has ordered me away for fear I shall get a nervous breakdown. I took the opportunity of driving my little pony buggy with its small pair of ponies, Adam and Eve, over the Eton Range. It was a very bad track to the wayside inn.

There was a stockman there holidaying for a few days. His idea was to ease his tired feet and he certainly did, for no matter where he was sitting his feet would go up onto the nearest chair or table. I often wondered whether he would one day put them onto my lap by mistake.

After a while Tom thought it would be better if I moved to another hotel nearer Thorndon, because he could then visit me and see how I was getting on. This was a good thing because I was actually dreaming of feet going up onto my lap and it was getting on my nerves.

ACROSS THE YEARS

This hotel was much more comfortable. We had a cottage all to ourselves, which at one time had served as a court house at Mt Britton, and had been shifted away when that town sank into oblivion owing to the loss of the gold reefs.

Drovers seemed just to call in at the inn and move on again after a few drinks. They kept an excellent table here, far removed from our usual corned beef. At breakfast we would get chops, cutlets and curried mutton. Mutton to us was a great treat. At night dinner consisted of roast mutton with mint sauce and poultry. As we got plenty of poultry at home I just revelled in the mutton.

I soon began to feel my old self again and decided that it must be the mutton diet. I was very surprised indeed when, the day before we were leaving for home, one of the children bounced in and said, "You have been eating goat not sheep."

We then began to fancy that we could taste goat on our food and could even smell the old billy, so decided to wend our way back to Woonon to our beef diet again.

I shall never forget coming down that steep range, which was so dangerous that Tom had to tie a big log onto the back to keep our brakes from slipping. I was so frightened that I hadn't time to pray while going down, but when we got to the bottom safely I said a thankful prayer. We gathered gum leaves on the top of the range because they make beautiful scented bags for clothes in the drawers and keep them free from insects.

I am much better again now and although I vowed that never again would I have another baby to lose, the stork is coming to see me again. Perhaps this is his last Christmas gift. Let us hope so anyway.

Love from your old clucky hen,

JANE

My Dear,

It is some months since I last wrote to you and I can tell you that I have shed a lot of tears in the meantime as I did not want another child.

Luckily I have a little friend who calls to see me three nights a week with her husband. She too, is expecting a visit from the stork. As it is her first she is delighted to show me her beautiful outfit, which must have cost a great deal of money. I myself have grown tired of spending money on baby clothes so am going to get the cheapest

TWO MORE SONS

outfit I can possibly buy. We are really running out of boys' names so have been looking through some books for suggestions. We do not like fancy names so have decided on Stuart after my little friend's husband, Alex Stuart.

I feel that it will be most unfair if I have another son so think that I must invite the stork again before I die to bring a daughter to balance things up. What do you think? Perhaps you do not think about it at all as you are not a married woman.

I have already been in Mackay for two months now waiting, so goodness knows when it will arrive. It is well past Xmas and here I am still. I'm all muddled up.

Please excuse this short letter.

Love from,

JANE

My Dear Althea,

I am home again now but that little wretch Stuart kept me waiting until 9th January.[29] Poor Tom got the measles while he was waiting for the advent, so between measles and babies I have had a worrying time.

You remember Nellie, old Peter's gin? Peter you know was the black who came back to Mackay after he had caught the young lubra. Well anyway, Nellie has now cleared off with a much younger nigger leaving him with a five-year-old boy. Poor Peter is a very old man now and lives on the bank of Plane Creek with the few remaining blacks of the district.

The other day the police came over to Woonon to say that old Peter was dying and that he was calling for his old master to come and take his son away. Tom's heart was very sore when he saw the poor old man lying there wasted away and dying from disease and filth, so brought the son back, in front of his horse, to the station. He was just like a little frightened animal and could not bear to sleep on his own so we let him sleep in front of our bedroom door until he lost the fear of the Devil-devil.

So now my family has increased still more. Wouldn't I feel embarrassed if I were to take my family abroad. The first child would be Pigeon, black; then Fred, white; Edmund, white; Leila, white;

---

[29] Henry Stuart Atherton was born on 19 January 1908. He died in 1952.

Stuart, white; and the last, yellow tinged with black.

I had a nasty experience the other day when my little brindle child ran to me and said, "Bigfellow tiger snake in garden." The only gun on the station at the moment was a shotgun. I had never used one before but knew that I should have to try as the snake had been seen several times already in the garden, and I was terrified that one of the children would be bitten.

When I got to the spot I found that the snake had crawled outside the paling fence with its head peeping through one paling. I took aim with the gun, pulled the trigger and then fell backwards — flat on my back. I had no idea that a gun could kick so hard. It left me with a shoulder and arm as black as thunder. Anyway I am very proud to be able to say that I shot the snake's head right off.

If it can be avoided we never let a snake get away. Oh, that reminds me that I must tell you another snake yarn. Mother was staying with me at the time, while she was waiting for Jim's house to be finished on his farm outside Proserpine — Cannon Valley — as she was going to live with him until Father got some work. One day she was dusting the sitting room and admiring our new suite of furniture when she saw a huge snake coiled round the legs of one of the new plush chairs. She called out "Snake", and I said, "You get a dipper of hot water to throw over it and while it is stupid I will kill it with a spade."

Mother went out to the kitchen but unfortunately could not find anything in the way of hot water other than the corned beef water on the stove. So she came in with this and threw the greasy liquid at the snake but mostly over the plush chair. I managed to kill the snake and then had to spend some time pacifying Mother because she was crying to think that she had ruined one of our good chairs. I can tell you that I felt more like swearing than pacifying.

We have a pet carpet snake which sleeps in the ridge capping in the kitchen. We will not kill him because he keeps all the rats and mice away. Sometimes, however, he gets into the woodbox, which is very annoying.

There seems to be such a lot of work to do on this property with its two thousand head of cattle, forty sheep, one hundred goats — I like goats now — and one hundred horses, than there ever was in the Gulf with its ten thousand head of cattle, four hundred horses and goodness knows how many pigs. Perhaps it is the continual dipping which takes place each month. We have no cattleduffers in this country though.

When we were in Brisbane, shortly after little Jim's death, we purchased a purebred jersey bull and two heifers to supply the house milk. They were inoculated for redwater disease by Mr Pound, the Government veterinary surgeon, six weeks before leaving Brisbane. They were beautiful animals, the bull cost one hundred guineas and the heifers fifty guineas each. The little heifers were so quiet that the children could crawl all over them, but alas! They only lived a month. Believe it or not, they died from redwater.

Really, being on the land is heartbreaking at times, for not only did we lose the heifers but we lost all we paid for the inoculation, which was no small sum of money. We did not require the bull any longer so sold him to a dairy farmer for fifty pounds.

I must away now as I have so much to do.

Love from,

JANE

My Dear Althea,

Stuart is growing into a very big child but he is so mischievous. We think he must be the last of the family the stork is going to bring. Tom spoils him terribly and if I should smack him he says, "Remember Mother, he is our last baby."

I have been at Tedlands again. It is a change away from Woonon. You have no conception of the numbers of wild waterfowl which live on the lagoon. Hundreds of duck and geese were shot and we practically lived on wild game. We were able to send sackfuls of the stuff to our friends in Mackay and Sarina.

At certain times of the year we have shooting parties ourselves and entertain Tom's old boyhood pals, such as J. Croker, W. Holyoake and J. Michelmore.[30]

I myself have sat for hours on the bank of a lagoon fishing, and at the same time holding my pea rifle so that I can shoot. I would always get a lot of wild fowl.

We were so afraid that Stuart would walk into one of the waterholes that we kept him tethered to the house by a long rope. Harry the nigger would mind him after he had had his afternoon nap.

I never play with the niggers now, they are far too civilised and cheeky. So when Harry yelled out "hey Missus, crocodile", I simply

---

[30] John Michelmore subsequently became Jane's second husband on 19 August 1937.

ignored him. The poor little fellow was nearly crying and said, "I am not joking, I really saw a crocodile near where you were sitting." He then pointed in the direction of what looked to me to be a piece of yellow wood and exclaimed, "There he is."

I knew that my pea rifle would be no use for killing crocodiles so hurried away from the bank. I then watched the crocodile's performance, which was very interesting. It began to crawl almost imperceptibly over to the opposite side of the bank and was obviously making for two birds which were sitting there peacefully. He went behind a pandanus tree and then we saw one bird fly away so concluded that he had got the other one. He then glided back into the water and floated motionlessly about, looking for all the world like a piece of wood.

It was nearly dark before the men returned from their day's mustering and they declared that all they had seen in the lagoon was a dirty piece of wood. I was furious to think that they would not believe me.

A few weeks later it was necessary to send a man from the homestead to Tedlands, and while this man was following the dry creek-bed he came upon a crocodile just leaving her nest of fifty-seven eggs. He brought a dozen home for which I was very thankful as it showed that my story was probably true.

Perhaps you will think that I romance a little too much but please believe me when I say that so many things have happened to me in my short life, anything might be true.

Lately we have been greatly troubled with swaggies who come to the homestead and ask for food. The trouble really is that our road is a better and more clearly defined one. However, as the local police station distributes ration tickets we have decided to cut out a lot of it.

We were sitting down to our midday meal the other day when Pigeon came in to say that there was a poor hungry-looking man outside asking for food. Tom told me to go to him as he said that he could not possibly refuse him food. However, I felt the same way about it myself so we decided that we would feed him but explain that it would be the last time.

Presently Pigeon came in again and said that the man had gobbled up his food like a wild animal, and that when she had asked him if he still felt hungry he had replied, "God I am." So Tom went out to him and had his plate refilled.

After lunch, Tom and Edmund went off to repair a fence about a quarter of a mile away. Our swaggie was so grateful for the meal we had given him that he insisted on our giving him the axe so that he could chop some firewood. We really did not want him to do anything.

Well, he began to cut the wood, and went on and on and on until at last I sent Pigeon down to him to tell him that he had cut enough. Pigeon returned to me looking very scared saying, "He looks so fierce and he keeps saying that he is a British subject, not a kanaka."

I told her that she was to shoot him if he came up and attacked me, and that even if he came onto the verandah I would phone the police.

So we were very thankful when we saw him hurrying towards the gate. Then suddenly he turned back in order to open the gate for Leila, who had been out riding. When her horse saw the swaggie it shied and pitched poor Leila on to the ground. We could see her lying on the ground, so ran at full speed to find her very shaken and with a broken arm.

The swaggie then went over to Tom and Edmund and said, "Your girl is dead." Tom immediately ran over, to find Leila sitting up crying with the pain in her arm. He then turned to the swagman who had walked back to us also and saw that he was really stark staring mad. He kept muttering, "I am not a kanaka, I am a British subject."

We of course telephoned the police and found that our swaggie friend was in truth a madman who had escaped from the Rockhampton Lunatic Asylum.

I will stop now. I suppose you think that terrible things happen every day here?

Love from,

JANE

Second daughter
Betty Clare — 23 May 1913

My Dear,

What do you think? But of course you will be able to guess. I have had another visit from the stork. I was so terribly ashamed when I found that after six years I was to have another baby. It seemed so terrible when I had a son of sixteen. I was very glad though that Fred and Edmund were at the Toowoomba Grammar School.

I really did not know how I was to face my lady friends. I was sure that they were laughing at me behind my back. Tom had to go to Brisbane on some business so that just suited me and I bought a beautiful brown, crepe de chine maternity coat and skirt.

We arrived back in Mackay during the week of the annual races so, as Tom was on the committee, I felt that I had to put in an appearance. I was very thankful for the new dress. Believe me it caused a little comment. One woman, after admiring my costume, said, "But why a coat and skirt?" She looked very knowing when she said it, too.

I went back to the station for a couple of months, then went on to Mackay, and surprised everyone, including myself, by having a little baby girl.[31] We have called her Betty Clare — not after any of Tom's former sweethearts either.

My letters, you no doubt think, are full of babies, woes and adventures. Well, I really think that this must be my last as I am now thirty-six. Anyway, no-one can say that I have not helped to populate Australia. I do not think that it is really my fault though.

Tom has been very ill and has been in Mackay for a month in the hospital. He returned two days ago but still has to continue with the treatment for gall colic. This consists of a cabinet steam bath and then lying down for an hour with a hot-water bag over his liver. I then have to give him a good rub-down before he gets into his pyjamas.

I really think that Stuart will end in gaol, he is still so mischievous. The other night, when Tom was in bed with his water bag, he lost sixpence and so struck a light under the bunch of pampas grass in the

---

[31] Betty Clare Atherton (b. 23 May 1913), later Betty Young.

sitting room to look for it. You may guess there was a commotion.

The governess we have for the young children was helping to clear the table while I was in the room attending to Tom. I of course immediately tore out to help extinguish the flames and called to Tom to come and help me.

Poor Tom had no clothes on and came to the door crying, "Where are my pyjamas?" In desperation he ran out with a blanket round him, but the flames were leaping so high that he had to use the blanket to put out the fire. I came along with a bucket of water and in my excitement threw the whole lot over Tom, quite missing the flames. Poor man, he was clad only in a singlet by this time, too.

Oh dear, I was so sorry but I simply had to laugh because he really did look so comical in his shrunken singlet. Tom was rather annoyed with me and did not see any joke at all and told me that I could put the next d—d fire out myself.

Suddenly we caught sight of the governess whose head was completely covered with the tablecloth. She, poor thing, was simply horrified at seeing a man clad only in a singlet. She looked so ridiculous that Tom just burst into roars of laughter and went off hugely enjoying the joke.

A few weeks later, when Tom was in Mackay, he met the police magistrate's wife, Mrs Magroity, who greeted him by saying with a twinkle in her eye, "I do hope that you did not catch cold after your fire." So the governess's face could not have been covered *all* the time.

The Pacific Ocean is only three miles from our home. Picnic parties, especially at Christmas and Easter, pitch their tents on the beach which has a dense scrub behind it. At times the picnickers stay for weeks at a time, and the women look after the camps while the men fish with net and line.

Early one morning word was brought to the homestead that a child of three years had been missing for nine hours, having wandered from the camp at sundown, and a party had been searching all night.

Immediately all hands left the station together with twenty men from Sarina, to search the dense scrub which fringed the beach for six miles long and a mile deep.

It had been raining hard all night so all little footprints would be quickly obliterated. The second night there was a lull in the rain and I could hear a child crying at the waterhole which was at the foot of the hill on which our house was built.

I lit up the house and took a lantern with me outside and began calling her by name, flashing the lantern everywhere. Then the rain

Jane and her daughters, Leila and Betty, July 1913. This photograph was taken about two months after Betty's birth on 23 May 1913. Of Jane's children, only Betty is still living.

came on again and I could no longer hear the crying.

When daylight came we went down to the lagoon but could find no sign of the child. The lagoon was dragged but there was still no sign so everyone put it down to my imagination.

It was not until several months later that a fishing party, who were camped on the steep banks of Plane Creek, found her body. It had been torn to pieces by the dingoes. It was only a mile from our home, too.

I hope all this does not make you feel sad. It certainly makes me feel that way.

I'll close now,

Love from,

JANE

My Dear Althea,

Tom decided after he left the Gulf, to breed Herefords only. He purchased first a bull and two heifers from Mr MacConnell of Cessbrook station near Brisbane. He also got bulls from Messrs Lumley Hill and Archer Bros of Rockhampton. His last purchase was a beautiful stud bull, Peter, from Cessbrook.

During the wet season after the drought a great many venomous snakes are often seen by the men out mustering. All hands carry a small lance and permanganate of potash which fits into a small case, about an inch long, which is tied to a string and worn around their necks. Just to be on the safe side, strychnine tablets and instructions for use are kept on the station.

One day one of the dogs went mad and ran underneath the bathroom. We of course surmised that he had been bitten by a snake, and we were anxious to try out our snakebite hypodermic syringe, so we pulled his tail through a wide crack in the bathroom floor and gave him a full injection.

The dog immediately came out and charged fiercely at two men who made off quickly for their quarters. The excitement was high when the dog turned round and ran into the house. The two men who had run away became a little more courageous and went with Tom into the house, armed with stout sticks. They followed him closely as he tore madly round the verandah yelping all the time.

The poor governess did not have time to shut the schoolroom door but luckily when she heard the cry of "mad dog", she and the children climbed up onto the table, otherwise I tremble to think what might have happened when the dog flew in.

A man stood at the door ready to clout him when he ran out again but missed him, only giving him a slight tap on the tail. We were certainly glad when we saw him scampering towards the lagoon at the bottom of the hill.

We then had a general muster of firearms, rifles, guns, pea rifles and revolvers, just in case he should return.

That night we all slept with closed doors and windows and rose at dawn armed with guns. Imagine our surprise when on going cautiously outside we saw the dog sitting there wagging his tail and asking for his breakfast.

The real reason why I have a governess now is because diphtheria has broken out at the Sarina school, and in West Plane Creek there is an epidemic of some disease, coastal or typhoid fever, which has killed dozens. It appears only to have attacked men though. So many very nice farmers died before the Government investigated the matter and ordered the whole of the residents of the town and district to be inoculated.

A relation of Tom's, Bernard Dupoy, died and left a wife and three young children. He had been surveying the main road at the time of his death.

We are not running any risks so we never go to Sarina nor do we buy any goods there. The doctors attribute the cause of the disease to the carriers who work in the canefields, where sanitary conditions are deplorable. So it was that the germs got into the water streams.

I think that I must finish now,

With love from,

JANE

My Dear Althea,

I am so glad that you like my letters. To me they seem more like the leaves from a diary than letters. I do not think that I am much of a hand at writing, I am sure that I am much better at talking.

We get a dry spell here from August to January. Woonon is looking very beautiful now. I think that it is really a land of milk and honey. As I mentioned before we are only a short distance from the main beach where the oysters simply hang in clusters from the rocks. We spend most of our weekends there, taking with us tea, sugar, milk, bread and butter. Each child has a small billy can and a frying pan,

---

SECOND DAUGHTER

174

to gather and cook their oysters in, if they prefer them cooked to eating them raw.

We have fishing nets and two small boats, and you would marvel where all the crabs came from. At certain times of the year hundreds of crabs are caught in the one day, in fact a small boat can easily be filled with them. Then on the other hand one can fish all day and not catch a single one. They just come in swarms and pass out to sea again.

It is a quaint sight to watch the turtles come into the shore by the hundreds at sundown, to lay their eggs in the dry sand of the little bay.

A turtle hunt was arranged one day, by Tom and the Sarina men. They waited till evening and when the moon was up they all rode to the beach, tethered their horses, and crept cautiously down to the beach, sitting on logs every now and again in order not to frighten the turtles. They finally arranged themselves in different spots along the high tide watermark. They worked in pairs but could not speak or even whisper and certainly not light a match. Can you imagine two men sitting on a log together for an hour or so without either speaking or smoking?

It was long after midnight when Tom really felt that he had had enough of it, so called out to his mates, "You're on a wild goose chase." He started to walk over to some of the other men and in doing so fell over what at first appeared to be a log. However, the thing moved and Tom got such a shock that he yelled. Yelling, you will recollect, was always Tom's long suit. Of course it was the only method by which you could get the blacks to do anything at times.

The whole party came rushing over at once, to find that the log was a huge turtle sitting on her eggs. They knew that the log, otherwise the turtle, had been there for at least two and a half hours, and had been not more than a few yards from them all the time.

After some little time they managed to get her onto her back to kill her. They then brought her home with some of the eggs. I tried to make a cake with the eggs but they were so gluey that even a second-rate cake became very second-rate with these ingredients. One leg alone weighed twenty-five pounds.

We had often had tinned turtle soup obtained from some place near Rockhampton but were always told that there was nothing like the real thing. If anyone ever tells you that don't you believe it. I have never in all my life tasted anything so vile. It was certainly not a scrap like the freshwater ones I had tasted in the Gulf country when hunting with the gins.

We hung the leg in a cool spot on the verandah and the smell crept through the walls of the rooms, permeating the whole house. Consequently the whole family was nauseated before finally the thing was carted away and burnt. However, we kept the shell to amuse the children. They used it as a cradle.

I am really feeling very well now and am always ready to enjoy a frolic with the kiddies.

Love from,

JANE

My Dear Althea,

I ended my last letter cheerfully, but I am afraid I am about to start off with the "moans" again. It is quite a time since I last wrote but somehow lately I haven't had so much heart to write.

Tom has been ill for many weeks past. He declares that it is the result of the wetting he received from me when I threw the water over him at the time of our fire, although it was over a year ago that this happened.

He and Murray Clark, who has a very bad limp, had some business to attend to on Suttar Creek. As a matter of fact we were selling him an empty run purchased from a Mr Hess.

Coming home they called at a wayside inn for the night. Only a double bed was available so of course Tom and Murray both slept in it. In the morning strange to say, Tom found that he had a limp like Murray's, in exactly the same leg. Murray, being a hasty-tempered man, accused Tom of mocking him, and it almost came to a fight. He was not convinced until Tom had to be helped onto his horse to go to Mackay for medical aid. It was then found that some cartilage had slipped in his knee. Shortly after this he had to be taken away in the ambulance because he had developed double pneumonia. This had been brought on not by the wetting he received at the time of the fire, but from having been in wet clothes all day when at Suttar Creek.

Really, he has had every complaint under the sun! Since we have been married he has had gall colic, typhoid fever, kidney stone, measles, malaria, in fact the doctor tells me now that there is nothing else left except baby's thrush.

While convalescing in the Lister Hospital he suddenly had a

brainwave and sent for Vincent Macrossan,[32] a solicitor, to talk over the injustices of the shareholders of the Plane Creek sugar mill, which they have been complaining about for years past.

After careful consideration the solicitor advised Tom to seek Council's opinion, which he did. The report was in their favour and the writ was issued on the mill owners for wrongful distribution of profits. When the articles of association were drawn up it was clearly stated that the profits were to be divided equally between the farmers and the shareholders. The latter had received nothing during the whole of the seventeen years the mill had been operating.

The law finally decided in favour of the shareholders, but alas! the farmers had spent all the money they had so wrongfully obtained and so were still poor. The only way we could have got our money would have been to put the whole of the Plane Creek district into insolvency and turn everyone off his farm. We did not want to do that so decided to take the accumulated sum of twelve thousand pounds, which had been held back while the lawsuit was in progress, and to be content with eight per cent on our shares.

Stuart is almost seven years of age and should be able to ride to school now. The only reason we are giving up the governess is because Stuart, being such a nervy child, is rather unmanageable at times.

We made arrangements for our stockman's son Teddy, who is ten years old, to lead Stuart's horse until he gained enough courage. Weeks went by and still Stuart had to have his horse led. Then one day the Sarina police phoned to tell us that Stuart and Teddy were having a buckjumping competition in the street. We subsequently learned that Stuart was by far the better rider of the two boys. So much for his nervousness. Next morning I felt glad to let every mother look after her own son and sent Teddy — who had been staying with us — packing. Stuart got a whacking I can tell you.

I have Pigeon sick at the present moment with toothache. She had very bad teeth. In fact she is the only abo I have ever come across with bad teeth, and I think that it must be her diet which is at fault. It is certainly not neglect because she is very careful about brushing them regularly with salt. Of course her forefathers always chewed bones and such like to give them strong teeth so perhaps that is the explanation.

I find it worrying at times to have a brindle family to care for. The

[32] This was Vincent Macrossan, one of the sons of John Murtagh Macrossan, M.L.A. for Kennedy and, later, Townsville, and Secretary for Mines on two occasions. J. M. Macrossan's sons included two future Chief Justices of Queensland as well as Vincent, who became a leading solicitor in Brisbane.

other day Harry came running to me and said, "Pigeon is always calling me a half-bred kanaka, I am not am I Missus?" I really could not tell him that a kanaka had a finger in the pie. He has yellowish frizzy hair and a light-brown skin.

I have never bothered about Pigeon's education as I have never forgotten Mrs Major Collis's case. She had a governess for her gin girl and had her taught music. She was really a beautiful musician. However, every now and again she would revert to type and run away to her native camp. She finally died from filth and disease among the abos. Anyway, Pigeon can at least read and write.

Well, I must get on with my work.

Love from,

JANE

My Dear,

Pigeon's teeth became very bad indeed and we took her into the dentist, and he advised extracting them all and getting her a set of false ones. We immediately went to the sergeant of police to see whether we could draw a small sum of money from her banking account — she has sixty pounds to her credit — for the purpose. The Government however, would not hear of such a thing. So although we are not obliged to do such things, we had her teeth seen to at our own expense.

She is a very valuable girl to me but has become tired of being nurse-girl for my seven children and is now housemaid and waitress. She looks so smart in her navy uniform, white apron and cap.

I wonder if you are feeling the strain of the war as we are here? The young boys of the district have simply gone mad and can think of nothing else besides getting into uniforms and going overseas to shoot Germans.

Fred, who is not yet eighteen, and to my mind far too young to shoulder responsibility, insisted upon going into Mackay with some of his mates to be medically examined. However, he has a knee which slips out of its socket every now and again and so he was told that this would have to be fixed up before he would be accepted.

He was going to Mackay again to have another try when the horse he was riding slipped, throwing him to the ground and injuring his weak knee, rendering him absolutely unfit for active service.

Edmund is only sixteen and is at the Toowoomba Grammar School still. He threatens to run away if we do not allow him to go to

SECOND DAUGHTER

the war when he is eighteen.

My brother Jim, who is forty, has enlisted. I think that it must be the Bardsley war spirit coming out as my great-grandfather and grandfather were officers, and my father a soldier in the Black Watch regiment.

After the railway passed through our run, we were forced to look for new lands to graze our cattle. Fred drew a selection in the Collaroy district, which he called Undercliff. It was forty miles from Woonon and we paid agistment to fatten our cattle. It took the best part of twelve months to build fences, yards, and a house, which had to be done before the stock could be shifted up there.

I gave Fred a cookery book and some lessons on how to wash with boiling water and soda before he settled into his new abode, where he would have to do his own domestic work. In his first letter home he asked why his woollen singlets went to glue when he put them into the boiling water, and stated that he had made a plum pudding but would like to know how to scatter the plums and raisins around the pudding next time.

On his first visit home, he brought a beautiful little animal which he had found in a creek. It was a platypus and had wonderful fur.

We were very surprised during the week to have a hawker's van drive up to the homestead. This sort of thing is very unusual as the township is so close.

The man left the van just off the road and started to walk towards the house, when suddenly his wife, who was in the van, called out, "snake". He immediately tore back to the van and began to throw its contents out onto the ground. We ran down to see what all the commotion was about.

After his van had been emptied, the snake was found and the man was able to kill it. The woman and I had stood by all the time armed with huge sticks. When all this was over, the man turned to his wife and they both began to jabber at the top of their voices. Their language was perfectly unintelligible but was obviously Italian, with a few English swearwords thrown in. I was feeling quite sorry that they were not speaking abo language because then I could have joined in.

Presently I said to the woman, "What you two feller yabber about?" She replied, "I don't know what you mean." So I had to use the word "talk" instead of "yabber". She then said, "That lazy b—, he says it was my fault! That I am too lazy to get out of my own way."

They then had to gather their pots and pans, men's clothing, scented soap, powder, pins, buttons and hooks and so on, for it was late and a thunderstorm was coming up.

ACROSS THE YEARS

I really felt rather sorry for the poor souls so sent word to them to come and have their supper in the kitchen. By the time they came up they had quite forgotten their quarrels and were in fits of laughter over the episode.

It is teatime now, and as all of us get very hungry, I shall have to stop.

With love from,

JANE

My Dear Althea,

I am sorry to have to tell you that our Pigeon has gone off the straight and narrow track. She has been mixing with white girls in Sarina who have had a very bad influence over her.

One day when Tom was camped out on the run, the police phoned me to know whether I was aware of the fact that Pigeon was in the town riding a chestnut horse. They stated that she had been there since eight o'clock, and asked me to be kind enough not to send her into the town on messages after dark, otherwise she would be sent to the Barambah mission station.

I have never sent her into the town on a message either during the day or the night. She is so cunning, she waits until I am alone, catches her own horse, brings it up into the cow paddock in the afternoon and ties it up there, and as soon as I go to bed she runs off to the township.

I was not certain of course, but suspected very strongly that Pigeon was pregnant. I asked her about the matter and she was very indignant with me and said, "I am a good girl." Of course I felt very mean then at having asked her such a question.

She never seemed to grow any different in form, and was always riding a horse barebacked and jumping off it before it had stopped.

One day we left her at home with a little white girl, while we went into Mackay. We arrived home at about seven thirty and a cold drizzling rain had set in. Aggie came to meet me and said, "Pigeon has had a baby and it is making a funny noise on the rubbish heap."

I immediately sent for Pigeon and demanded the full story. All she would say was that Aggie was telling a lie and that the baby was not hers but Aggie's.

You really cannot imagine what it is like looking for a baby on a rubbish heap on a cold wet night. I stepped high to avoid walking on it. Then suddenly something squarked like a frog.

SECOND DAUGHTER

I ran back to Tom to get his assistance. The rubbish heap was one of many years' standing and so it was like looking for a needle in a haystack. We eventually found a tiny mite wrapped in a flour sack, just breathing.

Tom acted as doctor and after setting the baby to rights, we removed it to a downstairs room and then sent for the ambulance to find out who the mother really was.

Well, Pigeon was the mother and we immediately sent her to bed and had a nurse in attendance for nine days. This seemed scarcely necessary as she had washed and polished two large rooms and cantered after the cows at milking time after her baby was born.

The baby only lived ten days and as Pigeon did not care for a bird's name it was called Doris. She did not know the surname.

They do say that if you look at a newborn baby you can tell who its father is. Well, the only person that I could see in Pigeon's baby was an old man who has a wife and six children, and who works at the slaughtering yards and delivers our meat.

So we had to send Pigeon away. We had to wait until a female prisoner was being sent from Townsville to Brisbane, for then the warder in charge of the prisoner could take care of Pigeon.

We had to wait for six months before a chance came. Then we only had two days' notice and Pigeon behaved very badly. She was so upset at the idea of being sent away that as fast as I packed her clothes she took them out of the port and began to tear them. I was alone with the governess and the small children, Aggie having left me. The strain of being accused of being the mother of a half-caste child was evidently too much for her.

At night, when she knew that the telephone service would be inoperable, she came into us with a gun and asked us for a cartridge as she wanted to shoot herself. Instead of giving her the cartridge we all hurried into one bedroom, and spent a dreadful night fearing that she would set the house on fire as she had threatened to do. She screamed hysterically, pleading not to be sent away as I was her mother.

In the morning she was calm but I was not. I had been crying all night so that my eyes were swollen and red. I had reared and nursed this girl almost from an infant and to have her going away was like losing another child.

I had to take her by coach to Mackay and when the time came for me to hand her over to the police, she screamed and flung her arms around my neck and cried, "Don't let them take me away, I won't do it again, I love you Missus, you are my mother."

ACROSS THE YEARS

Oh dear! I shall not forget in a hurry her poor drawn little face as she pleaded for my help. I had had her for nineteen years. I parted with her finally at the wharf and could hear her distressed goodbyes as the boat went out to sea.

She wrote me several letters from Barambah mission station, ending them with "your loving servant Pigeon". The last letter I had from her was to say that she had married a half-caste man and this time signed herself "Mrs Frank Smith".

My poor little girl died when giving birth to her second child, having the pneumonic influenza at the same time.

I shall end now,

With love from,

JANE

My Dear,

We do miss our little Pigeon. She was the person who knew where everything was and absolutely spoiled the whole family. She had such a wonderful nature and really helped others to be kind. I suppose it is just abo nature to stray in the way she did.

Well, I do not know how I am going to live through the next twelve months but we are to have a parson living with us. As you know there is now a Church of England in Sarina and as the parish is a poor one it has been suggested that we board the clergyman. I have had so little experience of such men that I have no idea as to how I should look. Should I go around with a sanctimonious face or just be natural? Fortunately I never swear in English, so that is one comfort. I shall be able to tell him exactly what I think him, if he annoys me, in polite aboriginal swearwords.

Of course before he came we began picturing what he would look like, and I started to teach the children grace.

When the idea of having this man was first mooted, Tom and I talked the matter over far into the night, and finally decided that the example of an English clergyman would be excellent for the boys.

The day he was expected, I put on my best bib and tucker, and dressed the children nicely. The waitress had her cap on, which she only wears on special occasions.

A dusty little man wearing a straw boater hat alighted, and approached me with an air of condescension. The boys were staggered, their ideal of an English parson shattered. He turned to

SECOND DAUGHTER

them and said, "Do you like horses? I do. They are my weakness."

When we were alone Tom asked me what I thought of him, and as I was so surprised I could only ask him what he thought. He replied that he did not see how he was going to stand the sight of him for twelve months.

I shall have to stop now, for between Tom, who is always moaning at the bishop and the Church, and kids and parsons, I am nearly off my head.

Love from,

JANE

My Dear Althea,

The twelve months had long passed and we still had the parson with us. Tom and I had such heated arguments as to who would be the one to tell him that the twelve months were up. Tom said that it was my duty, because it was my house, and although I felt brave enough for anything while the discussions were going on, in the morning my courage completely failed me. He really looked such a poor unwanted guest. I got so exasperated in the end that I threatened to pack up and go back to Mother. Even this would not move Tom.

However, the bishop arrived just in time to save the situation from becoming impossible, and we told him that now that the children were growing up they needed their separate rooms and that we would no longer be able to oblige the Church.

I have had a terrible experience. I know you think that I am always having them, and that by this time I must be a haggard old woman. But in reality I haven't a wrinkle on my face. Tom always says that the life agrees with me.

The police phoned one afternoon to ask whether the men were at home, and if not did I know how to use firearms, because two notorious blacks had escaped from Barambah mission station. They, the police, were certain that our two blacks must be feeding them as they were in hiding somewhere in the district. They asked me to keep a close watch on my abos, Peter and Maggie.

My abos cannot wash or iron so I have to drive into Sarina to fetch a woman out to do the washing. I do not really mind the trip as it usually fits in with the arrangements for picking up the groceries.

The washerwoman was here when the phone message arrived, so I told her that I was too frightened to take her back home that night and that she had better stay until the following day.

ACROSS THE YEARS

We gathered guns, revolvers and ammunition and put them in my bedroom, and barricaded the folding doors of the billiard room with buckets and old kerosene tins so that we should be sure to hear the approach of any enemy. We then started to fix up my bedroom, which has four light French doors. We pushed the furniture right up against the doors, but oh dear! I pushed the baby's cot right through the glass of one and smashed it to smithereens. I was so annoyed that I could have smacked my own face. By this time it was almost dark, so we put the children to sleep on the floor and I got into bed with the washerwoman. We were too scared even to whisper.

It was well towards ten o'clock when we were awakened from our troubled slumbers by the falling of the barricade. Mrs MacClarty, the washerwoman, grabbed a gun and I a revolver, and she started to call upon the Lord to save us. When a lull came in our prayers I heard a familiar voice say, "What's wrong, Mother?" It was Fred who had run out of tea and had come for a fresh supply. He also wanted the mail.

The police rang next day to tell me that they had spent the whole night underneath my bedroom guarding us and watching the movements of our niggers. They also said that they thoroughly enjoyed the joke when they heard our barricade fall in. Anyway, all's well that ends well, for it transpired that the blacks had gone right out of Sarina.

A week or so later Maggie said to me, "That fellow policeman, he big fool. Me been seen him sneak up under your house. Peter and me been give boys plenty tucker. We been leave it down at stockyards under sheet of iron when we bring milking cows up. That black boy say Pigeon send love longa you."

The truant niggers got right through to Burketown in the Gulf before they were captured and taken back to Barambah.

I forgot to tell you that my nigger Peter, who left the Gulf with his wife and family, had a daughter — the only one of three children who was truly black — which was adopted by Tom's mother. She used to sit at my mother-in-law's feet and run messages for her because she was a semi-invalid.

The girl grew up and was very devoted to her mistress and when Mrs Atherton died I believe it was heart-rending to hear her crying for her Missus. She died a week or so later, calling in her delirium for her Missus.

Love from,

JANE

My Dear Althea,

There are times when I actually envy you your single blessedness. I get so distracted with Stuart; his latest craze is to invite all his schoolmates to come on Saturdays to have what he calls a goat party.

We keep a mob of Angora goats, and a few sheep to kill. This provides a change of diet away from the beef. The old billygoat is one they cannot ride, for when he bucks them off, he makes a desperate charge at them, and they are afraid of being gored. He is so spoilt that we have to carry an umbrella every time we go to the lavatory, which is outside the paling fence. We open the umbrella in his face if he charges. It is laughable to see the way he scampers off.

Our old rouseabout man insisted it was our own fault and that he had not a bit of sympathy for us, and added that Billy never charges the men. He was watering plants the other day, where he had to step through a fence. I was watching him from the verandah and was so glad to see him, just as he was halfway through the fence, charged by Billy from the rear. He was sent flying, water and all, several feet through the fence. I had to laugh but poor Harry couldn't. He glared at me as if he would like to hit me instead of Billy.

I nearly adopted another child, but I could not as he was years older than I am. I had started off in a sulky to meet the children returning from the Sarina school, when nearing the front gate I met an old kanaka carrying a long grasstree stick. I said, "Where are you going?" He looked vacant and replied, "I go see my Mummie, she live up there." I can tell you I lost no time in turning the sulky round and galloping the horse up the hill to get to the house first, as I had left my baby and a little nurse-girl alone at the homestead.

Gathering them up I drove to the stockyards, where Tom and the men were at work. Jumping on their horses they lost no time in getting back to the house. The kanaka by now was seated on the kitchen verandah waiting, he said, for his Mummie to come and give him his supper. When I stepped from the sulky he bounced up exclaiming, "There is my Mummie." We phoned the police to take him to a lunatic asylum.

The heat is unbearable, I hope it does not mean that another drought is coming. I won't want to go back to the Gulf this time although they have no drought to upset their calculations. There has been a frightful fall in prices on the Gulf cattle market within the few years we have been away. Did I tell you A. H. Underwood sold Midlothian about five years after he purchased it from us for the lovely sum of thirty thousand pounds? He then bought a much larger property at a higher figure and this was his ruin when the cattle market slumped, but he has since built up again.

I'll stop now, sometimes I wonder if you find my letters a bit childish, when I write about all the silly doings that fill my days.

Love from,

JANE

Pigeon playing with one of Tom's cattle dogs, circa 1915.

Pretty Bend and Tondara
1917-1919   *1921-1925*

My Dear,

I am wondering what the year 1917 is going to bring us. We are on the move again, we sold Woonon to Atherton and Innis. I did not mind the packing up so much, but when it came to really shutting the front door and walking out, I did cry. My thoughts are the same as my Mother's must have been, when she broke up her home and wandered into a strange land where she would have to make new friends, and worse still, carry with her the nagging fear that it might not be a good move.

The menace of men and dogs chasing our cattle, and the abuse Tom received from some of the farmers for winning the lawsuit for the shareholders of Plane Creek Mill, became unbearable so we decided to shift our cattle to an empty property in the Bowen district, called Pretty Bend.

Don't think it is pretty because of its name. I think the person who named it so was looking through smoked glasses. We started a thousand cattle in our first mob, with Edmund as one of the drovers and Charlie Doherty in charge. They delivered twelve hundred, since many calves were born on the road.

Edmund then came back to drive Tom by car overland to Pretty Bend. Our Buick is the second in the Mackay district.

We, that is Mrs MacClarty, Stuart, Betty and myself, met Leila, who was returning from Ascham School in Sydney for her holidays, at Flat Top. I forgot to tell you we sent her there to finish her schooling. She had been at the Glennie School in Toowoomba since she had been eleven years of age. There were so many travellers on the road to Sarina that we were afraid to let her ride to and from school there, even though she was forbidden to pull her pony up and get into conversation with man or woman.

Well dear, I shall remember Flat Top Island as long as I live. It was so rough, we were unable to go aboard the boat by the gangway from the little river steamer which had taken us out to meet the larger vessel. We just had to do as we were told. First, we sat down on a round piece of canvas, packed as tight as sardines with the other

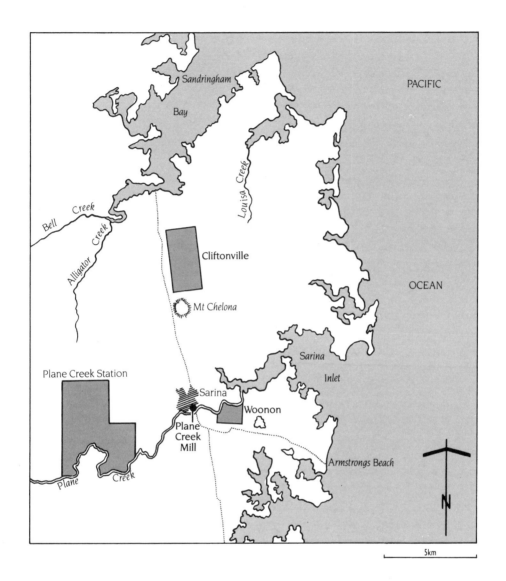

Map of the Sarina district showing the location of Plane Creek Station (founded by Henry Bell), Cliftonville (founded by Edmund Atherton II) and Woonon (originally called Atherton's Camp, founded by Richard Atherton in 1866, and sold to Thomas Arthur Atherton I in 1901). The area covered by this map is indicated on the general map of Queensland shown on p. xiii.

women and children, while the men stood in a circle round the canvas, holding onto the ropes which were pulled together to form an inverted parachute. We were then hoisted into midair and slung onto the deck of the waiting steamer. It took me some time to get my bearings and I had worked myself into a panic, fearing my two small children would be suffocated.

We arrived in Bowen before the car had arrived back from Pretty Bend, so stayed at the hotel. While we were waiting there, Mrs Lutzet, a neighbouring station-owner's wife, who was staying there, whispered into my ear to be very careful with all stores left by the previous owners as two cases of a deadly sickness, beri-beri, had lately come in from there to the hospital.

Can you imagine my plight! I felt like turning back with my little children, but it was too late, for the place had been paid for in cash and our cattle comprising two thousand four hundred head were there also.

Thank goodness for Mrs MacClarty the washerwoman from Woonon. She had come up, she said, as a favour to help us settle in. Actually, I think it was to meet her husband, who had strayed from her and was living in Bowen.

We arrived at the station at eleven in the morning and with the aid of Mrs MacClarty I scrubbed the kitchen and utensils inside out, threw out all eatables and cleaned the place up before I even made a cup of tea or tasted a mouthful of food.

I told Tom then what I had heard and how I had destroyed all the victuals. He was angry and said, "If I only could get at Mrs Lutzet I would tell her how kind she was to a neighbour, and also tell her I have heard of beri-beri and found it was the two bachelors who had owned the place and who lived mostly on rice, cooked for days, and that it was a form of scurvy they contracted from living on so rigid a diet."

The funny side about it was that Tom had hurried out to the station before I arrived and had the kitchen pots and pans scrubbed inside and out, and had thrown out all the eatables so that I would not see them. He had taken a small quantity of rations out, until the main load arrived, and so I had thrown our own food out.

Luckily I had taken bread, biscuits, tea and sugar out amongst my luggage. I am not liking living here. It is like back at the Gulf without the Mary-mary gins. We have no telephone here and I have to make our own bread and butter. It is so different to Sarina where everything was delivered to your door, and the railway was so convenient we used it in preference of the buggy.

ACROSS THE YEARS

Pretty Bend homestead, near Bowen, circa 1917. According to Jane, the property belied its name and she and Tom remained there for only two years. Indeed, for much of this time they preferred to live at Leyton, a property closer to Bowen that Tom bought for Fred to manage. When they lived at Leyton, Edmund was left to manage Pretty Bend.

At Pretty Bend station there are no women within miles, no church or Sunday school for the children, and it is thirty miles to Bowen.

I shall close this letter dear and hope my outlook is a little brighter next time I write.

Love from,

JANE

My Dear,

I am enclosing a photograph of the homestead taken soon after we arrived. The road out was terrible and the car had to be pulled over the Don River by a draughthorse. The sand was so loose, and it was fifty yards wide. There was only one redeeming point and that was that once across the river we were only half a mile from the homestead.

Edmund went back for the second mob of cattle almost immediately and Fred brought a hundred and fifty draught and race horses.

We stocked Pretty Bend with two thousand five hundred cattle, mostly breeders, as we had sold four thousand pounds worth of store bullocks to W. Hutton of Rockhampton a few months previously. A ring fence of ninety-five miles had been erected and our cattle had settled down very nicely when Mr Johnston of B—— and J—— arrived out and asked us if we would take thirty thousand pounds for the property. We thought it well over and decided to keep it as we had the boys to settle. Perhaps it was best, for if we had sold out, we would have probably gone into something on a much larger scale.

We have a family living on one side of us, who do not bear a good name. In the past they have been up before a judge and jury many times but so far they had not been found guilty.

The fence we built did not stop these thieves from doing their work in the moonlight, by taking the newly born calves away in split bags and rearing them on their own milkers. We had no idea that this was being done until the first muster, when Tom and the children could miss some of their cattle, especially Peter, a stud bull for which we paid one hundred and fifty guineas. We reported this loss to the police, but they took no notice as they were tired of always the same stories being reported.

A party of the surrounding station-owners arranged to meet at Lutzet's yards at one o'clock. Before the meeting one of the party went to Bowen and brought the stock inspector out. When they met, they found two hundred mixed cattle in the yard, with an extra lot of unbranded motherless calves which Tom claimed, as we are the only Hereford breeders in Bowen. The balance of the cattle, about a hundred and fifty, although bearing their brands, were unclaimed. A week later, a general muster was organised by the police and twenty-three men from miles around Bowen, Proserpine and Gumlu attended. They were all looking for cattle they had missed for years.

We found Peter with his ears cut off, looking very well indeed. In fact Tom was sure he had been fed. He was too valuable an animal for them to let get poor or die.

There were finally thirty-two different owners, when the cattle had all been checked. We did have cattleduffers in the Gulf but they had a hint of the gentleman about them, but how we are going to control these Lutzets is more than Tom can see.

I shall close now,

with love from,

JANE

My Dear Althea,

We never had cyclones in the Gulf, or even exceptionally heavy winds. However, we did have whirlwinds which seemed to go round and round, remaining almost stationary at times yet many feet up in the air.

Our washhouse there was covered by a bough shed which had a creeper growing on it with many years' growth of dead wood. One day one of these whirlwinds came along and besides gathering leaves, papers, sheets of old iron and tins, it lifted the shed into the air.

Now we have floods here. It is 17th January 1918 and the rain has been pouring down for days. This is our first experience of floods here so we were very interested in watching the Don River rise, creeping nearer and nearer to the house which is about fifty yards off. In fact we watched all through one night.

First of all the river came down in a roaring torrent from the Normanby Ranges, then the deep creek at the back of the house overflowed and met the flooded river. Our house quickly became surrounded by water, and rats, lizards, snakes and death adders were in large numbers over any piece of dry land to be found.

I can tell you that we were very glad to see daylight after that terrible night. The river was roaring, the wind was howling, and the rain was just beating down in torrents.

Then at eight o'clock a cyclone blew up, and the house swayed backwards and forwards. It took one of the verandahs away almost before we could get off it into the kitchen where all the blacks, piccaninnies, and stockmen were sheltered.

The rain blew in everywhere and we were soaking wet, but luckily the kitchen was on much lower blocks than the rest of the house and we felt much safer. As the morning wore on the gale increased to hurricane force. A lull came at two in the afternoon, and by four o'clock it began to die down.

The flower gardens were flattened to the ground, trees were uprooted everywere, and there was not a single leaf left on a tree for miles around the district. I must say that I prefer the thunderstorms we got at Woonon and in the Gulf.

I don't think that I have properly described our house to you. It is a four-room house made from adzed bloodwood, with horizontal slabs fitted into their positions. There are verandahs all round and it is built on very high blocks. The kitchenmaid's room, the bathroom and the men's dining room have been built in the same way, and connect to the main house by a long passage. I have already sent you a photo of it as it looked the day we arrived, but we are gradually transforming it into a pretty homestead.

First of all we varnished the main rooms and you cannot imagine how wonderfully the varnish brought out the different lights in the bloodwood. Then on one side we put leadlight windows and built our kitchen and dining room under the house, using the old kitchen for a billiard room.

Visitors simply rave about the beauty of the place, but of course I keep it quiet that we are overrun with cockroaches at times. Sometimes they are three inches long. An old miner from Normanby gold-diggings even brought me some cyanide but that was no good because they only seemed to get fatter on it. As for the boiling water we used, that only bathed them. I always think of the place not as Pretty Bend, but as Cockroach Villa.

I really think that I am lucky not to be in gaol now. I found an old tin of cyanide going to waste and the miner suggested to me that I should set baits for the possums who were eating all our fruit and vegetables.

Tom, of course, is on the shire council. In fact he was on it in Normanton, Mackay and now here. I often wonder about these shire councillors. Are they like Masons, with little secrets of their own? That reminds me of something which happened at Woonon. When Tom was coming home from his first Masonic meeting he was thrown by his horse, so he said, for he had bruises all down one side. However, my lady friends said, "Don't you believe it, he was thrown off the billygoat when it bucked."

Tom is a Justice of the Peace, so we had to wait our opportunity to prepare the bait. There is a fine of one hundred pounds or gaol for the unlawful use of cyanide.

Edmund and I went a little distance from the house to do our work. We had to keep on the side of the fire when boiling and preparing the pills, and I am sure that I changed my position at least a dozen times because Edmund would keep calling out to me that the wind had changed. We eventually had all the pills prepared and placed at the foot of every large tree near the house. I was very annoyed to find that I could not get rid of the smell, it clung so to my hands.

Next day Edmund and Stuart were up at daybreak and came rushing in to me to tell me that there were sixty possums dead.

The old miner had shown Edmund how to prepare and dry the skins, so they set to work. They spread hessian under the only fruit tree — mango — that we have for the preliminary work and put the skins in a small shed nearby to dry.

Halfway through the task they looked up and saw a policeman riding towards the shed. Everything was bundled up in a great hurry and put out of sight. The man soon left as he had only called in for his meal.

They decided that perhaps the men's quarters would be the best place to carry on their illicit work because it is only once in a blue moon that a stranger will pass there. But I'm blessed if a traveller didn't call and ask to camp for the night. So back went the boys and the skins to the mango tree once again.

By this time I was feeling nervous and I implored Edmund to throw the whole lot away, telling him that he had received two warnings not to go on with the business. However, he insisted on continuing and got more and more possums every day. He was greatly surprised therefore, when after having set baits he found them gone and no possums in their place. So you see there are possum duffers as well as cattleduffers.

I really think that I have told you all the news for the present.

Love from,

JANE

My Dear Althea,

I have finished with floods for the moment and want to talk about droughts. I must tell you something funny about the recent one.

We had a number of small calves whose mothers had perished in the drought. After dipping them we would leave them in the yards and Leila, who is very fond of animals, would feed them from feeding bottles made out of beer bottles. Of course they soon got to know her and led her a terrible dance because everywhere that Leila went the calves were sure to follow. Sometimes they would make a rush at her knocking her over, so that finally they had to be paddocked a fair way from the house. They never forgot Leila and even after a year would bellow and try to get to her if she passed the yard. The total cost for rearing the lot was nine pounds. She reared seven of them and sold them for six pounds each. Of course Leila is now away at school in Sydney you know.

We got over the business of the floods and cyclones safely, and the prices for cattle rose. We got eighteen pounds each for fat bullocks and twelve pounds for fat calves. So feeling a little more opulent we decided to have a trip to Sydney for the Easter holidays. We could attend the race meetings and see Leila at the same time.

After floods the crossing of the Don River was very treacherous even though it is only a short distance across. So we had to send a mob of cattle ahead of us in order to steady the quicksands. We went by buggy as there is no chance of taking a car across in bad weather. It was to be a long trip across deserted country.

Suddenly Fred, who was leading the mob, got into difficulties and his horse almost disappeared, in fact only its head and neck were showing. Fred jumped clear and he too began to sink rapidly. He kept quiet for a few moments until the sands settled and then crawled out on his stomach dead white from fear. It was quite ten minutes before the horse floundered out.

We had already had some experience of quicksand when bathing in the river. We don't do so in the nude now, but wear a pair of bloomers and a singlet, and if you happen to get into a quicksand you will lose your bloomers for they will be dragged off you. It is a most uncomfortable feeling being dragged down into the sand wondering whether you are ever going to stop, but after you have been made a fixture by the hardening of the sand you are able to scramble out.

On the boat we met a friend who was going to Melbourne to back a horse called Defence. Feeling quite opulent at the moment Tom put twenty pounds on it and it paid ten to one. Our bad luck had gone, we hoped forever.

We remained in Sydney and the Blue Mountains for three months. We took back with us a good present for the boys and a yearling foal for which we paid a hundred guineas. We called her Cannel Coal. We did all this without touching a penny of our letter of credit. Tom did not seem to be able to go wrong with his bets. Although he knew nothing whatsoever about steeplechasing he backed a horse one day and it paid ten to one. The only reason he had for backing this particular horse was that he had overheard two men speaking outside Jack Rice's stall, and had heard them say, "We'll pull this off."

Dear, it was just lovely to spend money and not to have to pause and say "Can I afford this?" I got such lovely dresses, hats and shoes, and two pairs of black stockings out of the first batch that came to Sydney. I had to tell everyone in Bowen that they were pure silk and cost twenty shillings a pair.

My hair was dressed over a hoop making my head look about three times its normal size, and hot irons were used to put in waves. The worst part of the business was having to sleep in a net and not being able to comb or brush one's hair for a week.

My hats were really a dream — just bunches of flowers and tulle perched on the side of my head and fastened with long hatpins. I also had a bright-red sunshade.

The wife of a neighbouring station-owner who has ten thousand head of cattle to our two thousand five hundred, was heard to remark, "I wonder how she dresses so well?" Of course she didn't know where the money came from.

Goodbye my dear, I am in high spirits now.

Love from,

JANE

My Dear,

Here we are back home again. The house is decked out in new curtains, and I have a silver coffee set and a Doulton tea set. I feel like an elephant in a china shop when I am using it. It is so different from the highly coloured set I had at Woonon.

We shut up part of the house while we were away and on our return we found that it was overrun with rats, mice, lizards and of course, cockroaches. We even found a snake in the corner of one of the rooms, so we had to work very hard to get it into order.

One day Tom was asleep on a double bed on the verandah. The two children were playing nearby when suddenly Betty came to me quietly and said, "There's a big black snake crawling along the iron railing at the back of Dad's head."

The little pea rifle was kept in readiness as we had already shot eleven snakes and five death adders since our return.

This particular snake was about two feet above Tom's head when I took aim at it. I really had no fear of missing it but thought it possible that the creature might fall on him.

It would really have been much better to waken him but he is such a nervous sleeper and always jumps up so violently when awakened suddenly. This of course is on account of the fact that he spent so many years among the blacks, where one must be forever on the alert against possible attack, that he has never been able to relax.

However, on this particular occasion I nearly killed him with fright. He jumped feet into the air at the sound of the rifle and had such a distracted face that it took us simply ages to calm him down. In fact I almost wished that I had left him to his fate because he declared in the heat of the moment that I had done it to amuse the children, because they, little wretches, were rocking with laughter.

We had a sick man — about forty-five years of age — call here and ask for food. The poor fellow looked so ill that I took pity on him and told him to stay in the men's quarters for a while, or at least until he was strong enough to continue his journey to Bowen.

My three and a half year old Betty took all his meals down to him, but would just put the tray on the doorstep and run home as fast as her legs could carry her. After a considerable amount of cross-questioning she finally blurted out, "Mummie, I might catch his one eye."

Our poor starved one-eyed friend soon recovered sufficiently to help me with the weeding in the garden, although he had to sit down to do it. Between attending sickrooms and trying to exterminate vermin I am feeling quite worried. We have had three one-hundred-gallon tanks made to store our provisions in so that they can be kept free from contamination. I am so afraid of beri-beri.

I shall close now,

with love from,

JANE

My Dear,

I feel very sad today. Our Edmund who is not yet quite eighteen years of age has gone to the war. Of course I feel very proud. He has to remain three months in camp at Enoggera, Brisbane, and then he will be home for two weeks' holiday, his pre-embarkation leave.

I must tell you some more about the sick man we had living here. He remained with us for six weeks before we finally decided to drive him to Bowen. He had always seemed a nice quiet man and would hobble to my flower garden and in a sitting position would fiddle about doing nothing all day. So imagine how we felt when we were forced to pay him two pounds ten shillings per week for the six weeks he had been with us.

I do not think that we shall do any more good turns to anybody, even if he is dying.

Love from,

JANE

ACROSS THE YEARS

My Dear Althea,

Edmund has been home and gone again many weeks. The mailman brought word to say that he was leaving Brisbane on a certain date and also a telegram to say that Leila was very ill and to come at once.

I was in Brisbane when the troops marched through Queen Street, but only saw Edmund through a mist of tears. I had had to go alone as the ticks were very bad and cattleduffers were very numerous.

While my train was waiting at Wallangarra Station, on the way to Sydney, I fancied that I could hear Edmund's voice in the passage outside my cabin calling me. I hurried out to see and found Edmund in his uniform with a bunch of Banksia roses in his cap. He looked very happy indeed. An officer stood by while we made arrangements about meeting in Sydney, and then he was dragged off to another train waiting at the same station.

The Sydney daily papers requested people not to disturb the lines of marching soldiers as they passed through the streets before embarking in the *Wyreema*.

I stood waiting and watching for the lads to pass. They all looked like lads to me, and amidst the cheering and the bustle I at last saw Edmund when he was still a fair distance from where I was standing.

I ran along the lines shouting "Edmund", when suddenly I was seized by a soldier in Edmund's line who said to me, "Come and see your Edmund, Mother, if you want to." So I was able to march in line with the soldiers for a few moments and could make a few further arrangements with Edmund.

Do you remember my sister Kate, the delicate one who spent nearly all her childhood with an aunt? You remember that she returned home when she was eighteen years old and married an accountant — M. L. Davies — of Burns, Philp & Co.

Her eldest son, Horace, was working on Jim's farm in the Proserpine district when war broke out. He enlisted and was a member of the 9th Battalion but was not in the first landing. He developed enteric fever and was sent to Alexandria Hospital where he was nursed by German sisters. Afterwards he was sent to France for two years. Then he was ill again and was sent back to Australia to convalesce. After six months he was again asked to report as he was to be sent back to France. The poor boy was not twenty-one years old and he put his head down on his arms and wept saying, "Why should I be sent back when there are so many who have not yet done their duty."

Herbert, his brother, then enlisted and he was sent to France also, very near to where Horace was and so they were able to see a lot of one another.

Jim also went to the war when he was over forty and sold a wonderful property, Cannon Valley, in order to do so.

Kate told me on no account to let Edmund see me looking sad because her own boys in their first letters said they would have preferred to have their last memory of their mother a happy one. So I was very busy biting my lip during the last half-hour with Edmund. But when the *Wyreema* broke her streamers I broke down and cried, and then when the band played "Nearer My God to Thee" I fled screaming away from the wharf down the street.

A woman ran after me and asked me what was wrong. I told her that I had a son who had just gone to the war and a daughter very ill. She advised me to seek Christian Science as an aid to my troubles and offered to accompany me down to the post office, where there was an office nearby. She then left me and I was left outside the door debating the point as to whether I should go in or not. As I was a member of the Church of England I really did not know what I would say if I ever did get inside the door.

To my relief a voice at my side said, "What are you doing here Mrs Atherton?" It was a friend, Harry Gordon, who had been manager of the Joint Stock Bank in Mackay, and who had just returned, on leave, after two years' service in the war. He could see that I was exhausted, so he took me along to the Arts and Crafts rooms where his wife was working, and she immediately made me lie down on a couch, and there I slept for two hours.

I then went out to see Leila who had been complaining of a pain in her side. We got her to Brisbane where Doctor Russell, who had just returned from the war, diagnosed it as fluid round the heart. She was in hospital for nearly four months.

Peace was declared while I waited in Brisbane. Edmund only got as far as the coast of Africa near Durban. Here all on board were stricken with pneumonic influenza and remained in quarantine for weeks.

Poor Kate's eldest son was blown to pieces just two weeks before the Armistice was signed. There was only his disc left to tell the tale. Herbert came back crippled and although he had held a good position before enlisting, he was not reinstated. The saddest part of it all is that Kate's only daughter died a few months before she was to be married and my sister was left a complete nervous wreck, from which she has never recovered.

Jim had been a prisoner of war and had been treated very badly by the Germans. He and his seven mates had to drag a huge plough while a German officer rode behind them with a whip to lash them if they dared to lag for a second.

By the time the Armistice was signed his mates were all dead and poor Jim was very weak and sick. He had not a hair on his head and he had lost all his finger and toe nails. They had been feeding him on cabbage roots from the garbage tins. It was quite twelve months after the war was ended before he returned to Australia.

I think I shall have to stop now because this is not a very cheery letter.

Love from,

JANE

My Dear,

I suppose you are getting very tired of hearing about droughts. It was after the 1918 floods, and the cyclone of 17th January, that we were again faced with a drought in November.

Our cattle were dying so a great many of them were turned out into the wild mountain country, which was covered with ferns that the cattle loved to eat, when the young leaves were just showing above the ground after a bushfire had cleared the spaces a little.

These zamia ferns spread rapidly after the aboriginals died out. The natives used to use the nuts to make their bread. However, the young leaves gave the cattle rickets, which of course affected their spines and hind legs. This disability rendered them practically useless for transport purposes, for of course they could not travel long distances with their hind legs dragging.

We have now purchased Belmore Downs, a small fattening property a few miles from the Collinsville coalmines. On our property coal can be seen in several places and can always be found by digging a few feet.

The range which had to be crossed between Pretty Bend and Belmore Downs was alive with brumbies — also there were many wild cattle. Some of them got in amongst the quiet cattle and would almost climb the stockyard poles trying to get out, and would charge the men who were trying to lasso them.

It was a great sport amongst the men this chasing up of the wild cattle. They would risk their lives by racing across mountain gorges

PRETTY BEND AND TONDARA

with a drop of hundreds of feet at the side. There was also the risk of being charged by an unseen beast and gored to death.

I remember once that Arthur Garbut of Townsville was out on one of these hunts amongst the Normanby Ranges which separated our properties. He had been following his beast for miles along the bed of a narrow steep creek, when suddenly a huge bull came round the bend and charged at him, throwing himself and his beast to the ground. The horse managed to get free but he was left with the infuriated animal which was frothing at the mouth, standing over him, scraping the ground with its great huge feet.

He was not able to stir or open an eye from fear. Then the black boy who had been riding with him took their gun and shot the beast dead. Luckily it fell sideways and only bruised his leg. Had it fallen on top of him it would certainly have crushed him to death, as it was such an enormous beast.

I feel so thankful when I see the men returning from these expeditions. I do not have an easy moment while they are away.

Love from,

JANE

My Dear,

Tom thinks that I have done my bit of pioneering so he has purchased a nice home called Leyton, three miles out of Bowen. It is so nice to be away from the worry of cockroaches and reptiles and then again I have Betty and Stuart living with me because they no longer have to board at the schools in Bowen.

The idea was to turn it into a tomato farm for Fred. Fred grew and packed two hundred cases and expected to get sixteen shillings per case, but alas! just as they were ready to ship, the wharf labourers struck and the whole consignment had to be buried. Things just went from bad to worse, and one consignment after another was buried. So finally we turned the whole forty acres into dairying land and managed to do fairly well out of it.

Of course the family just revel in the town life, but somehow or other even after all the grumbling I have done, I sometimes wish I were back in the bush again. They seem to lead such false lives in the city.

One thing that hurts me very much is the snobbishness that exists among some of the women in towns. One woman will say to another,

"Oh, I cannot be bothered calling on her, she does not really belong to our circle." In the bush there is no such thing as social distinction and everyone is like one big happy family, always ready to help a neighbour. It does not matter who's who in the bush, as there is a meal and a kindly word for everyone.

The annual show was an interesting affair. We were very interested in the cattle sections. Shorthorns are the breed in and around Bowen, but when we went to Pretty Bend we brought the Herefords into that district so that there was really good competition.

We exhibited a Hereford bullock for the heaviest beast section. The judge awarded the prize to Mr A. H. Cunningham for his Shorthorn. Tom was rather disgusted and bet fifty pounds that his bullock would weigh the heavier when killed, so at six in the morning the local butcher performed the operation in front of about thirty people.

By the time the beasts were killed Tom stood to win about two hundred pounds. I was not as worried about his betting habits as I had been in the days of the Gulf country, as we had recently sold a mob of fat cattle to the butcher at fifteen pounds per head. Anyway, our bullock beat the Shorthorn by at least eighty pounds.

The prize money was not accepted but given to the show committee for prizes for the following year's show.

During show week Leila made her debut at a ball. The only dances she had ever learnt were the foxtrot, tango and twostep, the old dances being forgotten. However, her party were old-time dancers so that meant that she had either to learn old-time dancing

Leyton homestead, near Bowen, circa 1919. Tom Atherton bought this property while living at Pretty Bend and intended it to be for Fred to run.

Post Office, Bowen, circa 1908. By the time Tom and Jane moved to the Bowen district in 1917, the town was substantial and prosperous.

herself or else teach her friends to jazz. It took about a fortnight to prepare her party of three girls and four men to attend the ball.

She entered the hall in her pretty white ball dress, and felt very pleased with herself to think that she had accomplished the task of teaching her friends to jazz. Imagine how small she felt when the MC told her, while they were doing the twostep, that he could not possibly allow such an objectionable dance to be performed there. Thinking that it was the twostep they objected to, her party tried a foxtrot but found they were not becoming any more popular with the MC. Finally in great disgust they finished out their evening by having a party at home.

The strange part about it was that the MC himself must have liked the dances because at their next meeting he revelled in them.

Well dear, I think I must close once more.

Love from,

JANE

ACROSS THE YEARS

My Dear,

I did not quite finish telling you about Edmund. There was great excitement when he arrived home about two days before Christmas. We had a lovely party with about twenty lads and lasses.

He did look so well. When he left home he weighed ten stone one pound, but on his return he weighed fourteen stone five pounds. He has really become thoroughly domesticated. Before he went to the war he thought a woman's work was absolutely nothing at all, but his ideas have undergone a complete change and now that we are without a maid he would not dream of letting me do the washing-up.

When washing day came around he wanted to help again, but thinking of his size and imagining that he would be very slow moving I was disinclined to let him. However, to my surprise he did the work perfectly, except perhaps when it came to hanging out the clothes. He hung articles like trousers by the legs, stretching them out along the line as far as he could, and then wondered why there was no room for the rest of the washing to be hung.

I get very tired of entertaining, but still I would not like now to go back to the Gulf as I have been too long in civilisation. But being in the town has its drawbacks. I would really like to go back to Woonon which seems to me now to have been ideal, because although not actually in a town it was still within easy reach of one.

The family have made it very plain anyway that they will not go back to the bush again. They are far too fond of the town life for that.

Well I must stop now.

Love from,

JANE

My Dear,

You will never believe it, but we are all back at Pretty Bend. I did not want to return under the circumstances we did, however it could not be helped. A slump came in the cattle market, so very suddenly too, that within a week we had shut up our town residence and got back here as quickly as possible.

The girls, especially Leila, hated the idea, but when it came to needs must, she fell in with all arrangements. We soared so high, while the war was on with bullocks at fifteen pounds per head. I suppose it was profiteering, we hardly gave a thought to the men who would require all our help on their return. We even bought a player

PRETTY BEND AND TONDARA

piano for three hundred and sixty-five pounds. It was the first in Bowen so attracted many, many visitors.

The player got on Tom's nerves so much that he threatened to chop it up if it was played before breakfast or after eleven at night. Although we included it in the furniture we brought back to Pretty Bend, it is a blessing to be free from the continual sound and back to natural sounds such as birds singing and chirping just as the sun rises.

We sold Leyton for two thousand pounds, the same as we gave for it. There was no slump in town houses. We have come out of it all with a credit of fifteen hundred pounds, so we are lucky don't you think?

Many of our neighbours are much worse off than we are, they dealt in buying store bullocks. One especially bought a thousand at ten pounds per head and had to be satisfied with about half the price.

Edmund had been six months on Pretty Bend after the war, and had kept the flower garden and the home in good order, so it was not as if we came to a deserted house.

It is ages since I went into Bowen last, not that I am ashamed as I could scarcely help the cattle slump coming, but when you realise bullocks bringing fifteen pound per head are now down to four pounds, you will know that we have not much cash to spare.

Leila is Betty's governess and we board Stuart privately in Bowen, from where he can attend the State school. We have no cook or maid now, I am back to two Mary-mary gins, but with a considerable difference. I have to be so careful with them not to offend them in any way, such as by calling them Mary-mary or black gin. The demand for their labour is so great and the supply of gins so limited that they can pick up a position at any time.

One of my gins has not long been married and has a small baby — no half-castes here, they are too smart — very like the father, whose name is Pompey. I have to call the mother Mrs Pompey as she objects to being called Bella.

I like my other gin, Maggie, and her husband. She is much older and has a lot of commonsense. I give her a sip of whisky often after washing day. The only satisfaction I have as far as Mrs Pompey — who talks such drivel — is concerned, is that I can swear at her, as she does not understand the dialect of the Gulf blacks.

I left her the other day to do the washing-up after our midday meal, while I took a little rest. I do get so tired, I suppose because of the life of ease I have led for so long. You can imagine my annoyance when I returned to the kitchen to find the dishes just as I had left them. Calling loudly and getting no reply I went over to their humpies and learnt that she had gone down the creek near the house. I followed her there to find out why she had left her work and found her and the six months old baby fast asleep. I yelled and shook her but could not wake either her or the baby. I felt like tapping her shins but dared not as I was entirely without protection.

I found she had swallowed a full bottle of chlorodyne that I had accidentally left in the dining room.[33] The blacks who had learnt the use of opium, now cannot procure it and so have substituted chlorodyne in its place.

The poor things have *bingy* (stomach) ache so often, we found it necessary to keep a supply, otherwise we would get no work out of them.

The show and races are to be held in Bowen in a fortnight's time. The pneumonic flu is raging in Mackay and is gradually creeping up the coast. I have tried to keep the family away from the town, but it is of no avail. Tom is the president of the race club so of course he has to go, and as his wife I have a duty to perform. My duty is to tie the ribbon around the winning horse's neck. It sounds like an excuse to go doesn't it?

All our niggers get a fortnight's holiday at that time each year and it is their only visit to town. The races, of course, are the event of the year. It takes a lot of preparations on my part, getting ready for this event. Dear, that sounds dreadful, you are not to imagine that because we are poor again, we go around in the buff on Pretty Bend. We have a neighbour however, a bachelor of course, who musters without his trousers. His station is amongst the ranges and there is no-one there but himself and a couple of niggers to do the stockriding.

It brings one back for the moment to the Gulf, when the gins had their race home without their trousers. I wonder, when our neighbour is chasing a beast, does his blue flannel shirt creep up under his armpits. You would never know him for the same man when he comes to town, dressed up in a suit, shirt, high collar and necktie. Poor chap, he does not know he is spoken of as "Without His Blooming Trousers".

I think it is one of Harry Lauder's songs. I'll close,

with love from your old friend,

JANE

[33] Chlorodyne was a proprietary preparation, available at that time without the need for a doctor's prescription. Its active ingredients were chloroform and morphine, dissolved in alcohol to make a tincture.

My Dear,

We have been to the show and races and are back home again. Everyone had a good time. We beat the first prize bullock again and this time by twenty-three pounds. The show committee insisted that we take the prize money this time.

I met Governor Sir Matthew Nathan at an afternoon tea party, and entertained him with some of my doings in the Gulf. I put the ribbon on the winning horse's neck. I did enjoy myself, but since we have come home we could all of us wish we had never gone to town.

Each morning of our gay week, we awoke and felt thankful, for the flu had entered the town. Sunday morning we were all ready to start for home, when we found Fred too ill to come down to breakfast. We called the doctor and he diagnosed it as pneumonic flu, and ordered him to be isolated in the Bowen hospital. He advised us to get back to the station without delay, but alas, when we were within a mile of the homestead Edmund was stricken down, and on reaching home was put to bed. He was running a temperature of one hundred and four.

When we were leaving Bowen the council gave us a pamphlet on what to do in cases of flu. One thing it said was on no account to give the patient any spirits.

Edmund was ill for a very long time and I was the next to get it, after being home three days. I did not get it very badly and was able to move about in a couple of days, well wrapped up in warm clothes. All the other members of the house wore carbolic handkerchiefs over their noses and mouths, and escaped.

The blacks arrived home in a frightful state, too ill even to make a fire for themselves. I, being the only one over the flu, went over to help them and was grieved to see poor old Maggie dying. She had a temperature of one hundred and six, and when she saw me she could just whisper "whisky"

I thought that there was no hope of her recovery so decided to let her die happy and gave her a good dose of whisky.

Next morning I crept over to the humpies, afraid of looking at death, when to my amazement she peeped at me over the blankets and said quite cheerfully, "More whisky please." So from then on I gave whisky freely to the patients and am glad to say that we never lost a case. At Strathmore station they kept strictly to regulation treatment and lost many blacks. In fact, some of them were in such a bad state that their limbs fell from their bodies before there was time to bury them.

ACROSS THE YEARS

In my calm moments I never really want to go back to city life, but when you have an awful experience such as I had last week it makes you long for civilisation and policemen.

The two gins had gone off to their huts for their midday sleep and I was alone with my aged father[34] of eighty-four years, and Leila. Did I tell you that Mother died soon after the war? The poor old soul lived in Brisbane all through the war and passed all her time knitting socks by the hundreds. She strained her eyes so much that she completely ruined the sight of one. So she went to a young eye doctor for advice. He wanted to charge her eighty pounds for an operation so she decided to consult another surgeon. She went to Dr Lockhart Gibson and when he discovered that the cause of her eye trouble was the war work she had been doing, he said that he would not dream of charging her a penny, and told her that he was in her debt for she had been truly serving her country.

This story is of course just by the way, but I thought you would be interested. I shall now get back to my terrifying experience.

Hearing someone call, I looked over the verandah of our two-storey home to see a fierce-looking man with a face covered with a thick growth of jet black hair, protruding staring eyes, no hat, no boots and clothes in rags. I asked him what he wanted and he said that he needed a feed, so I told him to wait a few minutes and I would fix something up for him.

The dining room and the kitchen are downstairs and by the time I got down there he was seated at the kitchen table with his elbows resting on it, and was muttering to himself all the while.

Leila, who had got the revolver loaded, went into the dining room where she could keep an eye on the man without letting him see her. As I moved about lighting up the fire and preparing his meal his eyes followed me around with what I though was a very sinister look. Finally with trembling body and shaking voice I said, "Your meal is now ready."

He then said, "Don't you go away, I shall want some more tea." Of course I knew that Leila was in the next room, but still I thought it possible that she might make a mistake and shoot me instead of the

---

[34] John Bardsley had deserted his family in the early 1890s when they were living in Normanton. He appears to have had no contact with any of his children until 1917 when he turned up at Leyton, Tom Atherton's second property, at that time managed by his eldest son, Fred. John Bardsley was sent to join the family at Pretty Bend where he was accommodated in the men's quarters. When the family sold out and moved to Maroona and afterwards to Tondara, John Bardsley left them and moved to Charters Towers where he died on 21 July 1923. Jane Bardsley senior, his wife, who had lived in Brisbane during the war, joined her elder daughter Kate in Cairns after 1918. She died there on 2 July 1925.

man. However, she told me afterwards that all she would have done in an emergency would be to knock the man out with the butt of the revolver and then kill him afterwards if necessary.

I shall never forget the way that man ate his meal. He just behaved like a hungry wolf, tearing the corned beef to pieces and biting huge hunks of bread out of the loaf. He quite scorned the use of a knife and fork.

As soon as he had finished his meal he demanded tea, sugar and tobacco. I can tell you that we were pleased to see him pass through the gate. In fact we were so hysterical that we put our arms around one another and wept.

I then went down to Father's room, which is apart from the main house, to find him sitting on his bed with a fully loaded rifle in his hand ready to shoot anyone who laid hands on me. I laughed hysterically, and I am afraid I quite hurt his feelings by suggesting that as his eyesight is very bad, he might easily have shot his daughter by mistake.

A fortnight later, when our men were looking for cattle in the ranges, they came upon an unknown camp and found in it a lot of new horse gear, such as saddles, pack-saddles, bags, a tent and many other articles. They looked about for the owner and found him in a steep dry gully where he had just killed a fat bullock. He was at that very moment preparing himself a nice piece of fillet steak.

Tom of course told him to get off the run, and said that if he did not do so the police would be notified in the morning.

A week later smoke was seen rising further up the ranges, and when Tom and another man were looking for a lost bloodmare they found the same man nicely settled in his quarters. He had killed another bullock and had his meat arranged over a frame where the sun could cure it.

Tom and his friend immediately ran back to the homestead to get a rifle each, while Fred went by car to Bowen to inform the police. The police arrived and brought the prisoner back to our homestead. He would not allow them to handcuff him in the night-time so they had to wait until daylight. He kept saying, "The king forbids."

The police recognised some of the goods that were found in the madman's camp as being those stolen from the Merinda meatworks. The meatworks had also lost two horses and so a search was started at once.

The man turned out to be an educated Russian. He finally refused to have any handcuffs on at all. On the second day Fred offered to relieve the police for a time with the watching of the man.

There was still no sign of the horses.

The hut in which the prisoner slept had a large room with three shutter windows and one door. There were several beds in the room to accommodate visiting stockmen from other stations.

The windows were all bolted and the policemen were fast asleep. Fred was sitting on the doorstep in a position where he could easily watch the prisoner. About two in the afternoon, when all was quiet, he began to feel drowsy and sank into a half-doze. All of a sudden he was aware of the fact that the prisoner had got out of bed and was creeping across the room to a heap of old brands that were kept in the hut. They were very near to where Fred was sitting.

For the moment Fred was fascinated and could not move, then suddenly he realised with a start what the prisoner was up to, as he saw him grab at the iron brands, and let out a yell that instantly brought the policemen to their feet.

The Russian halted and laughed an ugly laugh. "Did I frighten you?" he said, "I only wanted to go outside for a moment."

When questioned as to why he should want an iron brand if he was merely going outside, he replied that he wanted to feel his way with it. Of course we had our doubts about that.

The missing horses were finally found, tethered to a rope, right up in the ranges near a spring.

This has been quite a long letter hasn't it? There seemed to have been quite a number of things to tell you.

Goodbye for the present,

Love from,

JANE

My Dear,

It was lucky for us that when the slump came we had three thousand four hundred pounds, so that when we sold Pretty Bend and Belmore to a Mr Kelly we had thirteen thousand left from the wreckage of thirty-five thousand pounds.

We had longed for the bustle of town life so took a house on the beach — Maroona — four miles from Bowen, and remained there for twelve months. Then Fred got into difficulties with Tondara, a 60,000-acre block of land, so to get him out of his trouble we packed up and are once more in the bush.

Oh! dear, it is a very lonely place sixty miles from Bowen with no road fit to travel by car, consequently when we do go into town we leave the car at Gumlu siding. We have not even got a mailman and have to drive twenty-five miles by car each week to get parcels and mail.

Do not imagine Gumlu is anything special. I'll describe it so that you will know I have come to the last place on earth to live. It consists of a school, a few farms and a railway man's wife, who is in charge of the post office.

At first, I would go into Gumlu just for the run and to be away from the house. Now I have had to give that up through fear. The last time I had an unforgettable experience. I could see and hear from a distance of a few yards, two women having a heated argument with another woman, and then I saw one of them pushed off a low verandah. Fred was in the railway station, so I lost no time in bolting for the lavatory where I remained until I saw one woman depart, with a black eye.

Finally, I crept out and went to collect our mail; one of the women said, "You stayed a long time in the dunny. I suppose you were frightened I might give you a black eye too, but I tell you I know how to treat a lady." You may guess, I never took the risk of a punch in the eye.

I must tell you about a visitor we had the other day. He is a jackaroo on Strathmore station, his father is Lord Llewellyn, owner of John Lysaght Ltd Ironworks, and he has come to Strathbogie to attend musters.[35] We invited him to dinner and cards, but he arrived for afternoon tea. But instead of coming at four o'clock, however, he did not arrive until five-thirty. His only excuse was that his hair had not been brushed for a week and it had taken all that time to get it in trim, as he had heard there were two pretty girls at Tondara.

He caused great excitement on the station, for although able to ride well in the English poley saddle he was not able to stick on the ordinary saddle, and consequently had many falls when drafting cattle off a camp. He was about six feet two and wore size twelve boots, nevertheless, he could not be described as anything but a handsome man.

The Bogie River amateur picnic races are over for another year. There was a lovely house party, everyone was full of fun and all sorts of tricks were played. The governess tried to play a trick on Fred but had the tables turned on her. It was arranged — chiefly by the governess — to stuff a stocking and dress it to represent a gin and put

---

[35] In fact he was only a Baronet. Sir David Llewellyn, 1st Baronet of Bwllfa, Nas Chairman of Directors of John Lysaght Ltd.

it in Fred's bed. However, the host told Fred to take the stocking off and put it on himself and get into her bed. By eleven o'clock all were ready for bed and when the governess went to her room she thought the joke had been turned on her very cleverly. She took off her frock and was just about to slip out of her scanties when she heard someone cough, she let out an unmerciful scream and ran out into the room where the men were having their Dock and Doris.

Well dear, I must close now as it is time to see about dinner.

Love from,

JANE

My Dear,

We have had more bad luck at Gumlu. Tom has been beaten by the Labour vote in the shire council, after serving for twenty-five years. I tell him he'll be lonely without his secrets, and an excuse to have a few days jollification in the town.

Leila has gone nursing, she answered an advertisement in the *North Queensland Register* for a probationer for Innisfail. Poor Tom acted badly about parting with her. He could not understand her wanting to go and would not give her the money to pay her passage or to buy clothes, as if a girl could remain content looking at gum trees and nothing else all her life. Edmund, who is a jackaroo on Marathon sheep station, sent her twenty pounds and off she went with Tom's words in her ears: "You'll be back in a month's time".

She wrote in her first letter to me, that she could have easily run home the first day she arrived, but remembering Father's words, she would not allow herself to do so.

Betty is at school in Charters Towers and Fred has gone sugar farming in the Mackay district. We are alone with our wild lad Stuart and of course a lubra, Jessie.

Tom has built a nice home — I am enclosing a snap of it — with water laid on, so I put in my lonely days from 5 in the morning till 6 in the evening making a garden and attending to it. Oh! dear, it is such a lonely place, we are at the end of a road which leads to nowhere. My tears come at night when I pray to God to give me back my family.

The only thing I had left was a little Blue Mountain parrot, which I reared in the pocket of my overcoat. He had fallen out of the nest and was so small that I had to feed him with arrowroot biscuits and

Tondara homestead, on the Bogei River, 50 miles from Bowen, circa 1921. Jane lived at Tondara from 1921 to 1925. With most of her children gone, she was not very happy, and she devoted most of her time to developing a splendid garden.

honey by my own mouth. I had a little cretonne bag lined with flannel which I tacked low on the wall just outside my room. He would toddle off to bed there as soon as night started to set in and at daybreak would climb out and into our bed where he would go off to sleep again.

At times he would mate with his own parrots, and it was funny to watch him walk along the wire fence to them and with a cunning look

ACROSS THE YEARS

he would say "Pretty Joey", and screech and laugh when he saw them get a fright and fly off. We always kept one wing cut.

We missed him one night, for some reason he did not go to bed. Stuart and I called for him most of the night but he did not come. At dinner time however, he walked into the kitchen as usual and I fed him and put him on my finger and walked upstairs to have our usual camp. I do not know if I snore in my sleep but Joey, who was a great

PRETTY BEND AND TONDARA

mimic, certainly did snore in his. I was still holding him on my finger and loving him, for he was my only companion when Tom and Stuart were out of the house, when suddenly he dropped to the floor in a fit. I lifted him gently onto my bed and called Tom and Stuart. My poor little mate recovered from that fit but went into another almost immediately. His little heart beat faster and faster till he died.

If anyone had seen us I suppose it would have appeared funny. Stuart and I were on our knees bending over the little dead bird crying, and I am sure Tom brushed away a tear from his eye too.

A most peculiar incident happened when I took Betty to Charters Towers to instal her in the school. Staying at the Queen's Hotel in Townsville was a girl whom I had been at school with for years. We had not heard of each other for twenty years. She was the manager's wife of a very big sheep station and was in Townsville buying linen and other articles. I looked with envy at the beautiful linen sheets and pillowslips and said, "I have not possessed linen sheets since my trousseau which Mother bought me." She remarked, "I don't know the feeling of anything but linen." From what I could see it was far better to be a manager's wife than an owner's. I told her I was thankful to have cotton sheets and to be free of an overdraft.

The strange thing was I had not been home more than a few months when I heard her husband had died and that she will have to live on a very small income, so I guess she'll be down to cotton sheets.

What with the family all separated and little Joey gone I have got the blues properly.

From Jane, with love.

My Dear,

I quite forgot to tell you that during our stay at Maroona, after we sold out from Pretty Bend, we met some most charming English people; a Mr and Mrs Holder of Holder Bros England. They owned the Bowen meatworks and had great interests in the shipping world, and had come to Bowen with their own staff of servants.

It was election time, and if Labour had been defeated they were to purchase the Bowen Consolidated Coalmines, which would have put us in a wonderful position as we own many shares.

We called on them at the North Australian Hotel. Leila and Mrs Holder became very friendly, so during their stay in Bowen we saw a lot of them. They would come out to our sparingly furnished home and fit in as one of ourselves. There was no linen sheet ideas about them.

My black girl, of course, does all the work. She really is a scream, the way she annoys Stuart. She has been reared in a town and consequently is vastly different to the lubras of the Gulf. She knows all the latest songs and dances and whenever she sees Stuart will sing "I Want a Boy".

The other day Jessie Larry, as she is called, came dressed in her best to where Stuart and I were watering the garden and when within a foot of him began her song. He was so ashamed at my seeing such a sight that he immediately put the hose on her. Nearby was a fair-sized stake of wood which Jessie seized and then tried to hit him with, but as she tried to strike he watered her eyes until she at last appealed to me to make him cease.

She loves face powder so much that she appears at any time with a face like a flour bag. Knowing that it was my best powder being used I got the cheapest brand I could and kept it on my dressing-table and hid mine away.

If I had given her the powder she would have thought mine better and still have used it. She sleeps downstairs and when it is very cold I allow her to keep the stove going and she sleeps in front of it on the

Bowen, Meat Works, circa 1906. The meat industry was a vital part of Bowen's economy. Doubtless Tom and his sons sold many of their cattle for slaughter and processing here.

floor. We have enough wood for burning from the fallen trees just round the house to last us a thousand years. One night she knocked on my bedroom door and awoke me by saying that a large snake was near her bed.

Stuart and I went down with a lantern to look, but could not find it. At last we persuaded her to get under her blankets as it must have been only a bad dream. She slipped into bed then let out a yell and jumped clear of her bed. The snake had crawled between the blankets to the foot of the bed and when she put her foot down she felt the reptile. It was a huge harmless water-snake, and had come up out of the river.

Although Jessie has been spoilt by the town life she does like a hunt in the bush, and when Betty is home on holidays I am amused to see them start off for a walkabout. They take with them bread and butter, a frying pan, rifle and fishing lines.

Last week they returned home from their hunt loaded with rock cod, carrying them strung on a stout stick, each end of which was supported by a shoulder. Sometimes Stuart goes with them and brings back a sucking pig or a plains turkey.

Do not think for one minute that Betty is a little wild bush child. She does not play with dolls but having no other companion but Stuart this is to be expected. Her games are mostly mustering and dipping cattle. She is very fair with almost German white hair and large black eyes.

It was a very lonely little girl I left at the Blackheath Presbyterian School. She knew no other religion but the Church of England, and the other little girls gave her a bad time about her church. Her first letter home was imploring me to take her away from the naughty perspirations.

I'll be sorry to see her go back to boarding school again. She is only eight years of age, just a little innocent bush child. I fear her ideas will grow away from the life I am leading and I shall be left alone once more.

You would be horrified if you could see Stuart, he is so wild and venturesome. He seems to me to be friends with all the animals and birds of the bush. All his pets love him and he has a real menagerie.

During the dry season when the Bogie River was a bed of sand, he strung a strong rope from one side to the other, well above the reach of a flood. We all wondered what he was doing but now we know, to our dismay. We found him hanging from the rope over the flooded river yelling and screaming with delight.

I shall be glad when he is a man, he does make our hearts sore, we never know what he will be up to next. We could hear peals of laughter yesterday. Stuart had taken his rifle and two dogs down to the flooded river. The dogs Arn and Trim, whom Tom had got from Mr Peel of Antrim station in the Hughenden district, are a breed of cattle dog without tails. Thinking he would bring about his death by being too daring we ran at full speed to find him in the flooded river, holding on to a limb of a tree with one hand and with the other holding a huge boar which he was drowning by ducking every time it showed signs of coming to the top.

I cannot understand his nature, for he is so gentle and kind to both Tom and I, but I often say, "Stuart, I wonder what you will grow to and what kind of a husband you will make."

I'll close now, I am sure you must tire of hearing about the family, but I have nothing more to write about from this God forsaken hole.'

Love,

JANE

Last years with Tom
Torrington and Taronga 1926-1936

My Dear,

I do not long for town life, but if I could only turn back, say eight years, to when I had my family of five around me. Every minute was happy then. The meal times always brought laughter and argument and now we sit alone with our thoughts. I miss my little bird, although I have got another it is not the same and I have not the same interest in it. I also have the fear at the back of my mind that we shall lose Stuart some day.

We have had an offer for Tondara. The purchaser is fascinated by my beautiful garden. I have spent twelve hours of every day in it, I find it so soothing in my loneliness. I even hate to see the sun sink to rest, for then I have to wait until dawn before I can get amongst my flowers again.

Leila is liking her nursing very much better, but says she feels like a cooped up animal when she goes to the sleeping quarters, they have no privacy or any comfort.

The mail has just arrived and I am so anxious to know if the sale has been completed. It means so much to me. I'll let this note go and write you a long letter later.

Love from,

JANE

My Dear,

I am sorry to have kept you waiting so long for a letter, but I have lots to tell you about now.

We sold out from Tondara and are spending a few months in Brisbane. I am breathing freely to be away, I have no regrets and no sweet memories as I had when leaving Woonon. I had no regrets when we left Pretty Bend. It was so wonderful to be free of cattleduffers and cockroaches.

Our poor wild Stuart — who is loved by all — ran away with

Herbert Hall-Scott on the Port Hardy meat boat.[36] It was lying at
Bowen wharf with a cargo of frozen meat for England, delayed by the
waterside worker's strike. Stuart went as an ordinary sailor. There
were only thirteen hands on board when the ship sailed from the
Bowen wharf. By his letter he has had a fever when crossing the Red
Sea, which made him quite black for days, and he longs to be back in
Queensland again.

We cabled money to him through Burns, Philp & Co., and when
Mrs Holder heard he and Herbert Hall-Scott were on board, she had
them brought to her beautiful London home and gave them a
wonderful time, showing them the sights. She took them both to the
House of Lords, the House of Commons, the opening of Parliament,
the best hotels, picture shows and also to a hunt.

Mr Holder took them hunting deer, and had a good laugh I guess,
for during the hunt the deer went round a hill and Stuart took a short
cut over it and found the deer at a waterhole. He rolled his pants up,
took off his boots, and was holding the deer by the antlers when the
hunting party arrived. Mr Holder said, "How did you get there,
Atherton?" and Stuart replied, "I took a short cut of course." It was
just what he was used to in chasing pigs on Tondara. The deer was
killed and the front section cured and made into a nice ornament —
which now hangs on our wall — with the following inscription: Devon
and Somerset stag hounds, hind found Holland Moor, killed below
Marsh Bridge 27th February 1926. S. Atherton.

Mrs Holder loved Stuart too, and when she was saying goodbye
made him promise if ever he comes back to England, even if he is an
old man, he will stay with them.

Life is much more cheery. Leila is home after another long
period. She is engaged to Warren Shaw, a sugar planter, and Betty
goes to St Margaret's, Church of England Girls' School.

There must be something about my face, for when I met Sir
Matthew Nathan at St Margaret's fete, he looked at me, and
then said, "We met in Bowen did we not? I was most impressed with
your tales about the Gulf and would like to hear more."

Oh! my dear, we are so worried about Tom, he hates the sight of
city life and says that he feels he is sitting in a train, waiting for the
journey to end. Stuart is back from England, after paying a visit to
relations of Herbert's. They were two single old ladies and having tons
of money, gave the lads an extra good time showing them all over
Scotland, and they had the pleasure of a snowball fight.

[36] In fact Stuart ran away to sea. He had been left in the care of his elder brother, Edmund,
on the property their parents had given Edmund, but had quarrelled with him and left.

Tom is as happy as a schoolboy; having the excuse that Stuart must go on the land he has purchased a dairy farm, Torrington, for six thousand pounds. It is only four miles out of Toowoomba but I do not know how Stuart will like it on a dairy, it will be very different to chasing cattle. All I can do is hope it will turn out well.

Love from,

JANE

My Dear,

We have been here four months and have not seen a soul. I tell Tom we won't have anyone to follow our funeral if we should die here. I have heard that Toowoomba society wait to see who's who, and so far our pedigree is not suitable. The cold weather is so dreadful, the westerlies drive right through you, so perhaps our neighbours are merely frozen.

We have actually had our first social call today. After four months' sifting, our nearest neighbour called. She had found we are acceptable and have three grown sons. Our home is looking nice and we have a beautiful garden now.

Talk about dairying! I think the Lord should interfere. We have a man and his wife and their two sons, whom we pay fourteen pounds per month. They all get out of their warm beds at two o'clock in the morning to get the milk ready for the vendors who deliver it around the town. Stuart gets up at the same time and I feel it my duty to give him a cup of tea, so go to bed dressed in all woollens and even then I feel frozen inside and out, so God only knows how the poor milk boys feel. They seem to me to be always frozen, they drag their feet and speak with a drawl, so perhaps it is their tongues are frozen. It was so cold this morning there were icicles hanging from the water taps and on the clumps of grass.

When we were leaving Pretty Bend, Mr Kelly said it was quite our own fault that our neighbours stole our cattle, and if we had remembered the biblical quotation of "Be Kind to Thy Neighbour" and had taken them to dine at our table, they would have been better. However, I have just read in the *North Queensland Register* that Mr Kelly came across quite five hundred skulls of his cattle, who had been rushed over a steep bank, and all had a bullet mark in the same place. I do not know if he practised what he preached.

Well this is only a short letter again,

JANE

ACROSS THE YEARS

My Dear,

We have been here twelve months and have been rushed with visitors, some of whom are very nice people indeed, and had never heard of us until Tom became a member of the bowling club and I a member of the croquet club. I am sorry for all I said about them, but to our near neighbours I would like to say "buthue arrie arbeer" — a very bad swear in the Gulf blacks' language.

We have become acclimatised and are so well. Betty, who is a day scholar, has cheeks like roses and Leila has an English complexion, but poor Stuart is beginning to drag. his legs and has almost accomplished the milk boy's drawl. We worry a lot about him, he is so handsome and stands six feet high and has lost all his wild ways. We must try to sell out and get him into some other work, where life is bearable and he will have time to play cricket and tennis.

Later: A man turned up yesterday wanting to exchange his properties, a sugar farm and two houses at Bli Bli in the Nambour district, for our property here. The deal is made and we are off to Nambour in a week or so. Betty is to board at the Glennie, and Stuart has gone to Nambour.

Tom Atherton and Jane, Bli Bli, circa 1932. In 1926, Tom and Jane moved to Taronga, a sugar farm at Bli Bli in the Maroochy district, in order to help Stuart, their youngest son, get established. They remained at Taronga with Stuart and his wife, Edith Pugh, until Tom's death on 10 February 1935.

LAST YEARS WITH TOM

222

Some of the Glennie girls won't like Betty being a boarder since she always brought girls out for weekends — one little girl lost her mother while at school and was so lonely she often came out.

I'll say goodbye dear, I feel a little sad at leaving Toowoomba, as I have made some very nice friends and will miss my flowers so. The daffodils, snow drops and lilies seem to peep out of the grass without one ounce of care.

Love from,

JANE

My Dear,

The dairying was too much for Stuart, he tells Tom he would rather crack stones on the road than go back to that awful life. In fact he will not milk the one and only cow we own in the world.

Leila has married her sugar planter, Warren Shaw from Innisfail. Fred is married and farms on part of Woonon cattle run, which he purchased from some of the directors of Plane Creek Sugar Mill. Edmund is still a bachelor and farms in the same district as Fred. Betty is still at school.

Tom saw young B— whom we had known in the Gulf. He had sold his property up the Peninsula and had gone into sheep in the western part of Queensland. He was very prosperous and swell-headed. During his boasting Tom said "be careful young man", and he replied, "God Almighty can't keep me from being a millionaire now, I sold my property for forty thousand pounds and have purchased another for eighty thousand with half cash, and by the look of things I'm well on the road to a fortune." Tom met him such a short time ago yet already there has been a terrific drop in the wool market and we heard he was one of the first to feel it. Overnight he has become a poor man. I shudder when I hear folk tempting the Almighty.

You would just love the Nambour district, especially where our farms are situated on the bank of the Maroochy River, seven miles from Nambour. The river is gay at times with motor and speed boats, the fishermen drag their nets almost in front of the house, and oyster beds are close handy. There are crab nets set everywhere, and as there are no sharks hundreds of bathers come to swim in the river. Others of course prefer the breakers of Maroochydore which is only three and a half miles away by boat. I can lie on my bed and watch the feathery foam breaking at the beach.

ACROSS THE YEARS

On another side of the house we have the beautiful Buderim Mountain, where citrus fruit abound, overlooking the Maroochydore and Caloundra beaches. This is the lovely spot where the Duke of Gloucester spent part of his holiday when in Australia.

Leila has persuaded us to let Betty go up to her when she leaves school this year to give her a coming out dance. She is nearly eighteen and after being amongst a lot of girls at school for so many years she is lonely here when she is home on holidays. It would have been so different if she had grown up with the girls of the district.

Well dear, I must close now.

Love from your old friend,

JANE

My Dear,

I do miss Betty, she was home with me such a short while after she left school. She has been away six months now, staying with Leila outside Innisfail. She has now become engaged to Bill Young, a university lad who is a Master of Applied Science and we are expecting them down any day.

I hope Bill, when asking Tom for her hand will not have to go through a similar experience to Warren's. Poor man, it took him half a day to get ready and then when he had his speech half-finished, Tom, out of pure devilment said, "I beg your pardon." However, Warren was too smart for him and said, "Damn it all man, I'm asking for your daughter's hand."

Betty is far too young to marry yet, so will remain at home for about eighteen months before returning to Innisfail, or at least until Bill Young comes down in January 1934.

Stuart married Edith Pugh, the little motherless Glennie girl, and they have hopes of an addition to the family shortly.

I am looking forward to having Betty home. It will be such a pleasure to me to help her with her box. She is determined to do all her trousseau herself. She does beautiful work and I am so proud of her; but Oh! dear, I shall miss my baby.

Tom has not been well for weeks now. It seems sad to me that Tom and I will be quite on our own soon, just back to where we sat together a solitary pair on Midlothian at our first meal. Our large dining-room table has been made smaller, the bedrooms are all closed. All we have left is a black girl aged thirteen and Toby our cattle dog.

I sometimes wonder if you have not been wise in not marrying. You have missed the sadness of losing dear little children and of living to the age when they all drift away and have other interests so that their parents become just of secondary importance. Then again, of course, you have missed the years of happiness I have had with my children which counterbalances all the crosses I have had to bear.

Well dear, I must rush away to see the house is filled with flowers and all the rooms opened up to welcome Betty home.

Love from,

JANE

My Dear,

Betty has been home a full twelve months. The time has simply flown away. In a week's time she leaves for Innisfail with Bill to be married from Leila's home on 18th February, a bare eighteen days off. It is sad that neither Tom nor I will be at her wedding.[37] Stuart's wife is so delicate and Tom has not been well for quite a while.

Poor Edith, Stuart's little wife, has become so delicate since the baby's birth. The baby is a lovely child, fair-headed with dark eyes. They have called him Thomas Arthur, after Tom.[38] Our wild son has turned out one of the best, his life is devoted to his sick little sweetheart and his son. It is very sad; the doctor has told us that she will not recover and may pass away very soon. We are trying to keep the truth from her, she is so young to die and so devoted to Stuart and her little son.

A fortnight later.

My dear, I did not finish this letter as I was in such a fuss getting Betty off to Innisfail and now I cannot write for my eyes are blinded with tears and my brain numb.

Betty had gone ten days, her wedding was to be in a week, when Tom was seized with a haemorrhage. Both she and Leila caught the first train down, Fred and Edmund also hurried down, only to arrive

[37] Betty Clare Atherton married William Young on 16 April 1935 at Innisfail.
[38] Thomas Arthur Atherton II, b. 9 July 1935.

too late, for their poor old honourable pioneer father passed away a few minutes before they arrived.[39]

His faithful old cattle dog is breaking me up now. It would break anyone's heart to see him sniffing with his nose around the house, in Tom's room, even under the sheets of his bed, always looking for his beloved old master.

Love from your tired old friend,

JANE

---

[39] Thomas Arthur Atherton I died on 10 February 1935 at Nambour. The planned date of Betty's marriage and of the birth of Stuart's son, Thomas Arthur Atherton II, have been altered by Jane to create a more dramatic ending.

EPILOGUE

Following Tom's death, Jane's youngest daughter Betty, my mother, returned to Innisfail where she married William Young on 16 April 1935. A few months later, they moved to Brisbane where I was born on 18 April 1936. My grandmother remarried on 19 August 1937. Her second husband was an old family friend, John Michelmore, a merchant and businessman who had amassed a considerable fortune in the Mackay district. From then until her own death, Jane lived at Homefields, John Michelmore's Mackay home. It was in this period, I believe, that she prepared the first (handwritten) version of her book, and it is in the latter part of this period, after 21 February 1940 (when her solicitor wrote to her advising her to shorten the Ms and have it typed), that she completed the typed, illustrated first edition, from which the present edition has been prepared. (A second edition, without illustrations, was prepared by my mother in 1955.)

In February–March 1943, Jane and John Michelmore visited my mother in Brisbane. Jane suffered from hypertension and late-onset

Homefields, the Michelmore family residence, Mackay, circa 1904. In this house, between 1937 and 1943, Jane prepared the first edition of her book. By the time she came to live there, it was surrounded by fully grown trees and was considered to be a fine "gentleman's residence".

ACROSS THE YEARS

diabetes mellitus, and may have had some premonition of her impending death, since she made her will at this time as well as assigning her book to my mother in the hope that she would have it published after the war. She and John Michelmore took the train back to Mackay on Friday 19 March, arriving home the following evening. From Homefields she wrote a long letter to Betty, a passage of which is quoted below. It illustrates clearly that the style of her letters to Althea was in no way artificial — her eye for a good story, and the immediacy with which she could recount it, were as much a characteristic of her real correspondence as they are of her letters to Althea.

Homefields, Saturday (20 March 1943)

My dear Betty,
We have arrived home simply worn out. On getting ready for bed last night we discovered in the very next compartment were two men drinking rum by the bottle. One was an engine driver from Port Darwin who was returning home after holidays. He was about 6 ft 4 inches and had a voice like a fog horn. His mate was a nice fellow and did not drink much. The fog horn lasted in blasts until 11 pm. At 6 am, I was awakened with a smashing of glass near my head — it was the engine driver, who went to bed in his boots and who, in stretching his legs, put his boots through the wardrobe.

A naval officer joined the party and another rum drinker came along too, so then further noise was started up by each singing a solo, then duets — they had good voices! When arriving near Rockhampton, the last man to join the party went into the lavatory and bolted the door and went to sleep, and when the alarm was given an hour and a half later, the lavatory door could not be opened. The police arrived, and after about an hour of trying to get the fellow out, they pulled an almost dead man out. However, after he recovered and got some fresh air into his lungs, and the police were holding him, he let out a blow and caught the policeman fair in the face. He was taken off the train minus his luggage and I suppose he'll get six months.

At Rockhampton, a nice young pair got into our carriage. They had a dear little chappie, 20 months old, who had fallen down a flight of stairs and consequently was so cross he could scream by the quarter-hour without a stop. She could not hit him, as his poor head with a black eye looked so truly awful.

We were packed like sardines. However, at 8 pm two conductors gave us their sleepers and made us very comfortable. We started off in the last carriage of the train and ended up in the first from the engine, so you can know I was almost finished with blood pressure when I got settled. . .

LAST YEARS WITH TOM

Michelmore & Co., Sydney Street, Mackay, circa 1901. This prosperous general store, which grew to become Mackay's biggest "department" store, belonged to John Michelmore who became Jane's second husband in 1937.

I do miss the dear little boys, especially John.

Love to you all, Your loving mother,

JANE MICHELMORE

On Monday 22 March, Jane went shopping in her husband's department store and bought a dinner service and some wine glasses for my mother, luxuries in short supply in 1943, and wrote to her that evening describing the purchases. The following night she was stricken with abdominal pain and operated on for appendicitis. Although she survived the operation, the diabetes and hypertension from which she suffered had taken their toll. She went into surgical shock and died at 7 pm on 24 March 1943.

J.A.Y.
18 May 1986

ACROSS THE YEARS

EXPLANATORY NOTES

[6] This is a hitherto unknown eyewitness account of an infamous incident in the chain of events that led to the development of the "white Australia policy". Relations between Asian and European miners on the Australian gold fields, which had always been bad, became extremely tense in North Queensland at about the time the Bardsley family reached Normanton in January 1887. At this time the town had a community of Asian miners, chiefly Malays and Chinese, representing about one sixth of the town's population. On 14 June 1888, the Malay population celebrated a festival and, in the evening, a Javanese miner named Sedim ran amok and murdered three white miners in their tents on the outskirts of the town — these were John Fitzgerald, a carpenter, Christian Meriga, a labourer, and the Bardsleys' friend, Mr J. A. Davis, also a carpenter. The following day, a public meeting in the School of Arts led to violence and the formation of vigilante groups. Late in the evening, a great many houses and fishing boats belonging to Asians were burnt and their owners driven into the bush, where it was feared that they might be lynched. The police, aided by a force of special constables, rounded up all the coloured population except the aborigines and the Chinese (presumably because the latter were too numerous) and placed them under protective custody in an abandoned hulk called the *Rapido*, anchored in the Norman River just below the town. Although many of the Chinese were badly beaten, none appears to have been lynched, and some at least remained in the district when the trouble settled down. The refugees in the *Rapido*, however, were coerced into asking to be evacuated and were transported to Thursday Island. They suffered considerable privation there and were refused compensation by the Government for the loss of their possessions in Normanton. Sedim was tried for murder at the district assizes in Normanton in October 1888, convicted and hanged in Brisbane on 12 November 1888. The Normanton riots were widely reported in newspapers throughout Australia and were debated in the Queensland Legislative Assembly. Although the riots died down, racial tension remained high in the north, and political agitation led soon after to the expulsion of all Kanaka labourers from Queensland (from 1 January 1891). Asian immigration was effectively halted after federation, when the white Australia policy was formally implemented by proclamation of the *Immigrant Exclusion Act* on 23 December 1901.

It should be noted that Jane has compressed the time scale of the events she describes, making it appear that the riots took place soon after her arrival in Normanton, in January 1887. The true date, in June 1888, provides us with a clear explanation of why Jane's parents would have committed themselves to the expense of placing Jane in a convent in Brisbane from the start of 1889.

[7] There is a problem here with chronology. In the original typescript, the text reads "three years", but it has been amended in Jane's handwriting to read "six years". If, as she states, Jane left home just before her twelfth birthday (7 March 1889) she must have enrolled at her convent early in 1889, and, since her brother Jim enrolled at the Ipswich Grammar School for the quarter beginning on 5 October 1891, three years is clearly close to the correct figure for the time at which the letter was supposed to have been composed. Since Jane states later (p. 29) that her wedding (4 December 1895) took place just a year after she left school, it would appear that her final school year was 1894, giving her a total of six years at school. However, the archives at All Hallows Convent, Kangaroo Point, Brisbane,

record that Jane Bardsley of Normanton (parent's occupation "publican") was enrolled at the school for only one year — from 1 February to 31 December 1893. From her own testimony, it is quite clear that Jane attended a convent for much longer than one year, but it is possible, albeit unlikely, that she attended another convent (in North Queensland?) before going to All Hallows, and that this information was omitted when she compressed her original manuscript to its present size. This would still leave us with the problem of where she was in 1894. It seems more reasonable to suppose that the Convent records are incomplete. Although in several places throughout the text (e.g. p. 137) Jane writes of her seven years with the nuns, it is clear that the maximum period that she could have spent away from home was six years. It is presumably this figure that she had in mind when, erroneously, she amended her typescript.

SOURCES OF ILLUSTRATIONS

a = above, *b* = below, *l* = left, *r* = right

Mrs Yvonne Nurnberger
pp. viii, 37, 38 *a*, 40 *l* and *r*, 45, 105

John Oxley Library
pp. 2 *a* and *b*, 3 *a* and *b*, 6–7, 9, 11, 16–17, 18, 22, 25, 26–7, 32, 38 *b*, 43, 50–1, 84, 88, 89, 112, 114, 126, 144–5, 154, 158, 202, 212–13, 215, 228

John Atherton Young
pp. xiv, 34, 60, 74–5, 136, 138, 160, 171, 185, 189, 201, 221, 226

Maps by Alistair Barnard

INDEX

(numbers in italics indicate illustrations)

232